Mario Bava

Global Exploitation Cinemas

Also in the Series:
Disposable Passions: Vintage Pornography and the Material Legacies of Adult Cinema, by David Church
Grindhouse: Cultural Exchange on 42nd Street, and Beyond, edited by Austin Fisher and Johnny Walker
Exploiting East Asian Cinemas: Genre, Circulation, Reception, edited by Ken Provencher and Mike Dillon
The Politics of Nordsploitation: History, Industry, Audiences, by Pietari Kääpä and Tommy Gustafsson
The Mad Max Effect: Road Warriors in International Exploitation Cinema, by James Newton
Let's Go Stag! A History of Pornographic Film from the Invention of Cinema to 1970, by Dan Erdman

Mario Bava

The Artisan as Italian Horror Auteur

Leon Hunt

BLOOMSBURY ACADEMIC

NEW YORK · LONDON · OXFORD · NEW DELHI · SYDNEY

BLOOMSBURY ACADEMIC
Bloomsbury Publishing Inc
1385 Broadway, New York, NY 10018, USA
50 Bedford Square, London, WC1B 3DP, UK
29 Earlsfort Terrace, Dublin 2, Ireland

BLOOMSBURY, BLOOMSBURY ACADEMIC and the Diana logo are
trademarks of Bloomsbury Publishing Plc

First published in the United States of America 2022

Cover design by Johnnie Walker and Eleanor Rose
Cover image: Kill Baby Kill, lobbycard, (*OPERAZIONE PAURA*), 1966,
Dir. Mario Bava. Photo © LMPC / Getty Images

Library of Congress Cataloging-in-Publication Data
Names: Hunt, Leon, 1961- author.
Title: Mario Bava : the artisan as Italian horror auteur / Leon Hunt.
Description: New York : Bloomsbury Academic, 2022. |
Series: Global exploitation cinema | Includes bibliographical references and index. |
Summary: "A study of the Italian horror director Mario Bava, exploring issues
in authorship, genre, and film style, and examining the reception of
his films and reputation as cult auteur"– Provided by publisher.
Identifiers: LCCN 2021047855 (print) | LCCN 2021047856 (ebook) | ISBN 9781501356544
(hardback) | ISBN 9781501356537 (epub) | ISBN 9781501356520 (pdf)
Subjects: LCSH: Bava, Mario, 1914–1980–Criticism and interpretation. |
Horror films–Italy–History and criticism. | Auteur theory (Motion pictures) |
Motion pictures–Italy–History–20th century. | Motion picture producers
and directors–Italy–Biography.
Classification: LCC PN1998.3.B385 H86 2022 (print) | LCC PN1998.3.B385 (ebook) |
DDC 791.4302/33–dc23/eng/20211027
LC record available at https://lccn.loc.gov/2021047855
LC ebook record available at https://lccn.loc.gov/2021047856

ISBN: HB: 978-1-5013-5654-4
           ePDF: 978-1-5013-5652-0
           eBook: 978-1-5013-5653-7

Series: Global Exploitation Cinemas

Typeset by Integra Software Services Pvt. Ltd.

To find out more about our authors and books visit www.bloomsbury.com
and sign up for our newsletters.

CONTENTS

ILLUSTRATIONS

ACKNOWLEDGEMENTS

I would like to thank the Series Editors of the *Global Exploitation Cinema* series Austin Fisher and Johnny Walker for their enthusiasm for and support of this project. The following people provided support, either through advice, sharing ideas, reading drafts, recommending things for me to read or providing an opportunity to discuss ideas: Russ Hunter, Geoff King, Caroline Ruddell, Susy Campanale, Carol Jenks, Milly Williamson, Tamao Nakahara and the two readers of the initial manuscript. Before this project was even conceived, I had many enjoyable conversations about Bava and Italian horror with the late Peter Hutchings – we saw *La maschera del demonio* together for the first time at London's Scala cinema in the mid-1980s – and he wrote one of the best English-language essays on Bava, amongst an invaluable body of work on the horror film. Part of the book was written during a period of study leave at Brunel University, for which I am very grateful. Most of it was written during the Covid-19 pandemic, which meant having to adjust some of my original plans for the project. However, if Mario Bava taught us nothing else, it's that sometimes we must build our Viking ships out of pasta.

This book is dedicated to the memory of Margaret Hunt (1926–2020) and Lisbeth Hunt (1956–2014).

1

Between expendability and connoisseurship – situating Bava

*Back then Mario Bava was underrated. Now, thankfully, he's
overrated.*

MARIO MONICELLI (2007: 37)

Mario Monicelli's judgement of Mario Bava's elevated reputation might at
first glance seem like an inauspicious, or overly defensive, point from which
to begin a book on Bava. Certainly, it runs counter to the more romantic
narrative of an unfairly neglected filmmaker belatedly getting the recognition
he always deserved. A bit of context needs to be added here, therefore.
Monicelli acknowledges that the films Bava directed were not to his own
taste, not because he thought them poorly made but because he was not
interested in the cinema of fantasy and special effects. Rather, he preferred
to celebrate Bava's work as a cinematographer for films such as *Guardie e
ladri* (1951), the comic vehicle for Totò and Aldo Fabrizi that Monicelli co-
directed with Steno. But even without that declaration of taste, Monicelli
adds an important qualification to what might otherwise sound like a dig
at his former cameraman – 'thankfully' ('per fortuna' in the original Italian)
– which seems to suggest that Bava is more deserving of being over- than
underrated. There is a further layer to this, however, as far as reputations
go. Monicelli is still regarded as a major filmmaker in Italy, with a number
of classics to his name, but in spite of some notable international hits, he
never quite achieved lasting auteur status in Anglophone film culture, which
– if availability on digital media is anything to go by – has largely polarized
Italian cinema into arthouse/auteur cinema (Fellini, Visconti, Antonioni) and
cult/genre (Leone, Argento, Fulci, etc.).[1] Outside Italy, Bava, while still a cult
figure, is probably now better known and certainly more widely available
than Monicelli. This is not meant to sound like a validating victory for the

neglected 'artisan' because it has little to do with the respective quality of their output. But it brings us to some of the central concerns of this book. How do reputations – and particularly cult reputations – take shape over time and in different locations? How do we approach a filmmaker like Bava, whose achievements are often compromised by their production circumstances? How and where do we situate him and what issues do his films raise with regards to cultural value? To value is to 'rank or rate in an actual or imagined pecking order something or someone over another' (Hubner 2011: 1), but that pecking order is complicated by a filmmaker like Bava, who is simultaneously marginal and (cult-)canonical.

Mario Bava is the quintessential cult filmmaker, even though such a statement raises as many questions as it answers. According to Joe Dante, 'Before people knew what cult movies were, [his films] were cult movies' (*Mario Bava: Maestro of the Macabre*, 2000), while Alberto Pezzotta suggests that he can be seen as Italy's first cult director (2020a: 9). While a fuller interrogation of the different theories of cult is beyond the scope of this discussion, it is worth saying something about Bava's status as a cult filmmaker. The word 'cult' has been broadly used in two overlapping senses, as both a mode of consumption, a 'movement beyond reason' (Telotte 1991: 5) that can transform almost any commodity into a cult object, whether blockbuster or B-movie, and a type of textual classification that suggests the oppositional, the unusual or the niche, the counterpoint to its 'undefined and vaguely imaged Other' – the mainstream (Jancovich, Reboll, Stringer and Willis 2003: 1). The notion of the 'cult film' often operates discursively as a marker of compensatory subcultural distinction for films that 'failed' critically or commercially or whose earlier mass appeal has faded with time, but it also sometimes re-brands films that have passed from one cultural context to another. Which 'mainstream' does Bava stand in opposition to? The canonized Italian auteur cinema of the 1960s? The 'corporate' genre cinema of today? In either broad sense of the term, cult's battleground is that of taste, offering counter-canons to more 'respectable' or consensual ones and elevated positions to relatively marginal figures such as Bava. While cult can never be reduced to textual qualities, Bava's films are cult-friendly in a number of ways – in their chosen genres, their stylistic eccentricity, violence and eroticism and the fact that they have not always been easy to see. Add to this their perceived lack of 'legitimate' critical appreciation and the way that they lend themselves to an 'illegitimate' aesthetic appreciation that both challenges and reproduces certain hierarchies of taste.

Bava has been described as a major figure in 'world horror' (Hutchings 2016: 81) and was the subject of one of the most lavish books ever devoted to a single filmmaker (Lucas 2007). His cult reputation is that of a pioneering figure both in Italian horror and the *giallo all'italiana* or Italian-style thriller later popularized by Dario Argento, a master of special effects, an 'influence' (if not always an acknowledged one) on better known films by Argento, Fellini or Ridley Scott, a 'Serie B' director who made films look more expensive than they were, a cinematic stylist skilled in fashioning macabre atmospheres and luridly violent set pieces. In the area of Italian horror and the Italian thriller, only Dario Argento has received more attention and adulation, and unlike Bava, he received enough of it in his own lifetime to tide him through his later decline as a filmmaker (Hunter 2010). However, cult reputations are always qualified in some way, and Bava remains a relatively minor figure in the larger cinematic canon, even if he has some famous admirers. 'Mario Bava is one of those filmmakers that other filmmakers really like', observes Kim Newman in the British TV documentary *Mario Bava: Maestro of the Macabre,* and Bavaphile cineastes include the aforementioned Joe Dante, as well as Martin Scorsese and Tim Burton. These endorsements often come with similar caveats and an acknowledgement of the restrictions he faced, as if to answer their own question about why he is not more highly regarded. His heroic battle with poor scripts and low budgets is a prominent part of the Bava narrative, and perhaps one of the reasons why he is a filmmaker's filmmaker, seemingly confirming that it is possible for a director to transcend his or her material through sheer visionary zeal. Luc Moullet even wonders if Bava deliberately sought 'bad scenarios and impossible actors ... as if he were asking what he could do with such vile material' (1997: 51) – as Italy churned out genre films in the 1960s and 1970s, he would not have needed to look far. Scorsese and Burton make exactly the same claim about Bava's films. 'If you asked me to tell you the plot of any given Mario Bava film, I don't think I could', writes Scorsese in his foreword to Tim Lucas's book on Bava (2007: 13), while Burton claims not to remember the plot of even his favourite Bava film – 'I've seen *Black Sunday [La maschera del demonio]* I don't know how many times, but if you asked me what the story was (about), I couldn't tell you' (ibid.: 24). Both frame this as a positive, rather than a negative – Bava's art characterized as oneiric, atmospheric, visually expressive rather than aligned with storytelling – but we also recall Umberto Eco's claim that a cult film tends to be 'ramshackle, rickety', an object that you can 'break, dislocate, unhinge it so that one remembers only parts of it' (2008: 68). Bava's films often seem to be more easily remembered as parts than as wholes.

Bava's case has much to tell us about how the cult auteur circulates and is celebrated. He can be seen as an 'unstable auteur' in the same way that Valentina Vitali identifies certain genres as occupying an 'unstable position in the canon' (2016: 4). Significantly, Bava worked primarily in such 'unstable' genres – horror, the peplum or mythical-historical adventure film, the *giallo*-thriller, the 'sexy' comedy. Once difficult to see after (and sometimes during) their original release, Bava's films are now all easily available, most of them in prestigiously packaged Blu-ray editions. Then there is Tim Lucas's *Mario Bava: All the Colors of the Dark,* over 1000 pages long and providing the most detailed account of Bava's career to date, with an unprecedented amount of attention given to his earlier career as cinematographer and special effects expert. While lavishly produced, its only resemblance to a coffee table book is that it is large enough to use as an actual coffee table. It is one of only two full-length books on Bava in English, and Lucas approaches his subject as an erudite and dedicated cinephile-scholar – he edited the magazine *Video Watchdog,* which specialized in cult, exploitation and other niche cinemas. Peter Hutchings takes Lucas's book – rightly, I think – as clinching a certain status for Bava (2016: 79). But beyond cult fandom, critical and academic interest in Italian genre cinema (a cultish field within the academy), that status is still a limited one and I would venture is likely to remain so. Not only is Bava not Hitchcock – a critical and academic field in himself – he isn't even Sergio Leone, arguably the most canonical of Italian genre directors. A further instability lies in the tension between what we know of Bava's production context – a work-for-hire director in a precariously over-productive and chaotic sub-industry – and the claims sometimes made for him as an unappreciated genius-auteur. Auteurism has long had to negotiate such tensions, the figure of the auteur, as Hutchings aptly puts it, 'the phantasmatic outcome of cinephile activity' (2001: 29), rather than a working filmmaker in a particular production context. But this is exacerbated by several other factors in the case of Bava – the multiple versions of his films and the blurring of the different kinds of creative labour he brought to different projects (fully credited director, uncredited director and fixer of troubled productions, director of photography, special effects). Lucas's book is no less interesting or valuable for not being able to resolve the tension between Bava as artisan-for-hire and the claims he wants to make for him as a 'great, if underappreciated, cinematic artist' (Hutchings 2016: 89). On the one hand, he never loses sight of either the production context or the collaborative nature of filmmaking. He gives particular emphasis, for example, to the role of Ubaldo Terzano, Bava's camera operator and subsequently Director of Photography on his earlier films as director. Interestingly, while the Bava narrative often finds others taking credit for his contributions to certain films, here it seems to have been Terzano who felt that he was not getting enough credit for his creative labour, and Lucas seems to agree when evaluating the films made after *La strada per Forte Alamo/The Road to Fort Alamo* (1964):

> Seldom in Bava's later work will we encounter the kind of slow, insinuating tracking shots that Terzano piloted so capably, and never again will Bava's images be quite as sensuous in their interplay of light and shadow as they were during the tenure of Terzano.
>
> (2007: 591)

On the other hand, Lucas's investment in Bava-as-auteur sometimes leads him to overclaim; 'if it could be said of any individual, Bava *was* the postwar Italian cinema', he declares at one point (ibid.: 29). That is quite a claim to make for a filmmaker whose films rarely made much of an impression at the local box office, who worked mainly in genres marginal and 'foreign' to Italian cinema, and who was less broad ranging in his output than comparable directors such as Lucio Fulci or Antonio Margheriti. Sometimes, Lucas acknowledges that the best version of a Bava film is the one refashioned by others for a foreign market, while elsewhere it becomes a matter of concern that a particular version of a film 'hardly qualifies as "A Mario Bava film" at all' (ibid.: 692). The question of what exactly constitutes a 'Mario Bava film' is one I shall return to in the next chapter.

The notion of the auteur is a central issue in this book – books on directors are part of the legacy of auteurism – and yet my approach is not an auteurist one in the traditional sense. I am not interested in establishing whether Bava's films reflect his personality or some sort of authorial vision. It is relatively easy to argue that there is an unmistakable Bava 'look' or atmosphere in a number of his films, owing in particular to his artisanal skills as a cinematographer and special effects expert. But Bava's technical skills also leave him vulnerable to the accusation that he was somehow 'incomplete' as a director. According to screenwriter Ernesto Gastaldi, Ubaldo Terzano – who admittedly might have had an axe to grind – was heard saying on the set of *La frusta e il corpo/The Whip and the Body* (1963) that the film did not have a director, but rather two directors of photography, by implication himself and Bava (Acerbo and Pisoni 2007b: 89). There is certainly a distinctive approach in Bava's handling of the macabre, the violent and the fantastical, but this is less evident when the material is out of his comfort zone (his Westerns, for example) or working more successfully in a less familiar genre where he tries something different (the claustrophobic handheld camerawork in *Cani arrabbiati/Rabid Dogs*). Alberto Pezzotta characterizes Bava aptly as 'a professional who moves in different contexts, negotiating or surrendering his freedom every time. Without always having something to say, as the auteur theory wants, but holding onto the possibility of an outlet for moods, flights of fancy, visionary flashes' (2007: 102). For my purposes, Bava can be taken to be an auteur not so much because of any intrinsic property in his films – a 'personal' vision or style – but because his name is central to the way his films now circulate rhetorically and in their remediation as 'Mario Bava films'. In other words, what I mean by an auteur is any filmmaker – most commonly a director, but Bava is interesting in going beyond that – who facilitates a particular kind of connoisseurship, 'the pleasures of collectability ... and historical knowledge' (Church 2016: 2). One can collect Bava, accumulate expertise on his films and mansplain them to the uninitiated, track down his more obscure work, rank his films in order of merit and one has been able to read about him as a filmmaker of interest for some time. While the first full-length book on the director, Pascal Martinet's French language *Mario Bava*, was published in 1984, there was critical interest in him long before that. Nor am I invested in trying to elevate Bava's critical reputation, even though writing a book like this by its very nature establishes him as a worthwhile object of study and therefore in some way 'important' (and I am not going to pretend that I was not led to this project in the first place by my own love of Bava's films). My interest lies more in how canons and reputations take shape, and how Bava's critical reception marks certain mutations in cinephilia. The fact that there is more interest in Bava than before and that his films circulate widely in both best possible versions and their different release versions is not because we now have a better understanding of them (although greater access might make them easier to judge), but because a number of factors surrounding his films – technological, critical and cultural – have changed.

Here are a number of things we 'know' about Mario Bava:

1. Bava's is a cinematographer's cinema. Bava belongs to a lineage of directors of photography who became directors. A small number of these pursued directorial careers that equalled or surpassed their already distinguished work as DPs – Nicolas Roeg and Zhang Yimou, for example. But more often, DPs-turned-directors have been vulnerable to being seen as making visually striking films that lack the extra substance that a more accomplished director might bring. Mario Monicelli's view that Bava was a better cinematographer than he was a director was probably a common one in Italy, but most critical and fan work on Bava (Lucas is a notable exception) shows little interest in his work prior to his taking over *I vampiri* (1957) from Riccardo Freda, his work as a DP subsumed into his reputation as horror/exploitation auteur.

2. Bava's films are the triumph of atmosphere over narrative. Lucas calls Bava 'a mediumistic conductor, an orchestrator of macabre atmospheres', an 'inarticulate artist who spoke his heart by transposing text into image, circumstance into design and emotion into colour' (2007: 21). Ib Melchior, brought in by American International Pictures to try to impose some sense on the script for *Terrore nello spazio/Planet of the Vampires* (1965), seems to be making a similar observation – 'I think that he emphasised mood, rather than action … most of it was mood' (*Mario Bava: Maestro of the Macabre*). In films where dialogue must be easily translatable into (and often performed in) multiple languages, script pages were sometimes being produced on the day of shooting and different versions were prepared for different markets, one might expect narrative coherence to be a casualty. But even so, in some writing on Bava there is a willing away of narrative and a cinephile desire for Bava to move into near abstraction, the 'cinema-as-dream' that Tim Burton talks about in relation to his films (*Mario Bava: Maestro of the Macabre*). The review of *Ecologia del delitto/Reazione a catena/Twitch of the Death Nerve* (1971) in *The Aurum Film Encyclopedia* regrets that 'Bava doesn't quite manage to get rid of all vestiges of characterization or "psychological realism" so the film falls short of being the symphony of violence it might have become in a non-commercial context' (Hardy *et al.* 1985: 233).[2] It may well be part of the 'Bava effect' that fuels this desire to banish narrative and fall into atmosphere, spectacle and sensation – or to deploy it as strategic defence against critical dismissal of Bava as a poor storyteller – but it is worth looking more closely at how the films actually work.

3. **Bava was a pioneer.** While Riccardo Freda directed the first Italian horror film, *I vampiri*, in 1956, it is Bava (who photographed the film, handled its special effects and then completed the film when Freda abandoned it) who is more often seen as the 'father' of Italian horror. He would direct even more of another Freda film, *Caltiki, il mostro immortale/Caltiki, the Immortal Monster* (1959), but it is his official directorial debut *La maschera del demonio/The Mask of Satan/Black Sunday* (1960) that is usually seen as marking a distinctive 'Made in Italy' approach to the genre. He is also credited with creating a new genre, albeit one that would be popularized more fully by Dario Argento – the Italian-style thriller, the *giallo* or *giallo all'italiana*. These are both retrospective accolades that have a canon-building as well as reputation-building function.

4. **Bava was Italian cinema's 'Maestro of Horror'.** Bava worked in a number of genres and cycles, but horror occupies a privileged position in how he is understood and approached. Baschiera and Hunter suggest that Dario Argento was Italian cinema's 'first horror specialist', while others (including Bava) had to work their way through many different genres (2016: 12). Lucio Fulci, for example, is now often referred to as Italy's 'Godfather of Gore', but this accolade came late in his career. He did not specialize in horror until after the success *Zombi 2/Zombie Flesh Eaters* (1979) – most of his films up to the late 1960s were comedies, often starring the popular duo Franco Franchi and Ciccio Ingrassia (who Bava would direct in *Le spie vengono dal semifreddo*). Fulci did not even make a *giallo* until 1969. Horror and *giallo* fans have to be similarly selective about the careers of Antonio Margheriti, Sergio Martino, Umberto Lenzi, Aldo Lado and others. Bava, however, is a slightly different case, and this has helped auteurists map out his output into a more coherent *oeuvre*. Of the twenty-two films for which he is credited as sole director, either under his own name or under a pseudonym, at least thirteen of them are either clearly horror films or lean towards horror to some degree, as in the peplum, *Ercole al centro della terra/Hercules in the Centre of the Earth* (1961). This is notable because as a work-for-hire director, Bava was neither under contract to a studio specializing in horror (as Terence Fisher was at Hammer) or able to always freely choose his projects in the way that Dario Argento or some of his American contemporaries were able to. This suggests a degree of recognition by the industry that Bava's set of skills was particularly suited to this genre, or to fantasy more generally (which the peplum embraced), but at the same time this was offset by the recognition that horror was a commercially minor genre within Italian cinema for much of Bava's career. Its subsequent cult status notwithstanding, Italian horror

came in fits and starts, never really cohering into a sustained *filone* (cycle or trend) on a par with the peplum, the Western or the *commedia-sexy*. The viking movie *Gli invasori/Erik the Conquerer* (1961) earned twice as much as either of his first two gothic horror films and more than five times as much as his first thriller, *La ragazza che sapeva troppo/The Girl Who Knew Too Much* (1963) in Italy (Venturini 2001: 225) – any recognition of Bava as gothic 'maestro' was clearly tempered by industry pragmatism. Moreover, to take Bava as a horror specialist is to prioritize his directorial output over other kinds of creative labour that he performed in the film industry. If we broaden the picture, another genre starts to assume greater prominence in his output, namely the peplum.

5. Bava's films often exist in different versions, sometimes so different that they cannot be regarded as the same film. When does a film nominally directed by Bava film cease to be a 'Bava film'? At one extreme, there is the case of *Lisa e il diavolo/Lisa and the Devil* (1972) becoming *La casa dell'esorcismo/The House of Exorcism* (1975), where Bava's original footage was inserted into a new narrative about demonic possession; but is *Black Sabbath* the same film as *I tre volti della paura* (1963) when the episodes are in a different order, one of them has its storyline changed, the music score is different and there is new footage (possibly shot by someone other than Bava) of Boris Karloff introducing the stories? This ought to compromise Bava's status as a more traditional auteur, but the cult surrounding his films has found it relatively easy to incorporate this flexible view of his authorship.

6. Bava was critically ignored and/or dismissed in Italy before his rediscovery abroad. *Mario Bava: Maestro of the Macabre* begins with a familiar claim in Mark Kermode's opening narration, that where Bava was originally seen as 'an efficient jobbing director for hire', he is now regarded as 'a cinematic pioneer, a unique visual stylist, and a maestro of special effects', and asks, 'Why did it take so long for his artistry to receive the recognition it deserves?' Here is the familiar narrative of the neglected genius rediscovered that Lucas tells in greater and more nuanced detail. This raises a few questions. Firstly, it brings us back to the question raised by the Monicelli quote – how much recognition does Bava 'deserve' and of what sort? Secondly, is his status as an 'efficient jobbing director for hire' not at least part of the story of his career, and evident in quite a few of his films? And thirdly, was Bava quite as neglected as this romantic narrative suggests?

7. Bava made low-budget films that punched above their weight. Like Roger Corman, part of Bava's reputation is that of producing 'brilliance on a budget', to borrow the subtitle of a book on Corman (Naha 1982). At one level, this confers outsider-maverick status on both directors, but Corman's Poe films, made with an outstanding technical team, are amongst the few of his films to have been praised for their visual qualities in quite the same way as Bava's. Part of the mythology of *Diabolik/Danger: Diabolik* (1968), a bigger film than usual for a bigger name producer, Dino De Laurentiis, is that Bava used only a fraction of the budget allotted to the film, creating immense and expensive-looking sets using glass shots and maquettes. The view that the restrictions placed on Bava facilitated a particular kind of creativity is put most persuasively by Pezzotta (2013: 17), who sees him as a case study in 'the space of freedom and experimentation that unpredictable and bizarre directors could carve out within a chaotic system lacking strong controls'. But there is a flipside to this. According to producer Alfredo Leone, 'Give Bava a restricted budget of $500, 000 and he would come back and present you with a brilliant picture. Give him *carte blanche* and he was in trouble' (quoted by Lucas 2007: 896). Leone had *Lisa e il diavolo* in mind, the film for which he gave Bava considerable artistic freedom, but which proved theatrically un-releasable in its original form, where Leone was hoping to repeat the commercial success of their previous film together, *Gli orrori del castello di Norimberga/Baron Blood* (1972). In any case, the resources made available to Bava perhaps varied in scale more than his 'low budget' reputation suggests, particularly during the period from 1958 to 1963 when he was working in a number of capacities for Galatea S.p.A., the production company where his transition to director took shape.

8. **Bava introduced a new kind (and a new degree) of violence into Italian genre cinema.** Much has been made of Bava's official directorial career beginning with a beautiful but thoroughly evil woman being branded and then having a spiked mask hammered into her face. Four years later, in *6 donne per l'assassino/Blood and Black Lace*, a spiked glove destroyed the face of another glamorous woman, but as the Italian title (Six Women for the Killer) underlined, she was only one such victim – her fellow models were strangled, beaten, burned and drowned while bathed in pulsating colours. Some of Bava's earliest critical admirers sought the surreal and the Sadean, and these then-shocking sequences identified him as a filmmaker to watch. Alongside Riccardo Freda and Antonio Margheriti, Bava's films supported the view that Italian horror was characterized by cruelty and excess, sado-eroticism – those qualities that Dario Argento would most successfully channel into an authorial identity both 'personal' and Italianate. Inevitably, this applies to some Bava films more than others, and the period from the 1960s to the mid-1970s would see a range of 'new' forms of cinematic violence, from James Bond and Sergio Leone to the *giallo all'italiana* and the emergent 'gore' film. But this aspect of Bava plays a role in both his 'pioneer' status and the shaping of 'Italian horror' as a canon.

Bava in context

Mario Bava was born in Sanremo in 1914. It is well known that he was a *figlio d'arte* – his father Eugenio worked as a camera operator, director of photography, special effects expert and director during the silent era, as well as being a sculptor. He contributed to several of his son's films in the latter capacity, including fashioning the titular mask for Bava's official directorial debut. Bava inherited a family craft (which would pass in turn to his son Lamberto and his grandson Fabrizio/Roy), entering the film industry as a camera operator, director of photography and special effects expert. His transition to director seems to have been unintended, partly pragmatic and something that happened in stages. The main filmography in Alberto Pezzotta's monograph (2013), for example, adds to Bava's established credits as director six films prior to his official directorial debut on which he is believed to have done more than his recorded credits acknowledge. We can be confident in stating that he took over *I vampiri* and *Caltiki, il mostro immortale* from Riccardo Freda, the latter fairly early on during production, and played a role in completing *La battaglia di Maratona/The Giant of Marathon* (1959), credited to Jacques Tourneur; he is also thought to have directed (if that is the word for a film so reliant on stock footage) parts of *La morte viene dallo spazio/Death Comes from Space* (1958). Some have claimed that Bava co-directed the two Hercules films directed by Pietro Francisci, *Le fatiche di Ercole/Hercules* (1958) and *Ercole e la regina di Lidia/Hercules Unchained* (1959), which might depend partly on what we think constitutes 'directing' a film. In any case, even if his official credit as Director of Photography and Special Effects is fair and accurate (Francisci was an experienced director), both films display an unmistakable 'Bava touch' in their lighting and visual effects, most notably in his use of gels to light parts of the set in different colours. In addition to his film work, there is also a small but notable volume of TV work, which includes his work on the prestigious RAI-De Laurentiis series *Odissea/The Odyssey* (1968), credited as director of Ulysses' encounter with Polyphemus that is split between the third and fourth episodes, and *La venere d'Ille* (1978, first shown in 1981), co-directed with Lamberto for the TV series *I giochi del diavolo – Storie fantastiche dell'Ottocento*. He also directed some *caroselli* (TV commercials), including *I futuribili* (1970), made for Mobil Oil.[3]

There are problems with approaching Bava as though his career began in 1957, not only because it skips past nearly half of his cinema career but because if a director's visual style is seen to be informed by his work as a cinematographer, it could be argued that it is perverse to ignore so much of that work. Nevertheless, it is beyond the scope of this book to deal with that earlier career beyond a few references. The Bava that we are largely interested in now – Bava the *maestro dell'orrore*, Bava the 'father' of Italian horror and the Italian Serie B thriller, Bava the cult auteur – begins with those horror films and peplums where Bava's creative labour is clearly discernible. In addition to being Bava's first horror film, *I vampiri* also marks the point where different kinds of creative labour start to blur and combine. Some of this can be attributed to his friendship with Freda, who later claimed that he always planned to walk off *Caltiki, il mostro immortale* in order to force his unassuming DP into the director's chair, but even more important would be Bava's working relationship with Galatea, a significant production context for shaping his transition into a film director.

From the late 1950s into the early 1960s, the Italian film industry enjoyed a boom, boosted by state funding, credit from the Banca Nazionale del Lavoro, a thriving export market, American investment and co-productions with other European film industries, particularly France (Nicoli 2017: 9, 154). At the same time, it was precarious and chaotic, a boom that rarely seemed far away from the next bust – Italian cinema would face various crises throughout the 1960s. By 1960, Italy was second only to the United States for number of cinema screens (Corsi 2001: 115), peaking in 1967 with 7,437 cinema auditoriums, increasing to 12,975 screens if one includes more parochial, irregular and peripheral screening facilities, compared with 13,000 in the United States, 5,093 in France and 1,736 in the UK (ibid.: 125). But this inflation of screens ran parallel with a decline in box-office receipts, one that would hit harder in the 1970s as the deregulation of TV would exacerbate the situation. The production sector was equally chaotic, with production companies being rapidly set up and often dissolving after just one film – Christopher Wagstaff estimates that in 1967 forty-three such companies made one film each, capitalizing on the Western boom initiated by Sergio Leone's *Per un pugno di dollari/A Fistful of Dollars* (1964) (1992: 250). The fact that some of Bava's later films took two years or more to get a theatrical release can be attributed in part to the chaos created by fly-by-night production companies and the so-called *mercato di profondità* (Miccichè 1975: 118), the low-budget genre films churned out to fill a peripheral and mercurial exhibition sector. This unpredictable and crowded market arose from a hierarchical organization of exhibition that ranged from the more expensive *prima visione* (1st run) cinemas where more prestigious films were expected to go into profit to the more peripheral *terza visione* (third run) screens that required large quantities of cheaply made films in addition to the *campioni d'incasso* (box office hits) that had worked their way through the circuit. Many films went directly into the *seconda* (second run) and *terza visione* cinemas, where it could take up to five years for a film to go into profit both because of the lower admission prices and because of daily programme changes at the *terze visioni* (Ehrenreich 2017: 117).

In an influential essay, Wagstaff has characterized the *terza visione* audience as a highly distracted one, comparable to the way TV viewing was theorized before the days of binge-watching and 'appointment viewing' (but perhaps not so different from American drive-ins, grindhouses and other viewing contexts falling outside the paradigm of the more middle-class movie theatre), filmgoers going to their local cinema nightly without checking what was showing, not necessarily arriving on time, talking to friends, only attentive to individual scenes or moments that provided certain physiological gratifications – titillation, laughter, thrills and suspense – 'that were as interchangeable as plot lines' (1992: 254). We need to be careful before we map Bava's films too readily onto this film-going paradigm, even though the genres in which he worked were more the stuff of *il mercato di profondità* than the big city *prime visioni*. *Le fatiche di Ercole*, arguably the most successful theatrical film Bava worked on during this period, was the *campione d'incasso* of 1958 and the making of Galatea as a production company. It opened in *prima visione* cinemas but took off commercially in *seconda* and *terza visione* cinemas, making over 900 million lire (Venturini 2001: 63). Most of Bava's films opened in *prima visione* cinemas, if sometimes only for brief runs, and given Galatea's role in shaping his directorial career, one might speculate that insofar as they were in any way knowingly shaped for a hypothetical audience, something we can only speculate on, some of his films might have factored in having to work across different exhibition contexts – enough production value to pass in the *prime visioni* (Bava excelled in 'value added' film craft), but with enough physiological 'peaks' to register in the *terze visioni*. As Bondanella and Pacchioni (2017: 654) observe, there was always the possibility of a Serie B film becoming another *Per un pugno di dollari*, a breakout film that could take a *filone* (trend or cycle) into *prima visione* cinemas.

Italian cinema did not produce B-movies in the literal sense of being designed for double-bills, but then the term 'B-movie' has rarely been confined to its literal sense, referring more to a combination of a low-budget and a notional outsider status that allows a commercial film to somehow exist outside the industry 'mainstream'. Italian critics sometimes use the term 'Serie B', which derives from football leagues. Bava's films as a director were certainly not prestigious – to extend the football analogy, he was no Juventus or AC Milan. He was not offered the kinds of projects as a director that he might have been if he had continued solely as a director of photography, although he did do more prestigious work on TV. Might he have eventually come to the attention of an auteur director? *Diabolik* might have brought Bava closer to Serie A cinema, even though it was only a modest success, given that Dino De Laurentiis was the film's producer and it enjoyed greater press attention than usual because its comic-book source was already becoming a social phenomenon (see Hunt 2018). Instead, exasperated by De Laurentiis' interference and seemingly uncomfortable with the responsibility of larger budgets, Bava retreated into Serie B for his film work and probably did become a more marginal figure for the remainder of his career. Serie B's various *filoni* included genres and cycles that tend to be associated with 'exploitation cinema' – horror, sexploitation, cheap knock-offs of more prestigious films such as the Bond series. 'Exploitation cinema' is a term that derives from production, distribution and exhibition strategies specific, if not necessarily unique, to post-war North American cinema. But its broader sense as a 'a particular *kind* of movie' (Doherty 1988: 3) – cheaply and quickly made, sensational, geared to short-term trends and quick profits, often highly imitative – is suggestive of its applicability to production cycles in other places (although, not unlike cult, some films and genres became 'exploitation' as part of the process of their cultural transposition). It is particularly applicable to Italy, partly because 'Hollywood *sul Tevere*' sought to reproduce some of the practices of its more affluent model (and even to blatantly copy its box office hits, often the starting point for a particular *filone*). Moreover, Bava's films were often distributed, or even co-funded, by American companies associated with 'exploitation', most notably American International Pictures, and considered good drive-in or grindhouse fare by distributors. Thus, while I have not largely referred to Bava's films as exploitation films, they can certainly be understood in that way.

In spite of the chaotic industry in which he worked, there was a degree of stability to Bava's working contexts up to 6 *donne per l'assassino*, after which he became more of a 'jobbing' director. *La strada per Forte Alamo*, *Ringo del Nebraska/Savage Gringo* (1966), *I coltelli del vendicatore/Knives of the Avenger* (1966) and *Le spie vengono dal semifreddo/Dr Goldfoot and the Girl Bombs* (1966) look like the work of a director accepting whatever he is offered, regardless of whether they play to his strengths – two of these films were started by other directors and completed by Bava. From 1958 to 1964, a degree of stability and continuity was provided by three overlapping production or distribution contexts or alliances, two of which would resurface intermittently in his subsequent career – the production company Galatea S.p.A., the producer and agent Fulvio Lucisano and the American distribution company, American International Pictures (AIP) run by Samuel Z. Arkoff and James H. Nicholson.

Galatea was founded by Lionello Santi and Cosimo Conterno in 1952. Initially engaged solely in exporting films, they also moved into production in 1955, making over forty films in addition to buying or financing thirty others over the next ten years (Venturini 2001: 5). Bava would contribute to at least nine of them in one capacity or another. Often seen as a model of stability, Galatea was a medium-sized company making films in a number of modes and at a number of levels – they spearheaded the peplum boom, but also produced *cinema d'autore* (arthouse or auteur films) by the likes of Francesco Rosi and helped fund Antonioni's *L'avventura* – but nevertheless fell victim to one of several industry crises and closed in 1965 (ibid.: 5). The success of *Le fatiche di Ercole* – relaunched to even greater success as *Hercules* in the United States by Joseph E. Levine – fuelled their international ambitions and they forged a number of profitable alliances. One of these was with AIP, an alliance facilitated by Fulvio Lucisano as Arkoff and Nicholson were looking to improve the quality of their releases by purchasing foreign genre films that could be dubbed and retitled, if necessary – some of these films were still in production and in need of extra funding, which AIP would provide (McGee 1996: 153–4). AIP's earliest Italian imports were peplums, but a screening of *La maschera del demonio* would lead to an ongoing relationship with Galatea, and Bava's films in particular – AIP would remain an on-off distributor of Bava up to *Gli orrori del castello di Norimberga* in 1972, which they distributed under its English title *Baron Blood*. Simone Venturini suggests that if Galatea had such a thing as a 'house director' – which Italian production companies generally did not – it would have been Bava (2001: 136).

Nevertheless, this is the closest Bava got to an equivalent to Terence Fisher's relationship with Hammer films or Roger Corman's with AIP. What Venturini calls the 'Bava factor' was all over a number of their films, including peplums by likes of Pietro Francisci, Raoul Walsh and Jacques Tourneur and Bava's own horror films and thrillers. But just as productions from small to medium to (occasionally) bigger benefited from Bava's artisanal talents, so too his own films as director benefited from Galatea's recurring pool of talent, including Ubaldo Terzano, the editor Mario Serandrei and directors of production Massimo De Rita and Ferruccio De Martino. As *Black Sunday, La maschera del demonio* became AIP's biggest hit to date, and they become more closely involved in Galatea productions, a logical move given that Bava's horror films were performing better in the United States than they were at home – *La ragazza che sapeva troppo* and *I tre volti della paura* were both prepared in different versions, with some scenes (particularly the endings) unique to each. They were similarly involved in the production of two Bava films made for Lucisano's own production company, Italian International Film (founded in 1961), *Terrore nello spazio* and *Le spie vengono dal semifreddo*. While the latter seems to be no one's favourite Bava film, it provides a fascinating case study in fashioning a film for two different markets to the extent of being two different star vehicles – a Franco and Ciccio film for Italy and a Vincent Price film (more specifically, a Vincent Price *sequel*) called *Dr Goldfoot and the Girl Bombs* in its English-language version. Other producers would play important roles in Bava's career, not least Alfredo Leone, who had a hit with *Gli orrori del castello di norimberga,* was involved in the sex comedy *Quante volte ... quella notte/Four Times That Night* (1968 – released 1972), gave Bava the relative freedom to make *Lisa e il diavolo* before turning it into *La casa dell'esorcismo* and owned the rights to other Bava films for a number of years. But thinking about Bava as a Galatea filmmaker and an AIP director, as well as Lucisano's role in building Bava's profile abroad (AIP apparently tried to lure Bava to the United States on several occasions) confirm that for first half of the 1960s, he may have been working in Serie B, but he was by no means a marginal figure.

There are three 'What ifs?' in Bava's career. The first is: what if Galatea had not gone under in 1965, or moved away from genre films before that, and he had retained the stability of that working context? The second is: what if he had been lured to the United States by AIP, who seemed to regard him as either another Corman or even a B-movie Hitchcock. In *Mario Bava: Maestro of the Macabre*, Samuel Z. Arkoff claims that Bava would have been remembered as the equal of Hitchcock if he had been based in the United States and UK, and while that is questionable, he might have found a fertile working environment comparable to Corman.[4] Finally: what if Bava had capitalized on working with Dino De Laurentiis on two more high-profile productions, *Diabolik* and the TV series *Odissea,* to become a more mainstream industry figure, rather than (depending on one's point of view) retreating into more marginal productions or retaining the outsider status that is part of his cult aura?

Cult and expendability

In 2019, Martin Scorsese generated some controversy by declaring that Marvel superhero films were 'not cinema', but rather 'made to satisfy a specific set of demands ... designed as variations on a finite number of themes' (Scorsese 2019). The relevance of this statement is twofold. Firstly, Scorsese is undoubtedly the most critically celebrated of the filmmakers to have endorsed Bava, both because of his own reputation as a filmmaker and because he is known to be invested in the filmic canon – if he has not necessarily brought Bava *into* the canon, he has at least positioned him nearer to it. An endorsement from Scorsese is a different marker of distinction from, say, an endorsement from Quentin Tarantino, who champions films and filmmakers from the position of iconoclast and fanboy, building an alternative subcultural canon rather than renegotiating the existing one. Secondly, however, Bava's films – and the type of *filone* cinema within which Bava worked – were also made to satisfy a set of market demands and, like most genre films, were 'variations on a finite number of themes'. The battleground here, then, is not only the distinction between authored cinema and industrial cinema, but between the enduring and the ephemeral. One of the legacies of auteurism in its application to popular cinema is that the ground around these terms is forever shifting. 'Ephemeral' cinema has a history of not knowing its place.

According to Scorsese, Bava 'demonstrates the liberating side of working without prestige or significance hovering over your head' (2007: 13), and Pezzotta too suggests that there was a space for 'freedom and experimentation' granted by working in such a chaotic production context (2013: 17). But while it is appealing to think of Bava as an outsider artist transcending 'unimportant' projects and achieving unanticipated longevity, there is also some value in considering them as examples of what Lawrence

Alloway, the art critic and founding member of the Independent Group who first coined the term 'Pop Art', calls 'expendable art':

> Expendable art is consumed in use; it is operational for intense but short periods ... Movies, in their high topicality, intense participatory appeal, playful expertise, and freedom from the desire to encumber the future with monuments, can be regarded as continuing the tradition of expendable art.
>
> (1971: 34)

Alloway encouraged critics to focus not on the individual film, particularly those designed for lasting prestige, but cycles with a finite lifespan – it is unlikely that he would have been on Scorsese's side in the Marvel debate. Films were best read, he argued, 'in terms of a context of related movies', rather than what he called 'out-of-context overanalysis' (ibid.: 12). Alloway was writing mainly about post-war Hollywood as an exemplar of industrial art, and not all of this can be transplanted to Italy because it implies a level of industrial efficiency that is perhaps less applicable. But given his preoccupation with cycles, formulas and repetition, the notion of expendable art is a useful one for *filone* cinema – movies are a form of 'formulaic art', he argues, 'dominated by conventions' and 'grouped in cycles' (ibid.: 7). Writing contemporaneously with the rise of auteurism, Alloway advised critics to look to 'continually changing alliances of talent' rather than 'simple pyramids of personal authority' (ibid.: 6). The auteurist project was invested in critical elevation, invested in positioning cinema amongst more traditional art forms:

> The risk for film criticism is that the canon of individual authorship, applied to an expendable art form, will simply lead to the insulation of criticism within a kind of hobbies-corner specialism.
>
> (ibid.: 55)

Bava would probably be long forgotten without the benefit of 'hobbies-corner specialism' – a less flattering way of talking about cinephilia or cult connoisseurship. Cult cinephilia complicates the line between the ephemeral and the enduring because nothing is intrinsically ephemeral within the cult matrix. Lucas concedes that Bava probably intended *La maschera del demonio* (and this very likely applies to every other film he made) to be watched 'once, maybe twice, and then forgotten' (2007: 307), but cult cinephilia intervened. The cults of Bava, of Italian horror and Italian genre cinema belong to a very particular version of cult, one that is attracted to the cyclical, the formulaic, the ephemeral, movies that in their original context were designed to meet short-term tastes and trends, destined for obsolescence, at least in theory – Hammer films, Toho's *kaiju* movies, Shaw

Brothers *wuxia* and kung fu films, *filoni* such as the peplum or the Spaghetti Western, Roger Corman movies. This type of cinephilia is attracted to the ephemeral, while at the same time disavowing its expendability – identifying peaks in the cycle, glimmers of distinction in otherwise routine films, identifying auteur figures, canon-building, fuelling a collector's market of physical media for films no one expected to outlive their initial exhibition cycle. Nostalgia is one of its driving forces, too, as the 'pastness' of cultified films lends a veneer of the exotic to what might once have been formulaic and routine. One aspect of their ephemerality, in particular, enhances their cult appeal – they are types of cinema and film production that no longer exist.

Bava's reputation developed across two different experiences of cinephilia. The first is an 'old' one identified by David Desser that predates VHS, DVD and Blu-ray, one underpinned by a different kind of ephemerality because it was not yet possible for most people to 'own' a film. Thus, cinephilia was rooted in memory, impermanence and epiphanic 'moments'.

> The cinephile loves those moments in the cinema that rise to poetry, that inspire something in the cinephile, something that can only be experienced from the cinema.
>
> (2005: 208)

Bava's is very much a cinema of such epiphanies. Doubtless his cult began with such fleeting experiences with the sublime in the *mercato di profondità,* in grindhouses, fleapits, Midi-Minuit cinemas in Paris. It's easy enough to think of Bava 'moments' – Princess Asa scraping her nails along her tomb, breasts heaving, face studded with holes; Dr Eswai chasing a mysterious figure through a room, only to repeatedly find himself back in the same room and discover that he is pursuing his doppelgänger; undead astronauts tearing themselves free from plastic shrouds; Diabolik and Eva on a revolving bed of money; scheming killers gunned down by their own children just as it looks like they have eliminated all opposition. In the case of someone like Bava, we might also add the problem of seeing satisfactory versions of his films, which also pushed appreciation towards those moments. '(A)ll that remains today is threatened by time', wrote Luc Moullet in 1994, 'the prints of Bava's films are reduced to a predominant pink or wine-colour' (1997 [originally 1994]: 52). As David Church suggests, the tension between the *disappearance* and *rediscovery* of the ephemeral is one of the driving forces of cult connoisseurship (2016: 3), even though Bava's films never 'disappeared' to the same degree as the vintage porn films Church examines. D. A. Miller identifies one of the 'sacraments' of old cinephilia as 'the projection of a film that was *hard to see*', this 'hard-to-see-ness' founded not only on the limited number of prints of certain films but also on the decaying state of the prints themselves (2021: location 100). Reviving Bava via film prints was something of a challenge. In 1976, the Trieste Festival Internazionale del Film Fantascienza screened thirty Italian horror and fantasy films (from a wish list of sixty), none of which were held at the Cineteca Nazionale in Rome (Lippi and Codelli 1976: 17). The print quality was noted in the accompanying brochure, which became a bible of sorts for Italian-speaking fans of the indigenous genre cinema – the print of *Il mulino delle donne di pietra/Mill of the Stone Women* (1960) was tersely summed up as 'terremotato' (devastated, as if by an earthquake) (ibid.: 61), while others were 'mediocre'. Five Bava films were included at the festival – *La maschera del demonio* was only available in a 16-mm print of its dubbed *Black Sunday* version. The same year, the British Film Institute included Bava in a season entitled '12 Masters of Italian Cinema' (Lucas 2007: 29). During the 1980s, Bava films often surfaced in varying states of distress at London's notorious Scala Cinema – I saw the heavily cut *Revenge of the Vampire* version of *La maschera del demonio* there in the mid-1980s, and I have written elsewhere of my encounter with *Diabolik* at the Scala on a triple-bill with *Barbarella* and the 1966 *Batman* (Hunt 2018: 3–7). The 1990s saw Bava retrospectives in San Francisco, New York and Los Angeles, taking advantage of film prints collected by Joe Dante and others (ibid.: 29), while the Cinématheque Francais in Paris held its own Bava season in 1993 (Caputo 1997: 55), which might have been where Moullet saw Bava's vibrant colours turn to a less-than-shocking pink. In 1998, I attended the British Film Institute's Bava season, which included more or less everything in whatever print could be accessed, including the British Board of Film Censors' cut of *6 donne per l'assassino,* in which it was virtually impossible to discern how most of the *6 donne* actually died, and the *Evil Eye* version of *La ragazza che sapeva troppo,* as well as an uncut print of *La frusta e il corpo.* This is an admittedly anecdotal account of what became of Bava's films even as late as the VHS era – it was DVD that revolutionized access to his films as well as their print quality – and it leaves TV screenings out of the picture. But it is illustrative of the problems facing any notional 'Bava scholarship' prior to the DVD era. Pascal Martinet's 1984 book on Bava did not have access to *Lisa e il diavolo* and so had to approach it through its bastardized version *La casa dell'esorcismo* (and there is just enough of the former in the latter for that to work up to a point). Bava's reputation has flourished on VHS, DVD and Blu-ray, enabling closer analysis of 'unfamiliar modes of narration' (Vitali 2016: 72), and making it possible to not only 'own' Bava but to own the different versions of his films. Where 'old' cinephilia perhaps kept alive the fantasy that there might be a definitive version – and, indeed, it eventually became possible to see *Lisa e il diavolo*, if not necessarily in a definitive cut – new formats lend some support to Roberto Curti's impression of 'a body of work that never aspires to be definitive' (2014: 204). Blu-ray packages which present different versions of Bava films alongside each other are sold using his name, while reminding us of the many other factors shaping his films.

This is doubtless a bit too 'hobbies-corner' for Alloway, but the cult Bava is a genie that will not be going back in its bottle any time soon even if it is far from the whole story of his films. Expendability is easier to see in those films that fall outside his generic comfort zones, but even some of his best films mix inspired sequences with the visible haste of getting things finished on time. Not all of this is antithetical to cult. The cultification of Bava has found different versions relatively easy to accommodate into a notionally auteurist appreciation of his films because while they in some ways remediate the ephemerality of the films, they also reinforce Bava's collectability and the connoisseurship required to navigate their different incarnations. Engaging with a filmmaker like Bava means negotiating between two seemingly opposed and yet paradoxically overlapping understandings of his films – expendability and cult canonization.

Situating Bava comparatively: Fisher, Corman, Argento

Another way of situating Bava as a filmmaker is a comparative approach. I have selected three other filmmakers from three different film industries as points of comparison – the British director Terence Fisher, best known for his films for Hammer in the UK, the American Roger Corman who has a connection to Bava through AIP and the Italian director often seen as Bava's more famous successor, Dario Argento. The first two are chosen because we need to look beyond Italy to understand Bava's output, given that 1960s horror was often transnational both in terms of exchanging influences and production and distribution deals. What Bava's best films have in common with Fisher/Hammer and Corman's 1960s films (the Poe series in particular) is a cinema that was punching above its weight in terms of budget and production value. Bava was in demand in the early 1960s because his technical skills brought added value to modestly budgeted films, while Hammer drew on the production design of Bernard Robinson and the cinematography of Jack Asher (whose lighting had some similarities to Bava's) and had the advantage of stable production facilities at Bray Studios up to the mid-1960s. Corman, too, benefited from an outstanding technical team, most notably the veteran cinematographer Floyd Crosby and production designer Daniel Haller – when they moved to the UK for *Masque of the Red Death* in 1964, with a young Nicolas Roeg replacing Crosby, and Haller rejigging sets from *Beckett,* Corman would oversee one of the most lushly beautiful horror films of the decade. If one were to choose an Italian

director contemporaneous with Bava, the most obvious candidate would be
Antonio Margheriti (usually billed as 'Anthony M. Dawson'), whose career
followed similar paths and similar genres – between them, they made some
of the most memorable Italian gothic films of the 1960s, and if it was Bava
who initially made an icon of Barbara Steele, Margheriti would direct her
on one more occasion than Bava. Both brought certain artisanal skills to
their filmmaking and specialized in effects work. Margheriti would work
in a broader range of genres than Bava, looking less of a specialist in any
particular genre than someone happy to ride whichever *filone* came along,
from jungle adventure to martial arts. Perhaps a more versatile navigator
of Serie B cinema than Bava, and a capable, intermittently inspired director,
Margheriti's multi-camera production techniques lead to him often being
cast as less of a stylist and more obviously a journeyman.

Terence Fisher, not unlike Bava, was a self-effacing industry professional
with little interest in being seen as an auteur – he was, he insisted, 'only a
working director' (quoted by Hutchings 2001: 11). Fisher directed twenty-
four films before *The Curse of Frankenstein* (1957), but subsequently
became a horror specialist. There is nothing to suggest that personal choice
came into this – Fisher was working at a studio which began to specialize
in horror, albeit not exclusively, and he had directed their first two successes
in the genre. Fisher and Bava are now generally seen as horror directors,
even if that only accounts for part of their output (and Fisher directed
substantially more films than Bava did overall). Unlike Fisher, however,
Bava gives the impression of having chosen the genre at least as much as
it chose him – 'horror is my entertainment', he told *L'europeo* on the set of
Diabolik (Tornabuoni 1967: 57), a film he regarded as merely work. The
story goes that *La maschera del demonio* was Bava's reward for saving other
productions, but while Galatea put more resources into, and enjoyed greater
success with, the peplum, they were dabbling in horror in a speculative way
even before they formed the alliance with AIP that would make the genre
more profitable as an export. They had already produced *Caltiki, il mostro
immortale* and distributed *Il mulino delle donne di pietra*, alongside Bava's
debut, the most striking Italian horror film of 1960.

There has never been a critical consensus on Fisher's status as an auteur
because his most celebrated films were all made at the same studio, a large
number of them written by the same people and with a relatively stable
production team. A number of French critics, particularly those at *Midi-
Minuit Fantastique* who coined 'Fisherienne' as an adjective, regarded him
as one, while David Pirie discerned in Fisher 'a recognisable and coherent
universe' in his influential book on British horror cinema *A Heritage of
Horror* (2009: 67), but that is a less fashionable view of him now. Peter
Hutchings is more cautious in his monograph on Fisher, sensitively attuned
to how his films were shaped by different production contexts, sometimes
even at the same studio. 'Fisher' is often a way of talking about Hammer

more generally, the studio as auteur. Both directors' careers underwent a shift in direction and gear as the result of a genre 'boom', but a boom in different genres. Bava at Hammer is a more fanciful 'What if' than the ones proposed earlier, and one in which it is likely that the maverick stylist would have been expected to conform to a studio style. It is widely taken as read that while Freda's I vampiri predated Hammer gothic by a few months, Fisher's Dracula (1958) was the initial trigger for a modest filone of Italian horror films, several of them vampire films – by contrast, Hammer's Frankenstein films seem to have left no mark on Italian horror. The difference between Hammer and Bava, who was not necessarily 'typical' of Italian horror if anyone was, is often perceived in national-cultural terms – the sensation and sobriety of the Brits versus the excess and delirious illogicality of the Italians. And certainly, there are differences – Hammer's horror films are more writerly and actorly, solidly (if sometimes mechanically) constructed, with Fisher and others adhering to the script faithfully, whereas the Bava narrative has him overcoming weak scripts and either indifferent actors or actors left adrift by a director more interested in his camera and his tricks. But both British and Italian horror films were positioning themselves in the international market in different ways, rather than necessarily exhibiting some innate national character. Ultimately, Fisher and Bava present different versions of the director as working professional adapting to particular working contexts and commercial requirements as well as finding themselves, for better or worse, genre specialists.

Roger Corman's directorial career also connects him to a company with a strong public identity – AIP, the kings of the drive-in and the budget double-bill. But Gary Martin (1985: 3) reminds us that Corman was not an 'AIP director' in the way that Fisher was a 'Hammer director'. Rather, he was an independent producer and director, a 'one-man studio system' (Doherty 1988: 155) whose films were distributed by AIP and others. If Fisher's reputation as auteur is compromised by his association with Hammer, Corman's reputation as director is sometimes overshadowed by his subsequent reputation as a producer, particularly as someone who discovered filmmaking talents whose achievements would go beyond his own. Hammer and Fisher might have been the initial trigger for Italian gothic horror, but it would not be surprising if one were to learn that Bava never saw a Hammer film. Whether he ever saw a Corman-Poe film is open to conjecture, too – Bava seems to have regarded cinema-going as a busman's holiday – but there is a stronger connection both through AIP's involvement in several productions and because The Pit and the Pendulum (1961), often seen as the trigger for a second Italian gothic cycle, seems to have been a more tangible influence on a necro-morbid strain of Italian gothic that includes La frusta e il corpo and Freda's L'orribile segreto del Dr Hichcock/The Horrible Dr Hichcock (1962). Where Hammer and Fisher made horror films that were forward-moving and eventful, Corman's Poe films are leisurely, often conspicuously padded as short stories were stretched to feature-length, and *atmospheric,* that adjective so often applied to Bava. Narrative is secondary to atmosphere in both Bava's gothics and Corman's Poe films, but this takes different forms. Corman's films are actorly and character (and star-) driven, impossible to imagine without Vincent Price – 'atmosphere' functions as an expression of character, where it can often be an end in itself in Bava's films. The two directors share some production techniques – Evert Jan Van Leeuwen's phrase 'matte romanticism' (2019: 48) seems as applicable to Bava as it is to the Poe films. The vast torture chamber in *Pit and the Pendulum* and the underground hideout in *Diabolik* both fashion a great deal out of very little.

Bava and Corman share something else – an apparent tension between what often looks like a genuine artistic impulse and a pride in getting things done as quickly and cheaply as possible. Corman, at least publicly, took himself more seriously than either Bava or Fisher, with interviews that cited Freud, intellectualized about adapting Poe and rationalized his production techniques as being aesthetically suited to exploring the unconscious. Then there are *Masque of the Red Death*'s nods to Ingmar Bergman and *The Seventh Seal.* But while one could quickly become familiar with recycled sets at Bray Studios or Cinecittà, neither Hammer nor Bava recycled actual footage as shamelessly as Corman did even in some of his best films. On the DVD commentary for *The Tomb of Ligeia* (1964), Corman congratulates himself on not ending with a burning house (and the same recycled footage) yet again during the climax before realizing that he had in fact done precisely that. According to Robert Towne, 'he felt that if he didn't do it quickly he did it wrong' (quoted by Morris 1985: 5). Bava's haste or impatience manifests itself differently – the increasing omnipresence of the zoom, for example – but in both cases, a cinema of macabre atmospheres co-exists with a cinema of expediency.

According to Maitland McDonagh in her book on Dario Argento, Bava's films 'lack something' in comparison with the 'mature' work of the younger director often seen as succeeding or even superseding him (1991: 25). This is a familiar reputation-building strategy – sometimes one artistic reputation must be built up at the expense of another, and there is the matter of Bava's supposed 'influence' on Argento to be dealt with and exorcised. The reputations of these two filmmakers have long been connected, with Argento often prickly when questioned about the influence of *La ragazza che sapeva troppo* on his debut *L'uccello dalle piume di cristallo/The Bird with the Crystal Plumage* (1970) or Bava's non-naturalistic coloured lighting in 6 *donne per l'assassino* on the look of *Suspiria* (1976).[5] It is tempting, if probably only half true, to suggest that the 'something' McDonagh perceives as lacking in this comparison is a combination of money and privilege. While the two filmmakers are connected via genre, some shared stylistic characteristics and by an actual professional connection, they occupied very different positions in the industry – significantly, on the one occasion that Bava worked with Argento, he worked *for* him, contributing effects to *Inferno* (1980), while Lamberto Bava went from being his father's assistant director to being Argento's, as well as directing *Dèmoni* (1985) and *Dèmoni 2* (1986) for Argento's production company DACFILM. Both directors came to cinema via their respective families, but Argento's father Salvatore was a producer with influential connections – when Goffredo Lombardo, head of Titanus, wanted to remove the inexperienced Dario from *L'uccello dalle piume di cristallo,* Salvatore intervened on his son's behalf. *La famiglia Bava* were artisans, work-for-hire film workers with little power or influence – as a director, Bava had much in common with other *filone* directors who needed to work flexibly and quickly. Argento took what was then the most fashionable route into cinema – he had been film critic for the left-wing Rome newspaper *Paese sera* and his films would display an eclectic cinephilia, referencing both classic Hollywood thrillers and contemporary auteur cinema. Bava would cheerfully tell journalists that 'all cinema is made for infantile brains' (Tornabuoni 1967: 28), while Argento positioned himself knowingly as an auteur figure from the start, both in interviews and by placing certain markers of distinction in his films (the nods to Antonioni, particularly in *L'uccello dalle piume di cristallo* and *Profondo rosso/Deep Red,* the *flaneur*-like protagonists of his early thrillers, a growing self-referentiality). Argento was also a screenwriter prior to his directorial debut, and most of his films have been initiated by him and based on original ideas from Argento himself. Rather like Sergio Leone, Argento initiated a *filone* but subsequently stood at a remove from *filone* cinema. However, if Argento was above formulas and trends – or at least encouraged audiences to see him as such – one of the factors in his later decline might have been the need to conform to his own authorial legend, to continue to make 'Dario Argento films', rather than diversifying in the way that *filone* directors were forced to do. Any critical claims for Bava have to be qualified by the material conditions that shaped his films, but while there is an inevitable inconsistency in his output from the mid-1960s and some early critics felt that he never lived up to the promise of *La maschera del demonio,* his career is rarely framed as one of decline in the way that Argento's post-1980s output often is. And yet, Argento's perceived decline as a filmmaker does not seem to have compromised the reputation of his earlier films. Russ Hunter observes an 'entrenchment' of his reputation in the 1990s as his films appeared on DVD (2010: 67), following what he calls a 'cult insulation trajectory, which posits that his earlier work – and labelling as a cult director – has somehow acted to insulate him from being "dropped" as an object of critical attention and fascination' (ibid.: 71). If anything, his decline made it easier to build an Argento 'canon', distinguishing between 'major' and 'minor' works (ibid.: 69). While distinctions are clearly often made between 'major' and 'minor' Bava, they are framed less around 'early' and 'late' films than around genre – it is hard to think of a horror film or thriller directed by Bava that has not had a critical case made for it at some point. It has become almost impossible to talk about Argento or Bava without at least some reference to the other – they are the two pre-eminent figures in the Italian horror and suspense-thriller film. But they present two rather different cases in reputation and canon-building, a topic that I shall return to later in the book. How have they come to be seen as almost on level terms – the two canonical names in Italian horror-thriller cinema – given their rather different career trajectories and positions of power? One factor might be that, purely as a director, Bava's output is relatively small, easier to map as a canon than that of comparable *filone* directors, with horror acting as a thread of generic coherence (and visual coherence by allowing Bava to repeat various stylistic signatures).

In addition to examining Bava's films in their own right, this book also uses them as a way of exploring a broader set of issues, including authorship, genre, film style, reputation and canon-building. This is also a book about cinephilia and its relationship to cult appreciation, as the fascination with someone like Bava mutates over time. Sometimes the issues raised are more specific to him, but many are broader in their application to so-called journeyman filmmakers, cycles of generic cinema and the making and remaking of cult reputations and canons. Chapter 2 examines issues of authorship. As the title of Peter Hutchings's 2016 essay on Bava suggests, his films are seen as being sufficiently distinctive to give rise to an adjective, 'Bavaesque'. This might appear to push us towards auteurism – and, indeed, Bava has often been approached as an auteur, albeit with some qualifications – but there are other ways of approaching a filmmaker's career, even in the case of as distinctive figure as Bava. Another word recurs in discussions of Bava, particularly in Italian accounts – artisan, a word sometimes used to distinguish him from fully fledged auteur directors. Bava's standing as artisan and/or auteur raises questions of cultural value, while the different kinds of creative labour carried out by Bava, as well as the often radically different cuts of his films, pose the question of what exactly constitutes a 'Mario Bava film'.

Chapters 3 and 4 both focus on matters of genre. Bava's career was largely driven by generic cycles in the Italian cinema of the 1960s and 1970s, although mapping his films onto particular genres is not always as clear as it might first seem. Bava, then, is a fruitful case study in how genre operates both industrially and discursively, as well as its role in organizing an authorial canon. Chapter 3 examines three genres. The first is the peplum or mythological/historical adventure film, Italian cinema's first fully fledged post-war *filone,* high in volume and box-office success but lower in cult capital than horror or the Italian style thriller. Moreover, Bava's work on the peplum largely consisted of photography and effects work or fixing unfinished projects, drawing attention to his status as artisan. The second, horror, is both the genre most closely associated with Bava (along with the thriller or *giallo*) and one smaller in output, less popular with Italian audiences than foreign ones, but higher in cult capital. This section locates the films within contemporaneous cycles of production, both in Italy and elsewhere. The third genre is a problematic one for Bava – the Western, usually seen as a genre to which his talents were poorly suited. Chapter 4 confines itself to a single cycle or genre. Bava is often claimed as the 'pioneer' of a particular kind of Italian thriller, and the *giallo* or *giallo all'italiana* is a category that raises many interesting issues around the discursive construction of genre. What do we mean when we categorize this or that Bava film as a *giallo*? What sort of cult capital is embedded in the English-language usage of the term? Is it a brand (as it originated), a genre, a collection of loosely linked film cycles or a term whose 'generic function' (Mittell 2004: 15) is a cult canon-building one?

Chapter 5 turns to matters of film style, which loom large in the cult of Italian Serie B cinema, where 'excessive' uses of colour, camera movement, music and sound are mobilized against the aesthetics of the 'mainstream'. For those not fully convinced by Bava, style was sometimes his saving grace, while others viewed it less kindly. Setting aside matters of textual interpretation, how do these films actually work? What emerges out of the tension between 'high style' and material constraints? The chapter draws on a poetics approach to provide a detailed account of the 'Bava style', which can be seen as a combination of trademark visual signatures (coloured gels, spot lighting, mobile camera, glass mattes) and practices more widely used in low-budget *filone* cinema (the crash zoom, for example, one of Bava's more contentious stylistic choices).

Chapter 6 examines processes of reputation- and canon-building, particularly as they develop in different national and critical contexts, and over time. It takes Bava as a cross-cultural case study in historical reception and focuses on three sites of critical reception. The first is Italy, Bava's home country, where he is often perceived to have been critically neglected. For some time, Italian film historians prioritized neorealism and *cinema d'autore* at the expense of genre cinema, while the development of cult film studies in recent years has broadened the scope of the study of Italian cinema to include horror films, thrillers, science fiction and other popular film cycles. But just how neglected was Bava? At what point did Italian film critics acknowledge that there was such a thing as a 'Mario Bava film'? And how did they respond to his developing reputation elsewhere? The second site of reception is France, often seen to be more critically receptive in certain film journals to horror and fantasy cinema. France was also where the auteurist appreciation of commercial cinema originated, its critics playing an important role in the reputation-building of Hitchcock and other Hollywood directors. The first specialist film journal devoted to fantasy, science fiction and horror, *Midi-Minuit Fantastique*, was published in France from the mid-1960s to the early 1970s, and the first full-length book on Bava was a French language one. But was there a critical consensus amongst French critics regarding Bava, and what was his standing amongst directors making similar kinds of films? Thirdly, the chapter examines English-language reviews of Bava's films, including the American trade press and British specialist film journals such as *Films and Filming* and *Monthly Film Bulletin*, in which Bava was identified as a figure of interest. It also traces the subsequent cultification of Bava through retrospectives, the re-mediation and reissuing of his films and the writing of Tim Lucas and other fan-scholars.

Notes

1   Monicelli's episode *Renzo e Luciana* was removed from the anthology film
      Boccaccio 70 (1962) outside Italy, so that the remaining film was built on
      three internationally recognized auteur brands, Fellini, Visconti and De Sica.
      The current UK Blu-ray/DVD release restores the episode but its packaging
      still gives greater emphasis to the other three directors.
2   The *Aurum Encyclopedia* does not credit individual reviewers, but this entry
      reads most like Paul Willemen, credited along with Tom Milne as one of the
      book's two main authors.
3   *Carosello* was a half hour format for screening adverts on RAI that grouped
      together short items of around 110 seconds into a prime-time TV programme.
      Individual *caroselli* could only mention the product at the beginning and the
      end, the emphasis placed on entertainment (animation, children's stories, pop
      stars such as Mina) – in the early 1960s, it was the most popular show on
      Italian TV (Ginsborg 1990: 240–1).
4   Or a less happy one, like Tourneur.
5   Argento finally admitted to at least the former in his autobiography *Paura/Fear*
      (2019: 73), struck by Bava's use of the Coppedè district in Rome.

2

Artisan or auteur/artisan as auteur – Bava and authorship

Bava died on 25 April 1980. His last solo directorial credit was *Shock* (1977) – or *Schock (Transfert Suspense Hypnos)*, as it was named on some publicity materials – parts of which were directed by Lamberto, who would be credited as co-director of *La venere d'ille* in 1978. His final (uncredited) work – some trickery involving mirrors and a Mother of Darkness – was on Argento's *Inferno*. The headline of his obituary in *Corriere della sera* four days after his death declared him 'l'artigiano del cinema horror', using the foreign word for a genre rarely seen to fully belong in Italian cinema.[1] But 'artisan' is the word I want to focus on here because it recurs particularly in Italian writing about Bava. 'In other people's eyes, I'm kind of the last artisan', he told Ornella Volta in an interview for *Positif* (Volta 1972: 46). The word appears three times in the obituary, including the headline, but there is a subtle shift between different uses of the term – an appreciation of his technical skills but also a sense that he was little more than a craftsman. A distinction is made between his work as *artigiano* – his contributions to films by Rossellini, Steno, Monicelli, Walsh and Argento[2] – and his 'produzione d'autore', the films he directed himself. However, there is a strong impression that the word 'auteur' is not being used to suggest that he should be seen as part of *cinema d'autore*, the more prestigious and serious authored cinema. Even as nominal *autore,* he remains primarily an *artigiano* – 'the biggest part of (his films') merit was technical-artisanal', concludes the author of the obituary, summing Bava up as 'a talent perhaps limited but decidedly orientated, in the margins of storytelling, to a cinema nourished only by cinema-cinema' (Po 1980: 20). The phrase 'cinema-cinema' translates roughly as 'proper cinema', equivalent to the kind of 'pure cinema' once extolled by Hitchcock – an affective cinema fashioned by specifically cinematic means. Such a cinema can be celebrated for its aestheticism and affectivity – as Bava's films often are now – but can also be seen to prioritize such heightened sensations over substance, which is what seems to be implied here.

'Artisan' then carries two sets of meanings in relation to Bava. On the one hand, there is his craftmanship, his facility with the camera and special effects. When Bava was invited onto the TV show *L'ospite della due* in 1975, it was in the context of a discussion about special effects that also featured Carlo Rambaldi. When Simone Venturini calls him 'questo grande artigiano' (2001: 137), it is to stress the value of his creative labour within a particular industrial context – Galatea – and the importance of his collaborators, some of them also great artisans, as well as the guiding hand of production manager Massimo De Rita, who oversaw Bava's films at the studio. Bava the great artisan is not incompatible with Bava the auteur – Lucas goes into some detail about his various tricks and effects, which play no small part in the Bava cult. As Ruddell and Ward observe, the English word 'craft' can be extended into the adjective 'crafty', which 'suggests misdirection or deception':

> This connects us to a rich history of magic, witchcraft, sleight of hand and prestidigitation. If someone is being "crafty", then, they are not only "crafting" something, they are doing so with a view to deceiving or misdirecting.
>
> (2019: 1)

Similarly, in Italian, there is the word 'trucco', which means trick, but is also the word for make-up, the two linked by the implication of deception. Bava would combine both senses of the word in the ageing/deterioration effects used in *I vampiri, Caltiki, il mostro immortale* and *La maschera del demonio*, achieved through the same combination of make-up and lighting that had been used in transformation scenes in the 1931 *Doctor Jekyll and Mister Hyde*. 'The cinema is all a trick', he declared on *L'ospite della due* in 1975, often giving the impression that he thought it was little more than that. He was nothing if not a *crafty* filmmaker in all the senses given by Ruddell and Ward – we do not need to look far for the magic and witchcraft, from Princess Asa through to Baron Blood's nemesis, Elisabeth Hollë. In contemporary discourse, older craft skills are sometimes positioned against the digital (Ruddell and Ward 2019: 9), and Bava's *trucchi* – like those of Ray Harryhausen – can be similarly mobilized as 'old' crafts (several of them already old when he used them) against the contemporary reign of CGI, which would undoubtedly now provide *Diabolik* with a more digitally 'real' underground hideout but without the magic often discerned in the artisan's on-set ingenuity. There is a definite romance in this picture of Bava practising the crafty secrets of *la famiglia Bava*, cooked up in the family workshop, or re-staging effects that often dated back to silent cinema. Bava's was in many respects a cinema of problem-solving, of making a virtue of limited resources and technologies.

But then there is the other sense of the word 'artisan', that which separates the 'mere' craftsman from the artist or auteur. In this sense, it is synonymous with the notion of the 'journeyman' filmmaker, who *works* – competently or even skilfully – without managing to fashion an artistic identity. This is sometimes implicit, or even explicit, in the distinction between Bava the cinematographer (highly skilled and even distinctive) and Bava the director, who is not quite the finished article. A review of *Evil Eye* in the British *Monthly Film Bulletin* judges that Bava was 'always a better cameraman than director' (Anon. 1965b: 58), contrasting him with Riccardo Freda, a more fully formed – and admittedly much more experienced – director. Robin Wood, on the other hand, dismissed *Il rosso segno della follia/Hatchet for the Honeymoon* (completed in 1969 and released in Italy in 1970), released in the UK as *Blood Brides*, as a mere cameraman's film:

> Mario Bava's claim to attention arises principally from the fact that, since he usually photographs as well as directs his films, they are very consciously conceived in terms of the potentialities of the camera and as a result are, in a somewhat crude sense, 'cinematic'... The creation of elaborate effects through camera movement, stylised colour, focus distortion and the use of varied lenses is, however, no guarantee of quality; and the effects in *Blood Brides* appear merely self-conscious and self-indulgent.
>
> (1973: 29)

Carlos Clarens was most unkind of all, judging most of Bava's output as proof 'that if bad directors usually end up as photographers, the reverse of this axiom is just as valid and true' (1971: 230). Bava's status as cinematographer both amplifies his distinctiveness as a director and undercuts it by sometimes being perceived to be a substitute for directorial skill, as implied in Ubaldo Terzano's alleged jibe that their films together had two DPs but no actual director. Luc Moullet, a sympathetic critic, nevertheless attributes Bava's lack of interest in actors and characters to 'a rather common attitude on the part of a cinematographer', whereby the actor was 'the cinematographer's rival for the director's and his collaborator's interest' (1994/1997: 51).[3]

In the same issue of *Monthly Film Bulletin* that Robin Wood reviewed *Il rosso segno della follia*, he also reviewed (more positively) the film paired with it on a double-bill in the UK, the British *Creeping Flesh* (1973), which was also made by a DP-turned-director, Freddie Francis. Bava and Francis were making not dissimilar films during roughly the same period – *The Psychopath* (1965), in particular, looks like something that Bava might have made, with its sinister dolls and serial murders, and films such as *The Skull* (1965) and *Dracula Has Risen from the Grave* (1968) make use of colour filters and gels not unlike some of the effects in Bava's films, but without cohering into what might have been seen as a recognizable visual style. Francis's work as a DP was distinguished – more so than Bava's, in fact – ranging from *Saturday Night and Sunday Morning* (1960) and *The Innocents* (1961) to *The Elephant Man* (1980) and *The French Lieutenant's Woman* (1981), prestigious projects for which he was much in demand. But while there have been smatterings of critical interest in his work as a horror director (including from *Midi-Minuit Fantastique*), he is often regarded as a second-division filmmaker in British horror, particularly compared with Terence Fisher – 'variable' is how David Pirie sums up his horror output, while emphasizing Francis's lack of interest in the genre (2009: 106, 88). Francis made some interesting films, no doubt, but few commentators have been inclined to attribute their interesting qualities to him. Moreover, Francis, in common with Bava and Karl Freund amongst others, reinforces the impression that former DPs are thought to be well suited to directing horror – at least able to orchestrate atmospheric scenes and striking visuals, if nothing else.[4]

The distinction between art and craft, artist and artisan, carries less force than it did, but, as Larry Shiner puts it, 'hangs on in faded glory despite a century and a half of trying to overcome it' (2001: 289). But as Shiner demonstrates in his book *The Invention of Art,* that separation – the 'Great Division', he calls it – was already a relatively modern one, not fully institutionalized until the eighteenth century. 'Art', deriving from the Latin *ars* and the Greek *techne,* referred to 'the human ability to make and perform' (ibid.: 19) and the words 'artist' and 'artisan' were used interchangeably – 'the ideal qualities desired in an artisan/artist in the old system combined genius and rule, inspiration and facility, innovation and imitation, freedom and service' (ibid.: 111). The Great Division, created by such factors as the shift from patronage to an art market that fostered the aura of artistic 'independence', split these various qualities apart – the new category of *beaux-arts* or fine arts inherited all the elevated qualities, while 'the former virtues of rule, skill, imitation, invention, and service were gradually turned into reproaches if not vices' (ibid.: 115). Bava was fond of telling a childhood story, possibly apocryphal, of his father slapping him when he showed him a drawing of his own that he had signed – only real artists had the privilege of signing their work, he was told. The Bavas, for all their skill and invention, practised a trade, not an art.

Subsequently, the art/craft distinction was applied within modern mediums, such as that between art cinema and commercial cinema, 'a distinction between that which is understood to be *serious, substantial* and *important,* and that which is accorded the status of the *unserious,* the *insubstantial* or the *trivial*' (King 2019: 35). Auteurism would simultaneously complicate that line and reinforce it by re-casting directors within mainstream commercial cinema as serious artists. Lucas's book on

Bava provides a very detailed picture of the filmmaker both as an artisan in the sense of craft skills and as someone who had to negotiate his way through industrial constraints and an unpredictable working environment – he rarely turned work down because it was not always clear when or if it would be offered again. But he also bids for him to be seen as an auteur in the classic sense, which involves mobilizing certain markers of distinction. Bava's less-than-serious attitude towards his own work must be presented as a façade, just as Hitchcock's playful public persona had to be explained away by his original auteurist supporters. 'By diverting serious attention from his work, Bava was spared the embarrassment of admitting that he had been secretly expressing himself through (his films) all along' (Lucas 2007: 16). As this suggests, Bava's films, or at least some of them, are 'personal', 'challenging', *Ecologia del delitto* an 'audacious' and 'prophetic' work of art (ibid.: 850). All of this is arguable, of course, but it also operates within the terms of the art/craft distinction – Bava is *more than* an artisan, more than his coloured gels, his atmospheric lighting, his glass matte shots and eccentric camera movements, his artfully staged shock sequences. He is a rule-breaker, not a rule-follower, an innovator, even a *genius*. Pezzotta, on the other hand, is sceptical of auteurist claims for Bava, finding such analysis not only unconvincing but 'often pompous and a little ridiculous' (2013: 14). Rather than explain it away, he takes Bava's contempt for his material at face value – his disinterest, he suggests, would be evident even without those dismissive interviews, so contemptuous of any critic (particularly if they were French) unwise enough to take him seriously. Uninterested in narrative and character (a more familiar caveat about Bava), he puts maximum commitment and effort into the 'wrong' sequences 'which at the end are the most beautiful' (ibid.: 17). And yet, while Pezzotta steers closer to Bava-as-artisan – albeit an interesting and unpredictable one – this also makes him sound like an auteur of sorts, not the personal, compulsive artist that Lucas portrays, but a maverick whose experimentation arises out of boredom and disbelief that he has been left in charge of all the moviemaking toys.

Peter Hutchings discerns a 'key assumption' in auteurist writing, 'that all directors... are more or less the same in terms of the industrial function they perform' (2001: 25). The most obvious difference is between the arthouse director, whose freedom has its own economic limits (as does that of most 'independent' artists) but who plays a central role in initiating and shaping a film throughout its production and will likely approve its final cut, and the work-for-hire director who is operating within stricter parameters. But even within commercial cinema, there are varying degrees of creative control enjoyed by directors – the difference between the producer-director and the contract or work-for-hire director, or the difference between Bava and Argento discussed in the previous chapter. In this respect, it might be more useful to talk about varying degrees of creative agency, rather than the more polarized distinction between auteur and journeyman, or the once popular term *metteur-en-scene*, 'a talented director at the mercy of his script' (Buscombe 1981: 24). Director Florestano Vancini said of the Western *I lunghi giorni della vendetta/Days of Vengeance* (1967), 'I didn't make it in the real sense. I'm not responsible for it as its author, but rather in the sense of a professional service that was asked of me and which I supplied' (quoted by Wagstaff 2014: 151). A large part of Bava's career consisted of providing a 'professional service', but if he is not, as Pezzotta suggests, fully convincing as an auteur, nor does he fall easily into the category of journeyman. While the 'Bavaesque' or the 'Bavian' don't carry the same adjectival force as the 'Hitchcockian' or the 'Felliniesque', the fact that these descriptive terms exist suggests that *something* made at least some of his films stand out, even if Bava the cinematographer could not be easily separated from Bava the director (and perhaps cannot, or should not, be).

Bava operated with varying degrees of creative agency at various points in his career, from Galatea allowing him to play to his strengths and Alfredo Leone coming to regret giving him *carte blanche* on *Lisa e il diavolo* to being a replacement for another director at some stage during production and just having to get the job done, which happened more than once with varying results. A number of Bava films were initiated by him and shaped by him in pre-production, including script input, even if 'director's cut' was not a privilege he was likely to enjoy – as we shall see, a variety of cuts was closer to the norm. But the films initiated by Bava and those he took on as a jobbing director are not always as easy to tell apart as, say, the difference between *Lisa e il diavolo* and *Roy Colt e Winchester Jack* (1970). *La frusta e il corpo* is one of the director's most 'Bavaesque' films – perverse, provocative (it encountered considerable censorship problems, including prosecution and seizure in Italy), vibrant and colourful, 'the last word in over-ripe Gothic romance' (Rigby 2016: 130). But it started life as producers Ugo Guerra and Elio Scardamaglia asking Ernesto Gastaldi to write something along the lines of Corman's *Pit and the Pendulum* (ibid.: 130). Lucas, regardless of his investment in Bava-as-auteur, takes Gastaldi as the film's 'true auteur' (2007: 528). Certainly, Gastaldi had a track record with this sort of overheated sado-gothic – he had written the necrophilia-themed *L'orribile segreto del Dr Hichcock*, directed by Riccardo Freda the previous year, and similar themes would surface in 1970s thrillers such as *Lo strano vizio della Signora Wardh/The Strange Vice of Mrs Wardh* (1971). Whether this makes him an auteur or someone who knew how to wring multiple variations out of the same theme is another matter, but Gastaldi is certainly an important figure in Italian genre cinema. Gastaldi did not like what Bava did with the film, envisaging a dark psychological thriller more like *Les Diaboliques* – instead, 'Bava saw it as a baroque and decadent drama, and emphasised such tones beyond belief' (Gastaldi quoted by Curti 2015a: location 2807). In other words, Bava made what we now think of as a 'Mario Bava film' (even while working under a pseudonym as John M. Old). Meanwhile, *Terrore nello spazio* looks like something thrown together by Fulvio Lucisano, and further complicated by the involvement of AIP, without anyone asking whether they had the resources to do it justice, only for Bava at his *craftiest* to turn it into something worth seeing with the judicious use of dry ice, a few rocks and his signature lighting, colour and camera tricks. But Bava initiated the project before bringing it to Lucisano, obtained the rights to Renato Pestriniero's short story 'Una notte di 21 ore' (One 21-hour night) and sent detailed notes on the treatment during its development (Lucas 2007: 605–7). The extent to which he remained in control of it during production – perhaps in need of a Massimo De Rita to oversee it – is less clear, but it remains one of his most well-loved films.

Bava worked under a pseudonym several times – as John Foam (*Caltiki, il mostro immortale*), John M. Old (*La frusta e il corpo, La strada per Forte Alamo*) and John Hold (*I coltelli del vendicatore*) – generally at the behest of producers and much less frequently than Riccardo Freda/Robert Hampton or Antonio Margheriti/Anthony M. Dawson.[5] But he only asked to have his name taken off one film, *La casa dell'esorcismo*, even if he subsequently changed his mind. He is the credited director of the Italian version, but the American release identifies 'Mickey Lion' as director. The tangled relationship between *Lisa e il diavolo* and *La casa dell'esorcismo* will be explored in greater detail later in this chapter, but it is worth pausing over the question of credits. This refusal of authorship for one film seems to suggest that Bava felt at least a degree of ownership of most of his films, and *Lisa* in particular, which does give the impression of a certain level of investment in the film on his part, even if it is less likely that he saw producer Alfredo Leone as having painted a 'moustache on his Mona Lisa' (Lucas 2007: 8). Directors generally have their names taken off films to protect their reputations and put them in authorial quarantine lest they tarnish their developing canon, which sits incongruously with Bava's avowed lack of interest in his own *oeuvre*. His change of heart might suggest that he subsequently felt there was enough of *Lisa* in *La casa* for him to feel that it was sufficiently 'his', and he evidently directed at least some of the new footage (Lucas 2007: 929–32). There are, of course, other possible explanations. His falling out with Leone over the new footage could mean that removing his name was a simple fit of pique and that subsequently putting it back was a conciliatory gesture. Moreover, Bava was uncomfortable with the nature as much as the quality of the new footage (some of which was overseen by his own son), finding it blasphemous and disgusting. The initial refusal of authorship might be interpreted as either a matter of protecting an authorial legacy, albeit one that he claimed not to care about, or (more conservatively) just not wishing to be associated with the profanity and projectile vomiting and the blatant copying of other demonic possession films. Either way, it continues to pose the question of whether it constitutes a 'Mario Bava film'.

But what is a 'Mario Bava film'? 'Even when an individual has been accepted as an author', wrote Michel Foucault in his seminal essay 'What is an Author?' (1984: 103), 'we must still ask whether everything that he wrote, said, or left behind is part of his work'. Such a question is magnified by someone like Bava, making contributions large and small to a huge number of films, whereas his directorial output is a more manageable corpus and includes several films that are usually passed over unless one is writing a full-length book that commits to tackling his output film-by-film. Only Lucas has set out to cover 'the millions of traces left by someone after his death' (Foucault 1984: 104) with regards to Bava. Some of these traces are as phantasmatic as the ghostly hand at the window in *Operazione paura/ Kill Baby... Kill!* (1966) – Lucas's book frequently detours into what he calls Bava's 'Secret Filmography', films which he *probably* or *might have* worked on. Mario Bava's filmography is a complicated one, even in its more or less accepted versions (which already tend to include films for which he was not credited). The following factors come into play when determining the different levels of creative agency exercised by Bava in 'his' films:

1. Variations in film credits, sometimes adjusted for quota purposes or not adjusted to reflect those films that Bava 'rescued' (or might have directed large parts of). Even films on which Bava is credited as director can send out confusing messages, particularly across different release versions. The Italian releases of *Ester e il re/Esther and the King* (1960) and *La meraviglie di Aladino/The Wonders of Aladdin* (1961), for example, are credited as films 'by' Raoul Walsh and Henry Levin respectively, but 'directed' by Bava, while the English-language releases solely credit Walsh and Levin as directors.[6] These credits might reflect a degree of delegation or the misleading elevation of Second Unit work – Venturini claims that Bava directed a good deal of *Ester e il re* (2001: 55), possibly for linguistic as well as technical reasons, but that does not seem to have been the case with *La meraviglie di Aladino*. Ultimately such conflicting information might tell us more about the uncertain national identity of 'Hollywood *sul Tevere*' than they suggest that Bava should in any way be seen as their 'real' director.

2. The blurring of different kinds of creative labour that Bava contributed to films – camera operator, director of photography, effects and a tendency to slide across those roles as well as combining them. Accounts of Bava's career make different decisions about where to mark off his authored work. Pezzotta's filmography, for example, combines 'Official Direction and Principal Collaborations' into a single category, rather than isolate those he directed, officially or otherwise (2013: 140).

Thus, *I vampiri* and *Le fatiche di Ercole* often become 'Mario Bava films', at least to a degree, while the cover of the 2017 Arrow blu-ray of *Caltiki, il mostro immortale* calls it as 'A Film by Riccardo Freda and Mario Bava', neither of whose names appear on any version of the film except pseudonymously.

3. Bava the 'rescuer' of problem films and his close association with two other directors Riccardo Freda (two of whose films he completed) and Pietro Francisci, director of the first two Hercules films. These two directors occupy rather different positions in cinephilia and cult appreciation. While he has arguably been overshadowed by Bava, easier to situate as an auteur figure because of his generic predispositions and distinctive visual style – Freda was largely regarded as the better director in the 1960s, and his horror films and thrillers in particular still attract a cult following. What we know of the production of *I vampiri* (see Lucas 2007 and Curti 2015a) suggests that it would have been a much more interesting film if Freda had completed it – a lost subplot involving a severed head being re-attached to a reanimated body can be glimpsed in the stitch marks on actor Paul Mueller's neck. If it is easier to see Bava's touch than Freda's in parts of the film – in the ageing of Gianna Maria Canale and the lighting of gothic crypts and secret laboratories – that is partly because Freda might once have been a prime candidate for *metteur-en-scene* status, able to change style across a range of genres and subjects. Similarly, to see *Caltiki* as a Bava film, even if he shot most of it, is to be drawn towards the artisanal – the ingenious effects, including a variation on the 'ageing' effect as one victim of the titular *mostro* is drained in its deadly grasp. Francisci, on the other hand, while a very capable and experienced industry professional, was a less critically celebrated peplum director than someone like Vittorio Cottafavi. Lucas portrays Francisci as one of the people reluctant to give Bava the credit he deserved for his input into the Hercules films – a view evidently shared by Freda (Lucas 2007: 237). Certainly, the 'Bava touch' now seems discernible in the lighting, matte effects and use of coloured gels, even if we probably need to be careful about promoting him to co-director of the film. After all, it is by no means unusual for directors to be credited with visual touches that should be attributed to their DPs.

4. Bava the auteur and Bava the work for hire. As we have seen, these two categories are not so easily separated, but then there are those films where the jobbing Bava is visibly supplying a professional service in a genre that is not congenial to his talents. It is easy enough to write about *6 donne per l'assassino* or even *Diabolik* (a

work-for-hire film, but on a higher level than usual), but what are we to do with *Roy Colt e Winchester Jack* or *Quante volte... quella notte/Four Times That Night?* Pezzotta calls these films 'Bava meno "Bava"' (2007: 99) – the less Bava-like Bavas. The auteurist is fated to trip over these films – perhaps trying to find some tiny glimmer of inspiration and redemption, ignoring them or just getting past them as painlessly as possible – and no one to my knowledge has yet attempted a sustained re-evaluation of them. But they might have more to tell us about Bava the artisan, always 'negotiating or surrendering his freedom' (ibid.: 102) to some degree.

5. Bava films that exist in different versions, sometimes so different that it is not clear that they are the same film. This is the most substantial and interesting issue raised by Bava's filmography. It posed a particular problem for Bava scholarship that was reliant on film prints, and VHS tapes would partly inherit the problem (although *Lisa e il diavolo* and *Mask of Satan,* Galatea's original English version of *La maschera del demonio*, would both appear on videotape), but home media would find ways of capitalizing on, cultifying and monetizing the different versions of Bava. The remainder of this chapter looks at this matter in more detail.

Multiple Mario – versions of Bava

When a film travels across national and linguistic borders, it always to a degree becomes a different film without a single frame being added or removed. Dubbing, once a routine convention of preparing films for foreign distribution (and dubbed films are still a staple part of the Italian exhibition sector), is the most obvious example of this, one of the reasons why it has come to be seen as a marker of low quality, inviting audience laughter when poorly done (Olney 2013: 27). Dubbing removes part of an actor's performance, although that presumes that such a vocal performance was recorded in the first place, which is not always the case with Italian genre films (and some more canonical ones, too) with their multi-lingual casts sometimes only contributing to a guide track and their voice not necessarily in any version of the film. Such is the case for Christopher Lee in both *Ercole al centro della terra* and *La frusta e il corpo,* whereas Boris Karloff and Vincent Price can at least be heard in *Black Sabbath* and *Dr Goldfoot and the Girl Bombs* respectively, but not in their Italian versions *I tre volti della paura* and *Le spie vengono dal semifreddo*, a factor that complicates any decision about which is the most authentic. Which language track should one select on the DVD or blu-ray of a Bava film? Surely the Italian version is more authentic, but what if the dialogue was largely delivered in English and the lead actors are English speakers who dubbed themselves in their own language? Nor is the Italian dub necessarily always technically better. Elke Sommer's performance in *Gli orrori del castello di Norimberga* is already an aural monument to high-decibel scream queenery, but her Italian voice artist pushes it closer to torture than anything practised by Baron Blood – as the Baron's cries are heard during the climax of the film, she drowns them out by *screaming even more loudly*. On the other hand, subtitling carries the aura of authenticity and quality, but has to make certain decisions about translation, finding equivalent phrases rather than literal ones or condensing lengthy dialogue into something that can be realistically read onscreen.

But then there is the matter of more substantial changes that start to make the films look like different versions, not just different translations, or even different films. This should complicate auteur cults but often becomes a source of pleasure, of connoisseurship. A filmmaker like the prolific Spanish director Jess (Jesús) Franco could make ostensibly the same film as a horror film, a softcore sexploitation film and a hardcore porn film depending on the demands and censorship restrictions of different markets. There are the various cuts of George Romero's *Dawn of the Dead* (1978), including the Argento-approved cut released in Italy, that have been increasingly packaged together. Nor is the question of different cuts confined to marginal, low budget and 'exploitation' filmmaking. The cult around a big-budget studio film such as *Blade Runner* (1982) is invested in its different incarnations as release version, 'Director's Cut' and 'Final Cut' – Matt Hills suggests that they might even be viewed as a trilogy or '*a set of multiple film texts without cinematic prequels or sequels*' (2011: 6, emphasis in original). The Director's Cut and Redux version has become a staple part of both theatrical re-releases and, particularly, home media, while arthouse director Wong Kar-wai is notorious for screening provisional versions of his films at film festivals and then very different cuts for different markets. But while questions of textual authority and authenticity might seem to lean towards questions of authorship, the auteur is not always assumed to know best, especially when tampering with their own film rather than restoring an original vision compromised by the studio – George Lucas upgrading the effects in the *Star Wars* films (Klinger 2008: 41–2) and Walter Hill adding transitional comic book panels to *The Warriors* (1979) are cases in point. A less auteur-centred example is the upgrading of the effects in Terence Fisher's *The Devil Rides Out* (1967) for Studio Canal's 2012 blu-ray release – while even the film's most ardent admirers tend to concede that its original effects let it down, digitally improving them was seen by many to compromise the historical authenticity of the film. Its technical flaws had become part of its textual integrity, its overall quality perceived as overcoming them.

'What is a work?' asks Foucault, 'What is this curious unity which we designate a work?' (1984: 103). Larry Shiner historicizes the idea of a 'fixed work', as opposed to a series of performances, as something that developed out of the 'Great Division' (2001: 124). The *unfixedness* of Bava's films, including some of his most well-regarded ones, amplifies his artisanal status – a maker of *things* (effects, images, setpieces) more than a creator of *works*. But that does not necessarily erase the artist/auteur – rather, it points to the problematic legacy of the Great Division in making sense of creative labour in a collaborative medium. The best *filone* directors are perhaps best seen as artist-artisans in the pre-Great Division sense. At the same time, digital media has made a virtue of the unfixing of works by presenting different versions that facilitate cinephile and cult connoisseurship. Bava's films have benefitted enormously from their remediation – a small enough canon to collect (unlike the sprawling output of Fulci or Margheriti) but with enough variants to repay close and repeated attention. DVD, and by extension blu-ray, is, as Barbara Klinger puts it, 'an ambassador of context' (2008: 21), and Bava, like all Serie B directors, comes with an awful lot of contextual baggage. DVD and blu-ray paradoxically remediate the ephemerality of Bava's films while simultaneously canonizing them. Klinger connects digital home media to two types of cinephilia. The first re-articulates postwar theatrical cinephilia, 'a kind of aristocratic cine-literacy' that makes the unusual and the non-mainstream available for an aesthetic appreciation where high and low tastes converge (ibid.: 23). The second type of cinephilia, attracted to those 'perfect' DVD/blu-ray movies that lend themselves particularly well to the technical possibilities of the format (extras, commentaries, state-of-the-art image and sound), largely privileges the high-end spectacle and effects of contemporary cinema (ibid.: 29). But while they are unlikely to include state-of-the-art audio and high definition is not always kind to low-budget films, cult/cinephile-oriented labels are also able to fashion 'perfect' releases out of obscure and non-mainstream genre films – different release versions or title sequences, different languages, deleted scenes. The ideal Bava releases have been those that brought together different release versions.

A number of Bava films were altered for international distribution, with changes that varied from relatively small (*Blood and Black Lace* has a different title sequence to the meet-the-cast opening of *6 donne per l'assassino*) to more substantial.[7] Two of his films were not released theatrically in Italy (or anywhere in one case) – one became a completely different (and reasonably successful) film and the other had to be reconstructed over twenty years later, significantly in different versions. When determining which is the 'right' version to watch, two criteria may come into play. One is authenticity, which is not always a straightforward matter. It is easy enough to see *Lisa e il diavolo* as more authentic than *La casa dell'esorcismo* – the version that is closest to the film Bava wanted to make (and there is an array of auteurist discourses positioning the film as a personal project). But what happens when a film is made simultaneously in two versions which both seem to have been directed by Bava, as is the case with *La ragazza che sapeva troppo* and its American version *Evil Eye*? Even

Lucas sometimes admits to a preference for the slicker AIP cut of a Bava film to the more 'authentic' Italian version. He characterizes *Black Sunday* as 'a tighter, more polished work' than the 'flawed gem' that is *La maschera del demonio* (2007: 318). The other criterion is nostalgia – which version of the film did you first fall in love with? When Criterion released a huge box set of all fifteen Godzilla films from the Showa (1954–75) period in Japanese with subtitles, there were some complaints that they did not also include the American versions that first drew some fans to the series. When Martyn Conterio uses the AIP title for his monograph on Bava's debut film, it is not simply because that remains the name under which it is best known in English but because that is the version he has chosen to focus on (with *La maschera del demonio/Mask of Satan* as comparative versions) – 'the AIP version was – like a lot of folk – how I first became introduced to the film and the world of Mario Bava' (2015: 9), he writes. *Mask of Satan*, the English version of *La maschera del demonio* prepared by Galatea but rejected by AIP,[8] resurfaced on video and television in 1992. As a stronger version, it might have been expected to replace *Black Sunday* as the default, *authentic*, English-language version. Instead, the different versions co-exist on more or less equal terms, even though as a *title*, *Black Sunday* has the weight of exhibition history behind it to be the preferred English title.

The AIP Bavas

AIP were involved with seven Bava films, sometimes solely as distributors but in some cases, during production – *La maschera del demonio*, *Gli invasori*, *La ragazza che sapeva troppo*, *I tre volti della paura*, *Terrore nello spazio*, *Le spie vengono dal semifreddo* and *Gli orrori del castello di Norimberga*. Having had some success with the last of those films under its English title *Baron Blood*, they were very keen to distribute *Lisa e il diavolo* until they actually saw it. The first four films were Galatea productions or co-productions, the next two co-produced with Lucisano's Italy International Film, the final one made by Leone International Film. Five of them were re-scored by AIP's house composer Les Baxter – *Gli invasori* retained its Roberto Nicolosi score when it became *Erik the Conqueror*, even though AIP passed on the English-language dub (*The Invaders*) prepared by Galatea, and *Planet of the Vampires* kept its original score, in keeping with the minimal changes from *Terrore nello spazio*. English-language sources discussing *Black Sunday* have not always been kind about Baxter's score – the *Aurum Film Encyclopedia* calls it 'ponderous' (Hardy *et al.* 1985: 133), and David Pirie finds it 'ghastly' (1977: 160). While Baxter's score gives the impression that he might have been paid by the note, there is not a significant gulf in quality between his and Roberto Nicolosi's score – he even incorporates Nicolosi's love theme used in some of the romantic scenes between Katia and John Richardson's hero Andrej. Far from being ponderous, Baxter's score often seems playful, bringing the film in line with what seems to have been AIP's conception of the horror genre – spooky fun. This is even more evident in the end title music for *Black Sabbath,* which Kim Newman calls Baxter's 'worst excess' – a comic arrangement of Chopin's Funeral March interrupted by various other musical quotations (Newman 1986b: 24) – but otherwise Baxter's score for this film is a more brooding affair. Besides, the ending of *I tre volti della paura* was scarcely taking itself any more seriously as the camera pulled back to reveal Boris Karloff on a dummy horse, stagehands running in circles with tree branches to create the illusion of forward momentum, tinkly 'silent movie' music on the soundtrack. For the opening titles of *Evil Eye,* Baxter's theme replaces Adriano Celentano's 'Furore', one of those rare sequences that had placed Bava in the here-and-now of Italian popular culture. Celentano, the 'Italian Elvis', had made a cameo singing rock'n'roll in Fellini's *La dolce vita* (1960) as well as appearing in a number of pop-themed films – he performed 'Furore' for the Mina vehicle *Io bacio, tu baci* (1961) but it would only feature in the trailer for the film. Lucas is much kinder to Baxter than earlier critics and it is hard to disagree with his judgement that his *Baron Blood* score is superior to Stelvio Cipriani's – if Cipriani's opening title music is superficially appropriate for the jet-set air travel scenes that accompany it, Baxter at least seems to have registered that the destination is a gothic castle occupied by a re-animated ancestral sadist, not a luxury hotel with a pool. Ultimately, these are matters of taste – none of the scores Baxter replaced have the cult cachet that other Italian soundtracks have had bestowed on them (imagine him replacing Ennio Morricone's score for *Diabolik* or Piero Umiliani's for *5 bambole per la luna d'agosto*). While they vary in style – and, arguably, quality – their main function seems to be that of re-branding the films in the AIP style, pulling the gothic films closer to Corman's Poe films.

Galatea had already produced release versions – and English-language dubs – of *La maschera del demonio* and *Gli invasori* before AIP picked them up for distribution, trimming them and re-dubbing them for the American market. Something similar would happen with *Gli orrori del castello di Norimberga*, for which Alfredo Leone had produced an English-language version as *Baron Blood*. As with *La maschera del demonio,* AIP tightened up the film, toned down some of the violence (although less softening was required this time) and had Baxter re-score it. *Black Sunday*'s notoriety – including a censor ban in the UK – was achieved many years before it became apparent that Galatea's cut went further in terms of both violence (most notably, a spike through the undead Kruvajan's eye) and eroticism (more emphasis on the necro-erotic kiss shared between the revived Asa and a mesmerized Kruvajan). Some names are changed in the AIP version, but more importantly Javutich not only becomes Javuto but is explicitly referred to as Asa's serf, even though, as several commentators have observed, he does not dress like one and has his portrait alongside hers in the Vajdas's castle, which suggests a family connection. Publicity materials for *La maschera del demonio* supposedly referred to him as 'fratello della strega', the witch's brother (Conterio 2015: 78), but the film itself is more circumspect – the idea of him being a serf in *Black Sunday* seems to derive from the opening reference to him in the Italian version as Asa's 'servant of the devil'. Throughout the film, family ties are either broken (Asa repudiated by her brother before her execution, Katia's undead father telling her that he is no longer her father as 'the spirits of evil have broken that bond between us forever') or incestuously close – in the case of Katia and her father, both at the same time.[9] Often accused of being incoherent as a piece of storytelling – which in some respects it is – the film is all too clear in other ways.

La ragazza che sapeva troppo/Evil Eye, I tre volti della paura/Black Sabbath, Terrore nello spazio/Planet of the Vampires and *Le spie vengono dal semifreddo/Dr Goldfoot and the Girl Bombs* emerged out of collaborations between AIP and their respective Italian producers that in three out of the four cases produced different versions more or less simultaneously. *La ragazza* is discussed in further detail in the chapter on the Italian thriller, as is the episode of *I tre volti della paura* that was changed most drastically in *Black Sabbath, Il telefono*. It seems that Bava shot everything that is included in both *La ragazza* and *Evil Eye*, including their different endings. In the former, Nora wonders if everything has been a dream induced by the marijuana cigarettes given to her on the plane in the opening scenes and she throws them away. In the latter, where the drug smuggler on the plane has merely peddled illegal cigarettes, Nora takes onboard the recurring accusation that she is an over-imaginative female thriller addict and takes no notice as a man murders an unfaithful wife or lover on a cable car. But not everything in *Black Sabbath* was necessarily shot by Bava – it adds new linking footage of Karloff introducing each story individually, rather than simply introducing the film at the beginning and returning for his jokey sign-off. And it loses the end scene so beloved by Bavaphiles, a very literal illustration of his maxim that cinema is nothing but *trucchi* – and pretty silly ones at that – as Karloff signs off on his dummy horse ('Dream about me! We'll become friends!'). And the joins in the modified version of *Il telefono* – a newspaper story clearly seen in long shot that becomes a ghostly letter writing itself on the page – do show, suggesting that more work needed to be done to make the film AIP-friendly. Nevertheless, the Galatea/AIP relationship would appear to have worked more or less smoothly. Lucisano's Italy International Film, on the other hand, was a more downmarket concern than Galatea and their collaborations with AIP were evidently more chaotic. While *Terrore nello spazio* emerged relatively unscathed and remains a favourite with Bava fans, the next collaboration between Lucisano and AIP would pull in very different directions.

FIGURE 1 *'The cinema is all a trick' – Karloff and the dummy horse in* I tre volti della paura.

Due mafiosi contro Dr Goldfoot, or the film that came in from the semi-cold

We are Italian cinema. Our films travelled everywhere, unlike those of renowned masters like Fellini, Visconti, and Antonioni. Our films were reduced to 16mm prints so they could be shown anywhere, which didn't happen with Fellini, Visconti or Antonioni. And more than a hundred films in over ten years is no joke, even if they were cheap films made in a hurry.

Franco Franchi (Moscati 2001: 3)

Franco Franchi and Ciccio Ingrassia were something of an unstoppable force in 1960s Italian cinema, and continued into the 1970s even as comic trends changed with the rise of *commedia all'italiana sexy* and their relationship soured. Between 1961 and 1973 they made a minimum of five films a year, with a staggering eighteen in 1964, seven of which were episode films but still leaving a peak of eleven features. Critical disdain could not touch them; they were review-proof. In the documentary *Come inguaiammo il cinema italiano: La vera storia di Franco e Ciccio* (2005), film critic Tullio Kezich admits to laughing at their films while knowing that he was expected to give them bad reviews anyway. As a respected film critic, it would have been more than his reputation was worth to do otherwise. On the other hand, they attracted the attention of auteur directors, perhaps because they represented a dying tradition of Sicilian popular theatre. De Sica cast them in *Il giustizio universale* (1961) and Pasolini put them alongside Totò (another comic magnet for intellectuals) in *Che cosa sono le nuvole?*, an episode in *Capriccio all'italiana* (1968), even before Ingrassia's solo excursions into auteur cinema with the likes of Fellini (*Amarcord*) and Elio Petri (*Todo modo*). This is the 'vernacular cinema' Mikel Koven is seeking in the Italian thriller or *giallo* – 'largely formulaic' and reliant on 'pre-existing formulas' (2006: 38). As Franchi was keen to emphasize, 16 mm prints of some of their films were generated to allow them to penetrate ever-more marginal exhibition spaces – the essence of *cinema di profondità*. And it is probably also misleading to separate their films from their contemporaneous TV appearances, which were not under the same obligation to find ways of incorporating skits and routines into a narrative. When Franco demonstrates his mastery of disguise in *Le spie vengono dal semifreddo* (Diabolik has nothing to fear), it is a mere pretext for a rooster impersonation that would have been familiar from TV appearances. This is also a vernacular cinema in the linguistic sense. When Bill Dexter (Fabian) tells them that a secret agent needs to be able to speak at least four languages, Franco cheerfully reels off all the Southern dialects he knows, including his own Palermitano. The duo was often compared with other double-acts – Laurel and Hardy (Stanlio e Ollio), Abbott and Costello (Gianni e Pinotto), Martin and Lewis – but a more useful point of comparison might be the British *Carry On* films, at least if the latter had been churned out even more quickly and focused primarily on their movie parodies. Franco and Ciccio went after everyone and everything in Italian cinema, from Sergio Leone (*Per un pugno nell'occhio* 1961, *Il bello, il brutto, il cretino,* 1967), Visconti (*I figli del leopardo,* 1965), Fellini (*Satiricosissimo,* 1970) and Argento (*Due gattoni a nove code... e mezza ad Amsterdam,* 1972). Looking to international trends, James Bond was an inevitable target (*Due mafiosi contro Goldginger,* 1965), and eventually they found their way to kung fu (*Ku Fu? Dalla Sicilia con furore,* 1973).[10]

In English-language books on Italian cinema, with some exceptions, Franco and Ciccio rarely get more than a passing mention, even in discussions of comedy. Ironically, the most detailed (but rarely sympathetic) discussions of them in English tend to be in books on Bava and Lucio Fulci. Lucas is diplomatic and steers a careful course around them as he searches for the 'Mario Bava film' within *Le spie vengono dal semifreddo*. Troy Howarth seems to mellow towards them between the first and second edition of his book on Bava, but the most he can manage is to concede that humour is subjective and that 'the duo's popularity continues to this day in Italy' (2014: 89). In his book on Fulci, Stephen Thrower has to engage with the duo in more detail, given that the director made thirteen films with them before his later adoption as 'Godfather of Gore', but it is clearly a mission he would rather have avoided. Thrower acknowledges a low 'pain threshold' for them

(2018: 52), but thirteen films later has arrived at something approaching Stockholm Syndrome. 'I've laughed here and there', he enthuses, and 'felt more than a glimmer of what it is about Franchi and Ingrassia that inspired such affection in Italy' (ibid.: 89). Commentators often observe ruefully that *Le spie vengono dal semifreddo* was Bava's most commercially successful film as a director in Italy. During the first week of August 1966, it was one of two Bava films on release in Rome. *Operazione paura* was showing at the air-conditioned *prima visione* Corso cinema, while *Le spie* was screening at the less luxurious Dal Verme, but Franco and Ciccio would have the last laugh at the box office. In certain respects, it is arguably the most Italian of Bava's films, and certainly one of the few times he was in tune with Italian popular taste. Both Thrower and Howarth observe that comedy is a subjective matter, but it is also a matter of language and culture. Franco and Ciccio are sometimes seen as an insurmountable obstacle for Bava, but we could just as easily turn this around. Ingrassia referred to Bava as a 'great pal, great camera operator' who nevertheless 'didn't understand anything about comedy' (Moscati 2001: 49), suggesting that he was mainly chosen to direct because of the film's reliance on special effects.

If it was relatively easy for American and Italian producers to find common ground in the horror genre, Science Fiction and even the peplum (where Maciste could easily become Samson in the dubbing process), comedy was always likely to be harder. While Lucisano and AIP were both involved from the start, they were clearly not making the same film. AIP were making a sequel to *Dr Goldfoot and the Bikini Machine* (1965), a purely American production drawing on a number of AIP's popular cycles, including beach party movies and the Edgar Allan Poe series – its climax parodies that of Corman's *Pit and the Pendulum* and is filmed on the same set. Lucisano, on the other hand, was capitalizing on the fact that Franco and Ciccio had already made several spy spoofs, one of them featuring a villain called Goldginger, played by Fernando Rey. The title of *Le spie vengono dal semifreddo* plays on *The Spy Who Came in from the Cold*, but *semifreddo* takes on a comic double-meaning that does not translate – literally semi-cold, but also the name of an Italian dessert. Rather than a sequel to any particular film (least of all the previous Dr Goldfoot, even though it had been released in Italy with a Franco and Ciccio-like title, *Dr Goldfoot e il nostro gente 00-1/4*), *Le spie vengono dal semifreddo* is best seen as part of the vast *filone* of their films. According to Tim Lucas, *Dr Goldfoot and the Girl Bombs* 'hardly qualifies as "A Mario Bava Film" at all' (2007: 692). But the problem with trying to find 'Mario Bava' in either version – apart from his cameo as an angel (with harp) during the escape from Rome's Luna park in a hot air balloon – is not just that it was a 'professional service' rather than something suited to his particular talents or that the American version re-structured the film and added new footage (some of it a recap from the first Dr Goldfoot), but that it is futile to try to evaluate the film independently from its larger cycle. Franco and Ciccio's films operated more like episodes of a TV series in exactly the way that Christopher Wagstaff (1992) describes in his account of the *terza vision* audience. By 1965, 49 per cent of Italian families owned a TV set (Ginsborg 1990: 240), and while this was a dramatic rise since its introduction in 1954, it is indicative of the way in which cinema could still function as a primary source of entertainment, especially in the south where Franco and Ciccio were particularly popular. Television could be watched like cinema – gathering in a bar or café, or even a cinema, to watch *Lascia o Raddoppia* on a Thursday evening – and cinema could be watched like television (nightly, distractedly). And Franco and Ciccio were a considerable presence in both.

The question of which version of the film is most 'authentic' probably needs to put aside matters of authorship and look instead to stardom. While Vincent Price hated and regretted making the film – the ideal Bava role for him would have been Baron von Kleist seven years later – he comes out of both versions reasonably well, but inevitably better in the AIP version where he delivers what must have been his original dialogue (modified in the Italian dub). Moreover, the film can capitalize on his resemblance to Ciccio in a *Duck Soup*-like sequence where Ingrassia poses as his mirror reflection with the aid of a false beard. In *Dr Goldfoot*, as Price plans to divide up the world with his Chinese allies after they have provoked war between Russia and the United States, he lists Palermo as one of the places they can have (AIP's in-joke at the expense of the comic stars they felt Lucisano had forced on them?). But Franco and Ciccio suffer badly in *Dr Goldfoot*, if perhaps

FIGURE 2 *The two faces of Dr Goldfoot – Vincent Price and Ciccio Ingrassia in Le spie vengono dal semifreddo.*

not badly enough for some Bavaphiles. They have considerably fewer scenes and inevitably fall down the billing (behind Fabian), and the dubbing kills Franco's puns deader than the House of Vajda. In *Le spie* they literally get to end the film – Franco, trying to keep warm in a pan of spaghetti after the two of them end up in Siberia, announces to the audience 'The film is finished!' The final scenes of *Dr Goldfoot,* on the other hand, show more interest in Bill (Fabian) and Laura Antonelli's Rosanna. Antonelli, who fares much better in the AIP version, was clearly designed to be a larger presence than is the case in the Italian version of the film, where the two comedians probably carried most clout regarding screen time. There is a running joke about her slapping Bill every time he kisses her in *Dr Goldfoot*, but more importantly the film picks up a thread left hanging in *Le spie* – her replacement by a Girl Bomb replica of her. In the Italian version, she is abducted and later rescued by Bill, but it omits the scene most frequently represented as a still in Bava-centred accounts of the film – the Rosanna Girl Bomb, dressed in a slip and underwear, attempting to seduce Bill (one kiss from a Girl Bomb will trigger her to explode, although a champagne cork beats her to it as things heat up). Not only does the scene anticipate the sexier persona that Antonelli would adopt a few years later, but its out-of-context presentation in stills also makes *Dr Goldfoot* look more like a 'Mario Bava film', perhaps a sexy *giallo*-thriller. When she is subsequently reduced to a broken doll after an unfortunate encounter with an electric socket, we might feel even more that we are in Bava-land, amongst those mannequins that are forever eerily mimicking or standing in for live flesh and blood. But only briefly. And only in the AIP cut.

Lisa doesn't live here anymore

At one point in *La casa dell'esorcismo*, the film cuts from Leandro, Telly Savalas's sinister and literally diabolical butler, reflected in a puddle of spilled red wine, to a possessed Lisa reflected in a puddle of her own vomit. An unsympathetic viewer, especially one invested in Bava, might see this as an apt summary of the film – from a relatively artful shot from the original *Lisa e il diavolo* to the *filone*-jumping pea soup crudity and high-level obscenity (sample dialogue: 'There's your fucking daily bread... Eat it like you did those whores' cunts before you became a priest!') of what became of Bava's 'Mona Lisa'. It has become virtually impossible to separate *Lisa* from the narrative surrounding it – the desecrated 'masterpiece', the personal project taken over by the producer (although Leone rarely emerges entirely as the bad guy, regardless of what he did to the film), and then the 'lost' Bava found again (there would be another one of those to come). What might we think of the film if it had simply been released in 1973, probably to audience indifference but some cinephile appreciation? A 'late masterpiece' swimming against the tide or a film that would have been much better if it had been made ten years earlier when Bava was at the height of his powers and had the likes of Ubaldo Terzano and Mario Serandrei on his team, perhaps with someone like Daliah Lavi or even Barbara Steele in the title role. The *Aurum Encyclopedia*, citing critics who saw it in Spain, the only country to release it theatrically, calls it 'a hauntingly beautiful poem about decay and death' (Hardy *et al.* 1985: 258), but is forced to base this judgement on what survives of the original in *La casa,* admiring what could be seen of its 'morbid sense of necrophilia' and 'morbid romanticism' (ibid.). Heffernan (2007: 146) characterizes it as an art-horror hybrid, 'a wild mixture of the starkly original and the brazenly borrowed', while Pezzotta discerns signs of exhaustion in its lethargic zoom shots and a decline in the creativity that once characterized Bava's best films (2013: 118). When someone falls down some steps in an early scene in Toledo, the fall is lazily conveyed out of frame before the camera tilts down to his fallen body, while the same character's (second) death later in the film is accompanied by stage blood squirting clumsily into the camera lens. Nevertheless, for some (myself included), the film casts its own eccentric spell with its strange time shifts and plentiful evidence that Bava could still extract considerable aesthetic mileage from his beloved mannequins, here constantly turning into living (or once living) beings and then back. There are signs that the film wants to be taken a bit more seriously than Bava's 1960s gothics, although Savalas's amused performance suggests that we are probably not intended to take it *too* seriously. Whatever one thinks of *Lisa* now, it is not difficult to see why it was a tough sell – slow, not easy to follow in a single viewing, too slapdash in places to pass as an art film (although it supposedly played well at festivals), not thrilling enough to compete with 1970s trends in horror, although the version available now is probably tamer than the version intended for release (not all of the 'strong meat' in *La casa* had to be shot fresh). Thus, Leone tends to be characterized less as the crass producer than someone who not only gave Bava his head during production, but also found himself between a rock and a hard place – an intransigent Bava and unimpressed buyers (see Heffernan 2007).

If earlier critics had to judge *Lisa* on the basis of *La casa,* that might not have been quite as difficult a task as it sounds, even though the central premise – its central characters damned souls about to be carried away by the devil that Lisa first sees in a fresco in Toledo – and final twist go missing. Nearly two-thirds of *La casa dell'esorcismo* consists of footage from *Lisa,* including some material (in the form of longer versions of scenes) shot for the earlier film but not in the cut now circulating on DVD and blu-ray – a gorier version of Sophie's (Sylva Koscina) death, one of her eyeballs popping out under Massimiliano's blows, and a longer sex scene with her chauffeur earlier in the film. An even more explicit version of the latter scene, probably for more permissive markets, turns up without sound on some home media releases. In other words, the vulgarized version of *Lisa* also reminds us that the original film was not necessarily quite the refined art object it is sometimes made to sound. Leone's version, some of it directed by Bava, some of it by Leone with Lamberto's assistance, re-positions *Lisa* as part of the *filone* that succeeded the success of *The Exorcist* (1973) – such films as *Chi Sei?/ Beyond the Door* (1974), *L'anticristo/The Antichrist* (1974) and, inevitably, *L'esorciccio* (1975), a parodic vehicle for Ciccio Ingrassia. 'Such devilish acts!', as Leandro observes, but given that the film was already about the devil, there is a degree of logic in there somewhere, even if commercial logic was the stronger force. Leone's cut runs for ninety-two minutes, of which nearly thirty-four minutes (including opening and closing credits) consist of new footage. Not only must it add the *de rigeur* demonic possession setpieces – vomiting (she emits frogs at one point), profanity, levitation, plus a nude attempted seduction of Robert Alda's priest Father Michael – but try to make some sense out of what was already confusing in the original film. In *Lisa e il diavolo*, Lisa is the reincarnation of Elena, the woman who destroyed the Contessa's family by having both her husband and son fall for her, leading Massimiliano to murder both his stepfather and his adulterous wife. In Leone's version, Lisa is now possessed by Elena, still the seductress, although this is now put rather less delicately – she 'balled the shit out of' father-in-law Carlo because Massimiliano (Maximilian in the English dialogue) was impotent. 'Murder and adultery, an evil game played by the devil' – where in *Lisa,* the devil carries the damned souls away by plane, Leandro revealed as the pilot, in *La casa* it is the house itself that functions as their hell, but with Lisa taking Elena's place while Elena possesses her body. In terms of narrative coherence, there are Italian horror films that have grappled with worse, but it is the dramatic shifts in tone and style that might even have prompted unwitting viewers to wonder how this film came together – indeed, one reviewer felt that it was 'like two films spliced together' (Clarke 1976: 35), unaware that this was exactly what it was. And yet, Leone and editor Carlo Reali take unusual care with bridging the two sets of footage, sometimes in the form of sound bridges – 'Dinner is served! Dinner is served!' babbles the possessed Lisa/Elena, the final repetition overlapping with a transition to Leandro's banter with a stuffed hare before serving dinner at the villa. And then there is the aforementioned cut from *vino rosso* to *vomito verde*. Reali, retained from the original film, perhaps made the most accomplished contribution to the release version.

When *Lisa e il diavolo* returned from its exhibition limbo, a limbo rather like Lisa herself wandering lost in the streets of Toledo or finding, as in *La casa dell'esorcismo,* that she had been replaced by a foul-mouthed imposter, it should come as no surprise that at a certain point it was destined to sit alongside its once-despised variant rather than perform an exorcism of its own. Just as Matt Hills sees the different cuts of *Blade Runner* as a kind of trilogy, Heffernan sees the two versions of Bava/Leone's film as 'a diptych of two separate works of art' (2007: 160), remediated as 'a case study for historical, critical, artistic, and commercial reappraisal'. Recent editions of the films have added commentaries to both – an expert one from Lucas for *Lisa e il diavolo* and Leone occupying the auteur seat for *La casa dell'esorcismo*. He would play a key role in rehabilitating and re-building another Bava film, one as untypical as any of his jobbing assignments but carrying a very different aura of quality.

'Un thriller di Mario Bava'

In 1974, Bava made the most untypical of what might be considered his more 'authored' films, adapted from an Ellery Queen short story 'Kidnapped' in the back pages of a Mondadori *giallo*, as 'L'uomo e il bambino' (The Man and the Boy). Its untypicality lies in less familiar generic territory (a robbery heist and kidnapping, rather than colourful murder mystery or gothic fantasy), in its style (naturalistic lighting, handheld camera, the claustrophobic and tangibly sweaty interior of a car) and tone. Bava may have blanched at the obscenities added to *Lisa,* but *Cani arrabbiati* features a scene in which a woman, already manhandled and abused throughout the film, is humiliated by being forced to remove her underwear and urinate in front of her laughing tormenters. The enclosed space makes it rather more of an actor's film than one tends to associate with Bava, and while Aldo Caponi (former pop star Don Backy) and Luigi Montefiori (aka George Eastman) chew the upholstery in the back seat, Riccardo Cucciolla and Maurice Poli are particularly effective as two shrewder heads trying to figure each other out in the front. The film was complete bar some post-production work when its producer went bankrupt, and the raw footage was impounded. Stelvio Cipriani had partially recorded his score, but a relatively small number of music cues manage to do a lot of work in the version of the film that uses his original score. In 1995, actress Lea Lander, who plays the longsuffering Maria in the film, obtained the rights to the raw footage and a version of the film was put together under the title *Semaforo rosso* (red traffic light) and screened at the Brussels International Festival of Fantasy, Science Fiction and Thriller Films the following year. 'Un thriller di Mario Bava', announced the newly shot (and rather crude) opening titles. Several variations on this cut emerged and the one currently circulating uses Bava's original title *Cani arrabbiati* and a title sequence that provides a pastiche of 1970s Italian genre title sequences so note-perfect in its solarized images that it could pass as one prepared for the original release.[11] The only clue that the titles are not entirely authentic is in retaining the credit 'Un thriller di Mario Bava' from *Semaforo rosso,* a credit that situates it in an era in which the director's authorial cachet can be assumed to mean something.[12] In 2002, the film appeared in a revised version produced by Alfredo Leone for which Lamberto Bava shot new footage (supposedly based on his father's notes) and incorporated some unused footage from the original shoot as well as stock footage of traffic from the period (Lucas 2007: 954). Cipriani wrote a new, and rather bland, score, and the film gained a new title (or an old one, that of its original source), *Kidnapped*. Both versions can lay certain claims to being more 'authentic', but both are attempts to reconstruct footage shot twenty or thirty years previously. Both versions end on a freeze frame. The final shot of *Cani arrabbiati* is an unconscious (or possibly dead) child in the boot of a car. The final shot of *Kidnapped* is the face of an anguished mother, new footage shot by Lamberto Bava – the addition of the boy's mother, who also appears in earlier scenes, is the most significant difference between the two versions beyond which Cipriani score we might prefer or whether a certain rawness is preferable to a tighter and more professional edit.

The film opens with a heist at a pharmaceutical company, stealing the staff's weekly wages. One of the gang is killed by the police, but Dottore (the smart one, as his nickname suggests), Bisturi (scalpel) and Trentadue (32, a reference to part of his anatomy) escape with a hostage, Maria. They hold up a car driven by Riccardo, apparently trying to get his sick son Agostino to hospital. We spend a good deal of time in that car (real time in *Cani arrabbiati*, which does not cut away to the police operations in the way that *Kidnapped* does). Bisturi and particularly Trentadue torment Maria in the backseat, pawing at her, making crude jokes at her expense and generally humiliating her. They needle Riccardo, calling him the diminutive 'Riccardino', while he tries to keep everyone calm and encourages the more rational Dottore to try to control his two sociopathic accomplices. And indeed, when things go too far for him, Trentadue seemingly at the point of raping Maria, Dottore shoots him and the gang starts to unravel. At the same time, he is suspicious of Riccardo; sometimes not as worried as one might expect him to be, or (the most telling sign) rather surprised that the amount of money they have stolen is so small. Riccardo emerges as the sole survivor, killing the final two robbers with a gun concealed in Agostino's blanket, and a dying Bisturi guns down Maria. The final scene shows him making a call from a phone box to a Signora Derotto, revealing himself to be a kidnapper and the boy a hostage for whom he is demanding a ransom. Even for a director who specialized in horror and violent murder mysteries, this is nasty stuff. Again, one might ask how we would see the film if it had been released amidst the violent *poliziotteschi* of the mid-1970s. It may be untypical of Bava (or its nihilism might be read as more 'personal'), but it is by no means untypical of Italian crime films made during *gli anni di piombo* – the 'years of lead', the wave of terrorism, assassinations, kidnappings and political conspiracies that have provided a contextual critical framework for a range of cinematic forms produced in Italy during this period, from *cinema d'impegno* to Serie B.

Pezzotta observes that *Cani arrabbiati* is one of the few times that Bava seemed to engage with the wider world (2013: 123), but it could equally be seen as more of an engagement with trends in Italian *filone* cinema. If we are tempted to see it as 'personal' film, that might be more a matter of Bava attempting to re-orient his career – an unfashionable director who had just made an unreleasable film – than an opportunity to express some inner nihilism. In addition to fitting into the cycle of crime films made by the likes of Umberto Lenzi, Fernando Di Leo and Enzo Castellari, the film can also be seen as part of a smaller group of films that responded to Wes Craven's *Last House on the Left* (1972). Films such as *L'ultimo treno della notte/Night Train Murders* (1975), *Autostop rosso sangue/Hitchhike* (1977) and *La casa sperduta nel parco/House at the Edge of the Park* (1980) have psychopathic characters with a propensity for sexual violence encounter 'respectable' people who turn out to be at least as bad as they are. The latter two films feature *Last House* actor David Hess, who could easily have played either Bisturi or Trentadue, while Riccardo Cucciolla's Riccardo drops his meek 'Riccardino' mask to reveal himself as the coldest and cruellest kidnapper of the group. The urination scene, in particular, echoes *Last House on the Left*. In *No, il caso è felicemente risolto/No, the Case Is Happily Resolved* (1973), Cucciolla had played another citizen above suspicion, a college professor who murders a sex worker but is able to implicate a railway employee for the crime. This also resonates with the kind of readings that have been made of Italian crime films in the context of *gli anni di piombo* and particularly the *strategia della tensione* – the far-right conspiracy that aimed to use terrorism (often implicating the militant left, as in the 1969 Piazza Fontana bombing in Milan) to create panic and pave the way for a far-right government. In Bava's film, those who generate terror and chaos for a relatively paltry 100 million lire act as a distraction from a terror that wears a more respectable mask.

If *Cani arrabbiati* looks a bit more like a film that might have come out in 1974 – its rough edges a testament to the rush into release that often characterized *filone* cinema – Lamberto's involvement in *Kidnapped* adds another kind of authenticity, with his perhaps inevitable claims that it is closer to his father's wishes, but also the fact that he had been becoming more and more of a co-director with Mario during the latter years of his father's career, both officially (*La venere d'Ille*) and unofficially (*Shock*). Bava may or may not have intended Agostino's mother to feature in the film, but even if she was in his personal notes, the fact that no footage of her had been shot suggests the possibility that he might have changed his mind during production. *Cani arrabbiati*'s final scene hits harder, not so much because she is absent from that scene but because she has not appeared earlier in the film. Her first appearance in *Kidnapped* has her phoning the police Commissario to ask for news – 'So much time has passed', she says, which suggests that whoever she is concerned about has been missing for a longer period than the time that has elapsed since the robbery. In other words, *Kidnapped* rather overplays its hand, where *Cani arrabbiati* lays out clues that are more evident on a second viewing. But these are judgements – always debatable – that can only be made about the versions of the film that are currently available. Further versions could only result from the film being re-constructed yet again and could make no greater claim to being definitive. As is often the case even with films that were theatrically released, there is no 'original' version of 'Un thriller di Mario Bava'.

Bava often appears too much of an auteur to be a journeyman, and too much of a journeyman to be an auteur, but that perhaps says more about the 'Great Separation' of artisan from artist than it does about the filmmaker himself, who is far from untypical in popular genre cinema. Bava is a case study in the artisan *as* auteur, rarely (if ever) the author of a unified text, but enough of a discernible creative presence around which to organize a fluid canon of 'Mario Bava' films, not all of which need necessarily to have been directed by him. Moreover, his remediation for home media also encourages us to see him in this way by both re-articulating the cinephilia that attracted admirers to him in the first place (a cinephilia often based on *parts* of his films) and facilitating cult connoisseurship by both digitizing the provisional and ephemeral nature of his films while simultaneously canonizing them as cult classics. The figure of the auteur retains its currency because it is central to how films are marketed (often belatedly, in the case of the cult filmmaker), categorized, canonized and/or cultified. But the figure of the artisan brings us closer to what filmmakers actually *do,* the different kinds of creative labour they bring to the cinema, the different obstacles and limitations they face and the different ways they register on screen. Ultimately, there are worse reputations Bava could have than that of *grande artigiano*.

Notes

1   On the same day that Bava's obituary appeared in *Corriere della sera,* a more famous director died, albeit one whose artistic credentials were still being debated – Alfred Hitchcock.

2   The author incorrectly (but understandably) credits him with working on Fellini's *Toby Dammit.*

3   Some have suggested that Bava's credited DPs, when someone other than himself, were often really camera operators, with Bava himself in charge of lighting.

4   Of course, Nicolas Roeg would dabble in horror, too, both as a cinematographer (*Masque of the Red Death,* 1964) and director (*Don't Look Now,* 1973), but is never regarded as a horror director. *Don't Look Now* can be situated in close proximity to 'Italian horror', however, both because it was a British-Italian co-production shot in Venice and because it shares some

tropes with some Italian thrillers made both before (*Chi l'ha vista morire?/Who Saw Her Die?*, 1972) and after it (*Sette note in nero/The Psychic*, 1977).

5   When Freda signed the tatty *L'iguana dalla lingua di fuoco/The Iguana with the Tongue of Fire* (1971) as 'Willy Pareto', one senses that he did not even want Robert Hampton to be blamed for it.

6   Bava is not credited in any capacity on the English version of *Le meraviglie di Aladino*.

7   *6 donne per l'assassino* was distributed in the United States as *Blood and Black Lace* by Woolner Brothers. They had made more substantial changes to *Ercole al centro della terra*, re-ordering some scenes as well as adding a new title sequence and music. Not unlike some of the Galatea/AIP films, there are two English-language versions – *Hercules in the Haunted World*, the Woolner Brothers US cut, and *Hercules in the Centre of the Earth*, the UK release version that is almost identical to the Italian version apart from omitting its pre-credits scene.

8   There is one small difference between *La maschera* and *Mask* beyond the dubbing. The latter removes a short scene that seems to have been put in the wrong place – a daylight scene featuring Katia and Prince Vajda that appears in the midst of some night-time scenes.

9   See Jenks (1992) for more on the incestuous undertones of that scene.

10 'Ku fu?' means 'Who was that?' in Sicilian dialect.

11 Gomarasca and Pulici estimate that there have been five different cuts of the film, including *Kidnapped* (2004: 31).

12 'Un film di…' credits did appear on some *filone* films by journeyman directors in the 1970s, but never on any of Bava's.

3

Navigating *filoni* – from Hercules to *il gotico italiano*

Bava's transition from cinematographer to director was shaped in no small part by the emergence of a particular mode of cinema in Italy, the *filone* – 'the serial exploitation of one or more models of success, indigenous or imported' (Venturini 2014: location 1265). *Filone* cinema is usually seen to have begun in Italy with a film to which Bava made a substantial contribution – *Le fatiche di Ercole,* which initiated a prolific cycle of historical-mythological films now most commonly referred to as peplums, a term first coined by French critics. By the mid-1960s, the peplum had given way to a *filone* that enjoys a higher critical and cult status but occupies a more problematic position in the Bava canon – the Western all'italiana or Spaghetti Western. The peplum established two precedents for *filone* cinema. Firstly, as the counterpart to one of Hollywood's most expensive and spectacular genres, albeit one with its own traditions dating back to silent Italian cinema (Eugenio Bava worked on the 1914 *Cabiria*), it needed to find less expensive ways of being 'a feast for the eyes', as Michèle Lagny puts it, 'in the form of tableaux which rely on compositional devices, colour relationships... backlighting and *sfumato* effects' (1992: 173). It made a virtue of the 'arte del risparmio' (De Chiara 2016: 61) – the art of saving money – not only by recycling sets, costumes and locations (the beach at Tor Caldara is a particular favourite across a range of genres) or employing past-their-sell-by-date Hollywood names, but through the artisanal skills of people like Bava, who had made *Le fatiche di Ercole* look like a fair contender against its vastly more expensive rivals across the Atlantic. The formula of 'spectacular film at low cost' (Spinazzola 1963: 79) created a space for someone like Bava to experiment with colour and other visual effects – his creative labour is visible in films signed by Francisci, Tourneur and Walsh as well as the ones he directed himself. Some commentators have even found early traces of the sadistic murders of 6 *donne per l'assassino* in the death spasms of Queen Vashti (Daniela Rocca) and Keresh (Rosalba Neri) in *Ester e il re*, the latter's bare legs writhing as she is strangled amidst saturated colours. The 'Bavaesque' arguably took shape in the peplum and was easily imported into the gothic. Secondly, while *filone* films might open in *prima visione* cinemas, as had *Le fatiche di Ercole*, the more substantial profits tended to come (if they came at all) from *seconde* and *terze visioni*, making a profit over a longer period of time in the *mercato di profondità*. Moreover, *Le fatiche di Ercole* and *La maschera del demonio* were international hits, making foreign markets increasingly important and particularly vital for the horror film, which made very little impact in the domestic market.

Bava provides an interesting case study in how genre operates both industrially (cinema as 'formulaic art', organized into cycles of production) and discursively (retrospective categorization as connoisseurship), as well as its role in organizing an authorial canon. Genres also operate as 'systems of cultural value' (Mittell 2004: 15), and Bava's horror films (and thrillers) and peplums are a case in point. In industrial terms, the peplum was one of the two most important *filoni* during the time of Bava's career – between August 1961 and June 1962, nearly a third of the films to earn over two million lire were peplums (Spinazzola 1963: 75) – while the horror film was a minor one in terms of both numbers and domestic box office success – never more than half a dozen a year during the *filone gotico* of 1960–66, intermittent after that and rarely performing well. In his overview of *cinema di profondità* in the 1960s, Lino Miccichè does not even seem to think that the gothic *filone* is worth mentioning (1975: 119). *La maschera del demonio,* seminal in the *horror all'italiana* canon, was 109th out of 157 films at the box office in 1960 and was not even the most successful Italian horror film of that year, which was *Il mulino delle donne di pietra* (nine places above it), the only one of the five made in colour (Günsberg 2005: 138). The Italian gothic never produced a series akin to the Hammer Draculas or Frankensteins or Corman's Poe cycle, or the kinds of series characters that ran through the peplum (Hercules, Maciste) or Western (Django, Ringo, Sartana). But the Italian horror film is higher in cult capital than the peplum, is written about more extensively in a range of modes, from fan-cult to academic, more widely available and carefully packaged on DVD and blu-ray, and canonized as a national-generic brand. Bava, along with Argento, is the key figure in the retrospective cultification of 'Italian horror'. The peplum, on the other hand, occupies a more precarious status. There is no shortage of critical writing on the genre, much of it focused on the spectacle of the male body – see, for example, Lagny (1992), Dyer (1997), Günsberg (2005), O'Brien (2014) and Rushing (2016) – some fan guides and cult appreciation, and it was initially taken quite seriously by French critics, to the bemusement of Italian ones. But digital media suggests that this once-prolific genre has fallen into relative marginality – fewer than a handful (mainly Bava's) are available on blu-ray, otherwise 'the only surviving copies are terribly fuzzy, panned-and-scanned, 4:3 prints that were shown on American television in the 1960s and 1970s' (Rushing 2016: 112). The Italian DVDs of *Le fatiche di Ercole* and *Ercole e la regina di Lidia* – major box office successes in their day – are the American versions (in the wrong ratio) with Italian soundtracks. If the peplum has anything resembling a modest canon, it largely isolates the work of filmmakers associated with other genres, such as Bava and Leone – the French Cottafavi cult is a notable exception. If Horror is often framed as transgressive – and Bava as being one of the architects of that transgressiveness – the peplum is predominantly seen to be camp, the kind of thing Frank N. Furter invites his guests to watch in *The Rocky Horror Show*. Rushing admits to finding it difficult to avoid slipping into 'ironic and snarky amusement, sometimes affectionate, sometimes not' (2016: 2) when writing about the films. While the term 'peplum' arose from French critics seeking to take the genre seriously, that critical seriousness has not fully endured.

If we think of Bava and genre from an industrial point of view, he looks less like a horror specialist than a working director negotiating his way through around nine genres or cycles, largely the same ones that someone like Margheriti worked in during the same period. During the gothic *filone* of the early 1960s, Bava made only four films that were clearly part of that cycle – Margheriti made three, Freda two, although he had already put his name (or that of 'Robert Hampton') to two horror films before that.[1] Mary Wood observes the three year gap between Bava's first horror film and his second (2014: 314), diverted into more commercially viable Hercules and Viking films,[2] or trying out a Hitchcock-style thriller that seemed to fall on even more barren ground than the gothics in Italy. Galatea were unusual in returning to the horror genre more than once, perhaps, as Venturini suggests, a sign of their international outlook (2014: location 1114). But if we approach genre discursively – particularly because *filone* cinema was characterized by forms of generic contamination, such as the 'gothic peplum' – horror assumes a greater presence, never far away during that three-year gap between *La maschera del demonio* and *I tre volti della paura*. If we place the films Bava directed between 1960 and 1977 in the categories where they sit either as part of a cycle or discursively (where they are often seen to 'belong') – allowing films to sit in more than one category[3] – they might look something like the table below.

Inevitably, the reader will challenge some of these designations, just as I wonder about some of them myself – what is genre in its discursive sense, after all, if not the compulsion to categorize and re-categorize? I have placed *5 bambole per la luna d'agosto* in the horror as well as *giallo/thrilling* category, for example, even though it doesn't feel much like a horror film to me – barely interested in generating suspense, let alone fear or shock – but some of its original reviews referred to it as a horror film, and it sometimes appears in books about horror, such as the *Aurum Encyclopedia* (which only

Horror	Giallo/Thrilling	Peplum	Western	Comedy
La maschera del demonio (Ercole al centro della terra) I tre volti della paura La frusta e il corpo (6 donne per l'assassino) (Terrore nello spazio) Operazione paura Il rosso segno della follia (5 bambole per la luna d'agosto) (Ecologia del delitto) Gli orrori del castello di Norimberga Lisa e il diavolo/La casa dell'esorcismo Shock	La ragazza che sapeva troppo I tre volti della paura (Il telefono episode) 6 donne per l'assassino Il rosso segno della follia 5 bambole per la luna d'agosto Ecologia del delitto	Ester e il re Ercole al centro della terra Gli invasori I coltelli del vendicatore	La strada per Forte Alamo Ringo del Nebraska Roy Colt e Winchester Jack	Le meraviglie di Aladino Le spie vengono dal semifreddo Quante volte…quella notte Roy Colt e Winchester Jack

Science Fiction	Erotic	Cinefumetto (comic book)	Thriller/poliziesco
Terrore nello spazio (Le spie vengono dal semifreddo) (Diabolik)	Quante volte…quella notte	Diabolik	Cani arrabbiati

excludes *La ragazza che sapeva troppo,* out of Bava's thrillers). *Diabolik* was part of a *filone* initiated by an earlier attempt to adapt the comic of the same name that was abandoned but generated enough publicity to prompt other *cinefumetti,* such as *Kriminal* (1966) and *Satanik* (1968). But it also gets discussed as a science-fiction film because of its outrageous gadgetry and a setting that can be interpreted as futuristic or even dystopian (it resembles a police state, making Diabolik seem more of a rebel-outsider than mere thief). It is sometimes even categorized amongst the *filone spionistico* (secret agent films) because of its stylistic similarity to the James Bond films. Given the genre's proximity to the horror genre, it is perhaps surprising that Bava made fewer science-fiction films than he did Westerns (although the authorship of one of those is in doubt) – several unmade projects, including a *giallo* set in space and a Philip José Farmer adaptation, would have expanded that category in his output. What is particularly notable, however, is the expansion of horror from six gothic supernatural films (seven if we count *Lisa e il diavolo* and *La casa dell'esorcismo* as two films) to thirteen (or fourteen), including a gothic science-fiction film complete with resurrection of the dead, a peplum that pits Hercules against a character who is certainly vampiric if not an actual vampire (and played by an actor associated with the most famous vampire),[4] and several thrillers built on bodycounts, two of them unusually violent. But this is a generic discourse filtered through auteurism, confined to Bava's work as a director (even if the extent of his direction is uncertain in some of them). If we expand the focus to include other kinds of creative labour (photography, effects, fixing problem films), the peplum assumes a greater presence, even if that is harder to quantify because a good deal of this work is uncredited and ranges from the probable to the possible (Lucas's 'Secret Filmography' sets out the most extensive, if highly speculative, number of candidates for inclusion).

In examining the role of genre in making sense of Bava's films, I have chosen to focus on three genres here – the peplum, the gothic horror film and the Western – and will look in greater depth at a fourth, the Serie B thriller or *giallo all'italiana,* in the next. They each tell a different story of how a working filmmaker can be understood as an artisan, a 'master' or pioneer in a particular genre, and how a directorial output can be mapped and prioritized through genre.

Sword and sandal, viking and vampire: Bava at the centre of the peplum

Under a full moon, a circle of stones shrouded in mist surrounds an altar on a hill. We hear a scream, and the camera tracks to a young woman lying at the foot of the hill, clothes torn and legs bare – only later do we realize that

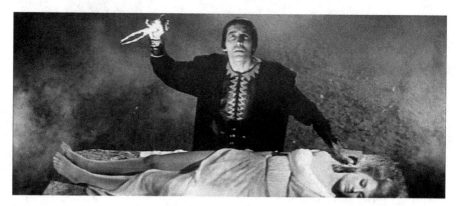

FIGURE 3 *Gothic peplum – the vampiric Lico in* Ercole al centro della terra.

she is Deianira, Hercules's intended wife. The camera tilts up to a cadaverous figure – if he puts us in mind of Dracula standing over one of his victims, that is partly because he is played by Christopher Lee.[5] He intones some ominous words about the Great Dragon devouring the moon and bringing eternal darkness as dense clouds fill the sky (some Bava trickery involving paint in a water tank) and lightning flashes. Cutaways reveal shrouded figures barely visible in the darkness, seemingly returning to their graves – subsequent shots find decaying hands lowering the lids of their sarcophagi, a sticky residue gluing the lids to their base. The opening credits roll.

Thus begins the first peplum solely credited to Bava as director.[6] *Ercole al centro della terra* is one of the more written-about peplums, alongside the two Francisci/Steve Reeves Hercules films and Vittorio Cottafavi's *Ercole alla conquista di Atlantide/Hercules Conquers Atlantis* (1961) to which Bava's film was a follow up of sorts. That can be attributed in part to its distinctive visual style, to Bava's name, and to the fact that it can be approached more or less as a horror film – the opening scene positively invites us to do so. The intended title had been *Ercole contro il vampiro* but Panda Film had already registered the title of *Maciste contro il vampiro* for its rival production. The year 1961 – the 'banner year' of the peplum (Bondanella and Pacchioni 2017: 170) – marked the arrival of the gothic peplum. Freda's *Maciste all'inferno* was released the following year, its opening scene, not unlike *La maschera del demonio*, featuring the burning of a witch who swears vengeance. Curti describes the peplum as the gothic's 'opulent and luckier twin' (2015a: location 362), while Spinazzola saw its eroticism and sadism as signalling a 'larger taste for the marvellous' (1963: 105), even characterizing it as a type of 'backwards Italian science fiction' (ibid.: 98). The vampire flitted particularly comfortably between the gothic and the mythological. Three of the five gothic films released in 1960 featured vampires – 'the sensation of the moment' after the success of Hammer's *Dracula* and the paperback anthology *I vampiri tra noi (The Vampires Amongst Us)* published by Feltrinelli the same year, and most likely where Bava first encountered Alexis Tolstoy's 'The Family of the Vourdalak' which would become one of the episodes in *I tre volti della paura* (Curti 2015a: location 1541). Above all, vampires haunted the *edicola*, the news kiosk, spawning pulp paperback series such as *I racconti di Dracula* (ibid.) – for reasons that are unclear, the vampire would enjoy greater popularity on the page than on screen in Italy. It is not entirely clear whether Lico is a literal vampire in *Ercole al centro della terra*. His intention to drink Deianira's blood is because of her royal lineage, so that he is the usual peplum usurper to the throne as much as supernatural presence, but then, in both *La maschera del demonio* and *I wurdalak*, Bava's vampires are inclined to feed on their own family members. The killing of Deianira's maid happens offscreen, but the memorable image of Lico's inverted reflection in a pool of her blood again suggests a vampiric presence. Deianira wields Pluto's stone like a crucifix to keep him at bay, and he finally dissolves not in sunlight but at the end of a lunar eclipse. Earlier in the film, we learn that not only does he have Deianira under his control but keeps her in a sarcophagus – the lid lifts by itself, and she rises on a Nosferatu-like hinge, leading to what will become one of Bava's favourite uncanny effects – a character who appears to float towards the (sometimes retreating) camera (*I tre volti della paura* uses this effect in two of its episodes). Establishing shots of the city of Ecalia, bathed in red light, show the altar and stones from the opening and closing scenes of the film to the left of the frame, as if the gothic and the peplum are immediate neighbours. When Hercules is reunited with his intended wife on his return to Ecalia, she stands morosely and semi-hypnotized by a fountain, recalling a similar scene with Katia in *La maschera del demonio* – Deinanira too is suffering the effects of a cursed family line and a relative who seeks power through her blood.

It is easy enough, then, to see *Ercole al centro della terra* as one of Bava's gothics, adding the saturated colours of the Francisci-Reeves *Ercole* films to the high gothic of his official directorial debut. But it is also part of the Hercules *filone*, which at this point still looked like a series more or less set in the same narrative world with a pre-established set of reference points and supporting characters, unlike the Maciste films which were free to go wherever and whenever they wanted, as had also been true of the original cycle of silent films – a flashback montage of scenes from previous films in *Maciste all'inferno* (where he turns up unexplained and barely dressed in sixteenth-century Scotland) seems unconcerned that he is visibly played by several different actors. Only the two Francisci-Reeves films follow on directly, even retaining some of the same actors in key roles, most notably

Sylva Koscina as Iole, who has become Hercules's wife in *Ercole e la regina di Lidia* – she has 'put me in chains', he jokes in an early scene. Deianira will be his love interest and/or wife in the next handful of films, one of the two roles played by Jayne Mansfield in *Gli amori di Ercole/The Loves of Hercules* (1960) where she meets Hercules (now Mickey Hargitay) for the first time. Bava's film was produced by Achille Piazzi for S.P.A. Cinematografica and followed two other Hercules films produced by Piazzi, both directed by Vittorio Cottafavi – if *Ercole alla conquista all'Atlantide* (1961) shows why Cottafavi was so highly regarded (it is often described as the best of the series), the tatty monsters of *La vendetta di Ercole/Goliath and the Dragon* (1960) suggest that sometimes even Cottafavi could only do so much with the material. Bava inherited Reg Park as lead from Cottafavi's second Hercules film, but it clearly does not follow on – he has yet to marry Deianira in *Ercole al centro della terra*, making it easier for Lico to control her, whereas they have been married long enough to have children (one of them an adult) in the two Cottafavi films. In chronological terms – perhaps a minor concern, considering how these films circulated, probably sometimes arriving out of order in *seconde* and *terze visioni* – it is more like a sequel to *Gli amori di Ercole*, even though it was made for a different production company and with different actors. The characterization of Hercules as someone who is tired of adventure and wants to settle down is often commented on in discussions of *Ercole alla conquista di Atlantide* – Elley (1984: 58) calls it 'the best-realised portrayal of Hercules in the cinema', and Park performs the role capably, especially considering his lack of acting experience. The two films support the popular view of Bava as being more interested in objects, colours, and effects than actors because one could easily think that his film was made first and that Park had improved as an actor for the Cottafavi film. Instead, he seems to have regressed, an inexpressive (if visually striking) muscular presence, suggesting that Cottafavi or someone else actually directed him, while Bava's interests lay elsewhere. Bava had photographed Steve Reeves several times, as Hercules or as Philippides in *La battaglia di Maratona* – 'The camera loved Steve Reeves', claims Rushing (2016: 45), and it was often Bava's camera that did the adoring. Park's Hercules carries out the required feats of strength – throwing a huge boulder to retrieve a magic apple in the Garden of the Hesperides or toppling the fearsome Procrustes – and is first introduced through a Tarzan-like dive from a waterfall. But perhaps as much as anything because the peplum was diversifying, being contaminated by other genres – and Bava was ideally placed to capitalize on this contamination – the film's preferred spectacle is less that of the male body than an extraordinary concoction of crypts and cobwebs, revolving door sarcophagi, gels and literally saturated skies, the vampiric and the pulp-mythological. Cottafavi 'aims higher', according to Elley (1984: 58) – a view commonly expressed about their broader output until more recently – but identifies the two Hercules films they made in

1961 as two of the finest examples of the 'genre-within-a-genre' he calls the '*fantastique* peplum'.

The 'peplum' has become the default term for a 'mythological, historical-mythological or pseudo-mythological action movie, usually based on a Greco-Roman legend, produced in Italy between 1957 and 1965' (O'Brien 2014: 2). They were neither the first nor the last historical-mythological films made in Italy – there is a cycle during the silent era, including the original Maciste films, and a 1980s mini-*filone* of sword-and-sorcery films prompted by the success of *Conan the Barbarian* (1982). But the term is most likely to conjure up images of Steve Reeves, Reg Park or Gordon Scott pitting their muscular bodies against despotic rulers, supernatural beings or men from the moon. While I do not intend to interrogate the term as rigorously – some might say, pedantically – as I will the *giallo* in the next chapter, it does require some definition of how it is being used here. The 'peplum' was never an industry term, or a word used contemporaneously by Italian film critics – rather, *Le fatiche di Ercole* generated interconnecting *filoni* and *sottofiloni* (sub-cycles) of costume adventure films, usually made on a modest budget at best. Lino Miccichè called them 'film romano-mitologico' (1975: 108), while Spinazzola, one of the few Italian critics who admitted to liking them, used the more common (and more inclusive) 'film storico-mitologici' (1963: 75). They were also known as *cappa e spada* (cloak and sword) films, roughly equivalent to the English 'sword and sandal'. Jon Solomon (2014) calls them 'Ancients', but even Italian writers now tend to use the word 'peplum' – it is the title of Francesco Di Chiara's 2016 book, for example.

O'Brien (2014: 2) and Rushing (2016: 1) see the term as less derogatory than some of its equivalents. It was first used in critical writing in a 1961 *Cahiers du Cinéma* review of Riccardo Freda's *I giganti della Tessaglia* (1960), although it was supposedly in use at the ciné-club Nickel-Odéon before that (Di Chiara 2016: 5). As with *film noir*, adopted generic terms bring with them a certain freedom of use, less likely to trip over (as with the *giallo*) pre-existing uses, and no two writers map the field in exactly the same way. Is it confined to films with muscular male bodies, as is the case in Rushing's book (2016) but probably wasn't for critics at *Cahiers*? How ancient does the history need to be and can it go beyond Greco-Roman settings to encompass Vikings, pirates, the Indian hero Sandokan, or the Thief of Baghdad? Might we include *Le meraviglie di Aladino*, even though it is primarily a comedy with Donald O'Connor in the title role and Vittorio De Sica as his genie? Is the peplum strictly confined to Italian cinema, or can it include any heady mix of mythology and muscles? Both Miccichè (1975: 109) and Frayling (1981: 71) attribute four to Bava without naming them, but they must presumably include at least one of his two Viking films. While blatantly modelled on *The Vikings* (1958), one of the ways in which *Gli invasori* distinguishes itself from Richard Fleischer's film is through its kinship with the peplum. Why cast the German Kessler twins as the respective love interest of the two separated male twins? One of the reasons is surely that they are dancers, capable of pulling off one of the required setpieces of the peplum – the dance performed by slave girls or in this case, vestal virgins (figures from *Ancient Rome!*). After an opening scene establishes the separation of brothers Erik and Eron when the vikings are lured into a trip by the villainous Lord Rutford (a classic peplum usurper), we are taken forward twenty years to what an onscreen caption calls 'the land of the vikings', a Bava-coloured cavern at the foot of a gigantic tree reminiscent of Omphale's crimson-hued cavern in *Ercole e la regina di Lidia* (or, at a push, Diabolik's hideout a few years later). A couple are tied crucifixion-style back-to-back on top of a large, wheeled platform decorated with skulls and bones, awaiting execution for the woman's infidelity to Odin. As the camera cranes up, the dancing vestal virgins emerge, but they are merely the warm-up act for a sword dance by Daja (Ellen Kessler) and Rama (Alice Kessler). There are similar scenes in most peplums from this period, part of what Michèle Lagny calls 'a seemingly unending series of dances, feasts, fights in the arena, chariot races and victory parades', a low-cost 'bread and circuses' for the audience (1992: 172). *Ercole al centro della terra* is a notable exception, unless one includes the Noh-like movements of the Sibyl, Ecalia too much of a cursed city for such festivities. Rushing claims that it is the female, not the male body, that is the body in motion in the peplum (2016: 51) and while such intriguing observations sometimes rely on generalizations, the casting of the Kesslers offers some support, even if *Gli invasori* is not short of male violence (a spear penetrates both a mother and the baby in her arms during the opening massacre) or the genre's requisite sadism (Daya threatened with a torture device that releases a deadly spider when its sand runs out). Italy produced a handful of Viking films, usually starring Cameron Mitchell (as is the case with both of Bava's) – perhaps seen as an affordable equivalent to Kirk Douglas. Bava is thought to have also worked uncredited on the first of the cycle, *L'ultimo dei vichinghi/The Last of the Vikings* (1960). To complicate matters, Bava's second Viking film, *I coltelli del vendicatore*, is a bit late for the peplum *filone* – it was started by another director in 1964 and abandoned when the money ran out. It is also rather different in style, often seen as a kind of 'Viking Western' – Pezzotta notes the incongruous harmonica on the soundtrack (2013: 78). Its hero Rurik (Mitchell again) is a lone rider and dark avenger with an unheroic past (he raped the woman he now protects in a misdirected revenge for the massacre of his family and is revealed to be the father of her son). Several confrontations play out in taverns reminiscent of Western saloons, the heavies unwisely taunting the hero as he drinks alone at his table (or he provokes them by deliberately sitting at the table usually reserved for their boss). And while Bava had yet to be connected to the initially troubled attempts to film *Diabolik*, audiences might have been put in mind of the 'Swiisss!' of Diabolik's daggers (like Rurik, two thrown at once) in the *fumetto*, a detail that would be played down in Bava's later film. A more engaging 'Western' than Bava's actual Westerns, a 'late' peplum or a film without an obvious cyclical home, another of Bava's 'rescue' films, *I coltelli del vendicatore* tells us as much about the unpredictable and precarious phase that Bava's career (and Italian cinema) entered in the late 1960s as it does about whichever genre or *filone* it might belong to. But it should be evident here that I am using the term 'peplum' in its broadest, but still specifically Italian, sense to cover a range of mythological-historical spectacle films. This is, after all, how cycles and *filoni* worked, branching off into *sottofiloni*.

During the same period that Bava directed *Ercole al centro della terra* and *Gli invasori* and made whatever contribution he did to *Esther e il re*, he is thought to have done uncredited effects work on several others. 1961–2 was a tipping point for the peplum in terms of prestige and resources – *Sodoma e Gomorra* (1962), signed by Robert Aldrich, was rescued by Sergio Leone in much the same way that Bava and Bruno Vailati rescued *La battaglia di Maratona*. Budgets fell away and Hollywood directors like Walsh, Tourneur and Aldrich were no longer attached to projects.[7] But initially peplums were often well resourced by local standards, and Bava was well paid for his contribution to *Le fatiche di Ercole* (Di Chiara 2016: 155). As Spinazzola recognized in 1963, Bava was one of the key architects of the peplum boom alongside Galatea and Lux as production companies, directors such as Francisci, Freda and Cottafavi, and writers like Ennio De Concini – 'the real father of the genre in its golden age' (Di Chiara 2016: 54) – and Duccio Tessari, who co-wrote both *Ercole alla conquista di Atlantide* and *Ercole al centro della terra* and would debut as a director in the peplum before moving on to the Western (along with another peplum artisan Sergio Corbucci) and other *filoni*. 'Bavaesque imagery' is the caption accompanying a still from *Ercole e la regina di Lidia* (a film directed by Francisci) in Derek Elley's *The Epic Film* (1984: 57) – Sylva Koscina as Iole, shadows falling ominously across her face and body, the black and white reproduction turning reds and greens into chiaroscuro. The most frequently reproduced still from the film – Sylvia Lopez as Omphale clutching Hercules's calf, seemingly in a state of perpetual arousal – is emblematic of the genre as well as forging another link with the gothic through its witches, enchantresses and scheming Amazon queens. Omphale is a vampiric figure, draining the energy of her endless lovers (Hercules loses his legendary strength along with his memory) before turning them into living statues – the fate of female victims in horror films such as *House of Wax* and *Il mulino delle donne di pietra*.

If the peplum exhibits, as Austin Fisher argues, 'a kind of tension with Hollywood cinema' (2017: 254), that tension is particularly evident in a more expensive film like *Ester e il re*, a Galatea film partly funded by its US distributor Twentieth Century Fox – a peplum closer in scale to the Hollywood Epic, with an American director attached (whatever the actual division of labour on the set). Thematically, it sits closer to the preoccupations of the Hollywood Epic, not least in its emphasis on Jewish persecution. The Bible was not a major source for the more modestly budgeted peplum, apart from recruiting Goliath to its Avengers Assemble of muscular heroes. But the film's titular characters are a dull pair, and it is the Italians who seem to be having most of the fun – Sergio Fantoni's silky Haman, 'a prince of festering corruption', and pouting Queen Vashti, played by Galatea regular Daniela Rocca. In the Old Testament 'Book of Esther', Queen Vashti is banished for refusing to attend the King's banquet and refusing to show him due respect. But the film escalates this into one of the peplum's trademark dance sequences, climaxing with the Queen removing her top. Admittedly, such sequences can be found in Hollywood Epics, too – Gina Lollobrigida's pagan dance in *Solomon and Sheba* (1959) is a notable example – but *Ester e il re* has barely finished a slave girl dance (which the King finds more tedious than the audience is probably expected to) before throwing Rocca and her more agile double at us.

Bava would return to the historical-mythological (and biblical) on a smaller screen. In 1975 he did second unit and effects work on the Italian-British mini-series *Moses the Lawgiver* (1974) – he had already parted *a*, if not *the*, red sea for Hercules and Theseus in 1961. But he made a more

FIGURE 4 Odissea – *Bava adds the gothic and his* trucchi *to the Polyphemus episode.*

substantial and memorable contribution to the prestigious *Odissea* in 1968. While mostly directed by Franco Rossi, Bava was assigned the episode featuring the cyclops Polyphemus – not a self-contained TV episode but roughly thirty minutes of narrative from the final minutes of episode 3 to just over half of episode 4. The onscreen credits for these two episodes highlight Bava's contribution – 'La regia dell'episodio di Polifemo è di Mario Bava'. Di Chiara situates the series somewhere between the 'cultural diffusion' represented by Roberto Rossellini's TV work and the more fantastical elements that the peplum traded on (2016: 82). Lagny has described the peplum as 'learned culture... reused by popular culture' (1992: 173), and while the 'learned' was emphasized in the Homeric verse that opened each episode, Bava was clearly recruited to terrify the audience. Without having to draft in vampires or witches, the episode plays as sheer gothic horror. While some of the more gruesome details are kept just out of view – one of Ulysses's men has his head smashed on a rock before being pulled in two and then eaten – the atmosphere of sheer terror is carried particularly by reaction shots of gibbering, and in one case fainting, onlookers and a more sparing use of the zoom than would become typical of Bava's later work. While Carlo Rambaldi (a veteran of both the peplum and the horror films) handled Polyphemus himself, Bava provided some of his most seamless effects work as human figures interact in shot with the giant monster. While the series accorded auteur status to Rossi, the artisan Bava might have left its younger audience with lasting nightmares about gigantic hands and the sound of cracking bones. Watched by an average 16.6 million viewers per episode during its original transmission on RAI between March and May 1968,[8] it now seems fitting that some of the most widely seen work by the 'forgotten' or 'neglected' Bava once again married the peplum to horror.

Il gotico 'Made in Italy'

If one had tried to determine the style and preoccupations of *horror all'italiana* on the basis of films released in 1960, it would not have been unreasonable to conclude that a mixture of mild and derivative thrills and even milder titillation would be Italy's contribution to a genre otherwise dominated by British and North American films. This formula is best represented by the English title of *L'ultima preda del vampiro* (1960), *The Playgirls and the Vampire,* which throws together bloodsuckers, ineptly staged dance sequence, some brief nudity and babydoll nighties – one of its opening shots focuses on the bare thighs of one of the 'playgirls' as she adjusts her stockings. The recipe is put together rather better in *L'amante del vampiro/The Vampire and the Ballerina* (1960), which is more eclectic in its borrowings. Hammer's influence is more visible (a Dracula-like silhouette in a bedroom balcony doorway, gruesome disintegration in sunlight), and there is an unexpected echo of Dreyer's *Vampyr* as a newly turned vampire awakes in her coffin and watches her own funeral through its window. *Seddok, l'erede di Satana* (1960) is not, despite a throwaway comment about its titular monster being an 'atomic vampire',[9] a vampire film, but its lead female character is a stripper, allowing the film to open with her undressing. Screenwriter Dardano Sacchetti claims that Italian audiences did not realize that Hammer films were meant to be frightening – 'people went to see them because you could get a peek at the actress' breasts as Dracula attacked them!' (quoted by Bini 2011: 63). While most likely a generalization, this certainly seems to be the assumption made by the 'sexy' vampire films of 1960. Mainly remediated now as paracinematic retro-kitsch on cult DVD labels, these films tend to be marginal to the 'Italian Horror' canon which forms above all around *La maschera del demonio,* invariably seen as the seminal standout Italian horror classic of 1960 and entirely untypical of the output of that year. Once again, Galatea were instrumental in fashioning a genre cinema that practised the art of *risparmio* but also recruited the artisans with the skills to add markers of quality. *Caltiki, il mostro immortale* had been their first foray into the genre – famous for its amorphous creature fashioned out of tripe by Bava (how tempting a metaphor that might have been for unsympathetic critics if they had known) – but more money and resources were put into Bava's official debut. Galatea also distributed *Il mulino delle donne di pietra,* the first Italian horror film in colour and thus closer to the then-influential look of Hammer as well as re-elaborating the premise of *House of Wax* in a mock-Netherlands setting. The vampire is the most conspicuous thread in the initial Italian gothic, from *I vampiri*'s updating of the subgenre to the comedy *Tempi duri per il vampiro* to the three films released in 1960 – more vampire films would follow over the next few years. Bava claimed not to know about vampires prior to making *La maschera del demonio,* and they are entirely absent from his initial treatment written in 1959 under the title 'Il Vij', after Gogol's story (Gomarasca and Pulici 2004: 20).[10] Bava's plea of ignorance may or may not be true but adheres to the popular view of the gloomy gothic as a 'foreigner' in sunny Italy. 'As good Mediterraneans we don't have any sympathy for horrors,' claimed a dismissive Italian review of *The Bride of Frankenstein* (quoted by Venturini 2014: location 67). But if Bava was prepared to play the part of the 'good Mediterranean', he obviously knew his Wurdalaks, if not his vampires – might he have first encountered the undead in Tolstoy's story, thus approaching the vampire story as a folk tale, rather than an attempt to marry Hammer to Teaserama?

While earlier traces of 'Italian horror' can be retrospectively identified (Venturini 2014; Hunter 2016), *I vampiri* is undisputed as the start of the genre proper in Italy, occupying a pioneer status that is sometimes a mixed blessing for a film's reputation. But not until 1960 does *il gotico* look like a *filone* with a sudden blossoming of five films – six if we include the comedy *Il mio amico Jekyll*. Horror was also a generic presence at the *edicola* with cheap paperback series, such as *I racconti di Dracula* and *KKK – I classici dell'orrore* better able to disguise their Italian origins by pretending to be translations of foreign originals.[11] None of the films made any great impression at the local box office, and *La maschera del demonio*'s seminal status can partly be attributed to its international success. Whether it can be credited with making 'Horror Made in Italy' a generic brand depends on the degree to which its Italianness was registered abroad – one or two reviews did mistake it for an American or British film. As Baschiera and Hunter observe, the 'Italian' in 'Italian horror' is hard to identify satisfactorily, often reduced to 'extreme, visceral content', which is by no means unique to Italy (2016: 2). Nevertheless, notwithstanding *I vampiri*, Italian horror, as it is taken to be widely understood, is often seen to begin with a mask, a large hammer, and a woman with extraordinary eyes, the start of a road that leads to Argento, Fulci and Lamberto Bava, whose collaboration with Argento, *Dèmoni*, has been identified as an end point in a great tradition of Italian horror (Gomarasca and Pulici 2004: 4).[12] The father–son angle gives this narrative a pleasing circularity – with Argento as both successor (to Mario) and mentor (to Lamberto). That it is ultimately just that – a narrative – does not detract from its force in making sense of the Italian horror film. Graphic violence, then, is one of the elements that identify *La maschera del demonio* as the curtain-raiser. But this is not a consistent feature of either Bava's other horror films or other Italian gothics. The Italian gothic did not produce anything that violent again until Margheriti's *Le vergine di Norimberga* (1963) nor did Bava until *6 donne per l'assassino*, which featured a different kind of violence that has not lost its ability to shock.[13] Then there is the film's conspicuous style, its fluid camera movements and highly expressive lighting, but while that is a marker of Bava's earlier films in particular, thus his reputation as a stylist and (because of Argento) Italian horror's reputation for being 'stylish', it is not a consistent feature of Italian gothic horror either. Margheriti's more workman-like approach with multi-camera set-ups is a case in point. In terms of *il filone gotico* of 1960–6, its most significant feature is its iconic star.

The 'woman as the motivating force of the storyline' (Bini 2011: 54) is often identified as distinguishing Italian horror from this period from its Anglo-American equivalents (Günsberg 2005; Curti 2015a) – *I vampiri* sets the precedent. Early Italian horror films struggle to find a compelling male vampire – Walter Brandi is particularly underwhelming in *L'amante del vampiro* and *L'ultimo preda del vampiro*, and while Arturo Dominici's Javutich is formidable enough, he is subordinate to Asa in *La maschera del demonio*. Barbara Steele, as much a *filone* in herself as star or icon, would emblematize this and prove to be as instrumental in Italian horror's presumed distinctiveness as any director. She made as many gothic films as

Bava, Margheriti and Freda combined during this period. Finally, there is the relationship between narrative and spectacle, evident in both derogatory comments in reviews about weak scripts and the claims of contemporary admirers that they cannot remember the plots and that therefore the films are all about the images. Rushing's characterization of the peplum in some ways applies equally to the Italian gothic:

> There is, strictly speaking, not much narrative in the sense of unfolding and concatenated events, each a consequence of what went before. Rather, there is a series of setpieces.
>
> (2016: 16)

In some ways, this is even more true of the gothic horror film – generally, more a genre of atmosphere, sensation and spectacle than narrative complexity. Italian horror often seems to exhibit an uncertainty about who it is addressing. A local audience, a 'European', or an international one? *Prima visione* or *il mercato di profondità*? As producers and short-lived production companies tried to second guess public taste – and often foreign taste – artisans tried to keep things interesting for themselves and the audience. Editor Mario Serandrei allegedly obtained a writing credit on *La maschera del demonio* by virtue of compiling the most coherent version of the events and setpieces that De Concini and others wrote and Bava and his team filmed – if we are not always even sure whether it is day or night, the film's basic scenario is straightforward enough and largely makes as much sense as it needs to. We are not invited to worry, for example, about why Javutich is able to resurrect to full strength at Asa's command while she can barely move from her tomb even after drinking Kruvajan's blood (which was supposed to restore all her strength) until she has absorbed Katia's lifeforce, which makes thematic if not narrative sense. Thus, we might remember the film in a very particular way – as a basic (and relatively familiar) genre set-up and as a series of more memorable setpieces and images, which give the impression of being what the film is really 'about'. On the other hand, *La frusta e il corpo* is more carefully structured and paced, even if its murder mystery plot is probably not what most will remember about the film, and the individual episodes in *I tre volti della paura* either exhibit a narrative tightness less evident in Bava's feature-length plots (*I wurdalak*) or allow a very simple premise to be an exercise in sustained atmosphere and shock tactics (*La goccia d'acqua*).

Bava returned to the gothic in what Venturini calls the *filone*'s hinge year, 1963 (2014: location 966). Both *La frusta e il corpo* and *I tre volti della paura* were modelled in different ways on the Corman-Poe series, the former an attempt to capitalize on the success of *Pit and the Pendulum*, the latter both Bava's final Galatea film and the last of his original gothics to be re-packaged by AIP. In the same year, Margheriti made *La vergine di*

Norimberga and *Danza Macabra* (the latter, starring Barbara Steele, released early in 1964), and Freda made *Lo spettro,* also with Steele. If the Italian vampire cycle wrestled with Hammer or ignored them as *La maschera del demonio* seemed to do, the Corman series resonates to a greater or lesser degree in nearly all of the 1963 gothics. *Danza Macabra* features Poe as a character, while *La vergine di Norimberga* elaborates on the torture devices of *Pit and the Pendulum* (in which Steele ended up in an Iron Maiden). Both *La frusta e il corpo* and *Lo spettro* adopt the leisurely pace and nocturnal wandering of the Poe films. And just as Corman's *Pit and the Pendulum* throws *Les Diaboliques* into its gothic mix (a fabricated haunting as cover for an extramarital plot), both films feature 'ghosts' that are not supernatural beings – a projection of the heroine's desires (*La frusta e il corpo*) or a husband faking his own death and pretending to come back for revenge (*Lo spettro*). Peter John Dyer's anonymous review in the British *Monthly Film Bulletin* called *La frusta e il corpo* a 'prankish' simulation of British horror (Anon. 1965a: 40), perhaps because of the presence of Christopher Lee, whose whipping of Daliah Lavi's Nevenka also reminded the same reviewer, in a different publication, of Gainsborough's brand of period cruelty in films such as *The Man in Grey* (Dyer 1965: 5). But from the opening scene, Tor Caldara stands in for the eerie coastline in *Pit and the Pendulum*, both films exemplifying 'matte romanticism' (Van Leeuwen 2019: 48) in their hill-top castles. The corridor-wandering often marks time in the Corman-Poe films, where Hammer are more impatient to move their busier plots forward. But one of *La frusta*'s greatest setpieces – a *tour de force* of Bava's lighting, Terzano's camerawork and, above all, Lavi's performance – finds Nevenka wandering the corridors of the castle in an attempt to trace what sounds like the crack of a whip. The camera remains tight on her face for much of the time, capturing the light and shadow, the filtered colours and the play of emotions on her face. When she enters a room full of furniture covered in dust sheets, the zoom lens seems to swoon in the reverse shots between her and the furniture, her eyes filling with tears. When the 'whip' proves to be merely a vine lashing the window blown open by the wind, her disappointment registers more strongly than any sense of relief. Bava is often thought to be more interested in objects than people – Pezzotta cites a circular tracking shot in the same film around a vase of red roses as two characters engage in some dull exposition (2013: 64). But Lavi's face is the most constant object of attention in the film. The Corman-Poe influence makes this a much more coherent body of Italian gothic films than the releases of 1960, even if that influence manifests itself in different ways.[14] *I tre volti della paura* takes Corman's *Tales of Terror* as its model in its three-story structure, its use of an established horror star, and claimed literary credentials (genuine in Corman's Poe adaptation, misleading in at least one of the Bava episodes). While Vincent Price was the face of the Corman-Poes, Boris Karloff appeared in three AIP gothics in 1963 – Corman's *The Raven* and *The Terror,* and Jacques Tourneur's *Comedy of Terrors. I wurdalak,* the most substantial episode of *I tre volti della paura,* is surprisingly faithful to its literary source, the story of a peasant family who fall victim to their vampire-father – like Prince Vajda in *La maschera del demonio,* a father who is no longer a father but retains his paternal authority, the wurdalak/ vourdalak a vampire that devours those it loves most. One scene comes straight from the page as Gorka lurks in D'Urfe's room, the latter anxiously awake and sensing his presence – when he sits up suddenly, the vampire patriarch seems to have disappeared until a fast zoom finds him staring hungrily through the window. The face, or hand, at the window is an image that comes to epitomize the 'Bavaesque' gothic – in *La frusta e il corpo, Lisa e il diavolo,* and above all, *Operazione paura* – a repeated trick that never lets the films down.

Science fiction was even more marginal to Italian cinema than horror until the success of *Star Wars* prompted an imitative cycle in the late 1970s, but by the mid-1960s Antonio Margheriti was its most productive director, due to four films primarily aimed at American television often referred to as the 'Gamma Space Station' series, starting with *I diafanoidi portano la morte/ War of the Planets* (1965). Juvenile and mainly enjoyed now for their kitsch retro-futuristic designs, they otherwise stand in contrast with Bava's *Terrore nello spazio,* which Philip Strick called 'a cheerily relocated *Haunted Palace'* (1986b: 59), that is to say a science fiction re-working of an H.P. Lovecraft adaptation that was originally packaged as a Poe film. Often reduced to being cast as the Serie B forerunner to *Alien* (1979), what it shares with that film is taking the gothic into space. *Filone* films often 'participate in, rather than belong to, genres' (Günsberg 2005: 2) and *Terrore nello spazio* is a case in point. It can even be seen to take the peplum as part of its space cargo, with one of the spaceships named the Argos and an alien landscape reminiscent – probably by necessity as much as design – of the Underworld visited by Hercules and Theseus (the travellers are warned in both films not to be deceived by appearances). The film was loosely adapted – a complex process involving both Italian and English-language writers – from a short story by Renato Pestriniero in the science-fiction magazine *Oltre il cielo (Beyond the Sky). Una notte di 21 ore* is a mixture of *Forbidden Planet* (some cod-Freudian talk about the planet acting on the Id) and *Invasion of the Body Snatchers,* to which the film adds two (or should that be three?) alien races, the antagonists seeking control of the crew of the Argos and the remains of a more ancient, and gigantic, species that has already fallen victim to the planet's disembodied inhabitants. Possession, the undead and doubling structure the film – two spaceships (the Argos and the Galliott), the crew and their possessed reanimated doubles, and a crew that we take to be from earth (the English dialogue refers to them as human) but turn out to be from a more advanced civilization that merely resembles ours. Giorgio Giovannini's production design reflects the hybrid identity of the film – the futuristic and the archaic, the pseudo-science of Meteor Rejectors and the future-gothic of polythene shrouds and metallic grave markers.[15]

Made at the end of the 1960s gothic cycle, *Operazione paura* is a little harder to situate. The last Barbara Steele gothic, *Un angelo per Satana*, was released the same year, and the Corman-Poe films had run their course, although AIP continued to exploit the Poe brand. The different titles of the film in some ways speak of its cyclical 'homelessness'. The word 'operazione' was ubiquitous in Italian film titles during the 1960s, including re-titled foreign ones – one of the Bond films, *Thunderball* (1965), became *Operazione tuona* (Operation Thunder), for example. As this suggests, the word conjured up the *filone spionistico*, rather than gothic horror. The American title *Kill, Baby... Kill!* makes it sound like a sequel to *Faster, Pussycat... Kill, Kill!* with its promise of titillation as well as thrills, although it would have served as an effective English title for any of Bava's thrillers. The UK *Curse of the Dead* is more apt, but only because almost any Italian horror film up to that point could have been called *Curse of the Dead*.[16] Strangest of all is the German title *Die toten Augen des Doktor Dracula* – the Dead Eyes of Dr Dracula, which also seems to nod to Edgar Wallace and even Dr Mabuse. Eschewing the violence of *La maschera del demonio* and the perversity of *La frusta e il corpo*, made on a much smaller budget (which apparently ran out) than the earlier gothics, and with a score consisting of recycled music cues, it is nevertheless a favourite with Bava connoisseurs, supposedly Martin Scorsese's favourite of the director's films and its reputation bolstered by its similarity to (and possible influence on) Fellini's *Toby Dammit*. Starting in the key of Corman-Poe – a coach driver refuses to take the hero all the way to a cursed destination that gives him a hostile welcome – its scenario mixes rehashed clichés with bizarre inventions, its colour scheme and camerawork are more subdued and it is in no rush to get to its best-remembered sequences. But it shares one affinity with all of Bava's gothic films. Just as much as women are at the centre of things (which is particularly applicable here – a ghostly child, a benevolent witch, an evil medium/mother, a heroine returning to her uncanny home) – so too is the family.

'We all want to know where we come from, and from whom', says Peter von Kleist at the beginning of *Gli orrori del castello di Norimberga*, and he will learn to be careful what he wishes for. The tainted family line is a familiar gothic trope and variations can be found in *La maschera del demonio*, where Asa preys on her descendants, the women fated to resemble her, and *Ercole al centro della terra*, where Deianira, the heir to the throne, is preyed upon by her uncle in his quest for power. But from *La maschera del demonio* to *Shock*, all of Bava's gothic films – *Terrore nello spazio* is an exception, its Sci-Fi DNA winning out – are to some degree about the family. The family is fragile in *La frusta e il corpo* – dead mother, ailing father, disinherited son, fraternal rivals, arranged marriages – and, as in *Lisa e il diavolo*, female desire gives it just the push needed to topple it over. Incest lurks in the

FIGURE 5 *Woman as 'motivating force' of the Italian gothic – Ruth confronts the Baroness in* Operazione paura.

green or red shadows of the Bava gothic – the father trying to feed on his daughter (*La maschera del demonio*) or his whole family (*I wurdalak*), a young man who has murdered his mother in a possessive rage (*Il rosso segno della follia*) or to escape her possessiveness (*Lisa e il diavolo*), a young boy play-wrestling with his mother and suddenly exhibiting unmistakable sexual pleasure in dominating her (*Shock*).

How might we account for this thematic thread? While Bava's own career and reputation as a filmmaker is strongly connected to being part of a family line, this kind of biographical auteurism is not the most productive way of approaching this question, tempting though it might seem. First, the family is there for the taking in the gothic as a mode – in the literary source that *I wurdalak* is adapted from and more contemporaneously with the Poe series, which began with the most famous of tainted gothic families, the Ushers, and re-wrote *The Pit and the Pendulum* as a story of a protagonist doomed by his masculine lineage. Even Hammer, their titular character absent from *Dracula*'s first sequel, turned *The Brides of Dracula* (1960) into the story of a vampire first overindulged and then imprisoned by his mother before escaping and feeding on her – 'He has taken the blood of his own mother', observes Peter Cushing's Van Helsing with undisguised revulsion. In *I wurdalak,* the family is suffocating, vampiric, ruled by a dead father, literally consuming itself. All of this is in the original story, but the film makes more of Sdenka's desire to escape – she actually leaves with D'Urfé, a departure from Tolstoy's story, but the undead family will not allow the tie to be broken ('No one can love you more than we do'). They surround her and close in on her ('floating' towards her, one of Bava's signature effects). D'Urfé is played by Mark Damon, who had attempted to free Madeline Usher from her family line in Corman's *House of Usher*. Closer to home, the family was one of the central institutions of the Christian Democrats, but *il boom*, Italy's 'economic miracle', would inevitably re-shape the Italian family as urbanization had the effect of privatizing the family unit as collective festivals and gatherings became less common – it 'closed in upon itself' (Ginsborg 1990: 243). But at the same time new freedoms became available for younger family members, that which Sdenka seeks with the wealthy and worldly D'Urfé. However, while some of Bava's films might lend themselves to this kind of symptomatic reading, it risks being rather too schematic as the socio-historical key to the films, particularly as it preoccupied the horror thriller genres more generally between the 1960s and 1970s. Nevertheless, Bava's gothic films (and some of the thrillers with which they overlap) suggest that it was being reworked a little more in Italy than in comparable cycles of the period, a theme that *il gotico italiano* could explore with varying degrees of intensity. And if the gothics did not themselves appear to resonate with Italian audiences, there is reason to think that the family as a site of violence, perversion and murder probably did.

Richard Dyer argues that the family is a central force in the Serie B thrillers of the 1970s which present the family as 'at once endemically perverse and violent and something to be defended from the degeneration of modernity and non-reproductivity', its members often called upon to kill 'to help one another out' (2015: 191). In these films, killing often boils down to matters of inheritance (ibid.: 187), which is true of two of Bava's thrillers, *La ragazza che sapeva troppo* and particularly *Ecologia del delitto*, but Kurt in *La frusta e il corpo* has been disinherited, leading us to think that he might have come back from the dead (or faked his death) in order to take revenge on his father, whereas Nevenka is revealed to be the killer. Bava of course blurred the lines between the gothic and the *giallo*, adding the grand guignol of the former to the intrigue of the latter in *6 donne per l'assassino* and *Ecologia del delitto* or moving from the story of a serial killer to a ghost story in *Il rosso segno della follia*, so we might expect some thematic spillage. Dyer traces the multiple killings of the *giallo all'italiana* to the memory of Leonarda Cianciulli, the *Saponificatrice* (soap-maker), who turned the bodies of three women into jam, cakes, soap and candles; she was convicted in 1946. Having lost most of her fourteen children during adolescence, she believed that the Madonna had told her that she must make human sacrifices to save her son (ibid.: 183–4). It would not be too much of a leap from La Cianciulli to Baroness Graps in *Operazione paura*, who communes with the spirits of the dead at her dilapidated villa and attributes the deaths in the village to their control over the ghost of her daughter Melissa, taking revenge for allowing her to die during a festival. But the Baroness turns out to be the controlling force, staring at herself in a distorted mirror, driving Melissa to kill – does Melissa seek revenge herself or is she merely the weapon of her insane mother? If most of the deaths are motivated by revenge, her most curious intended victim is Monica Schuftan, who left the village when she was one-year-old and has returned to visit her parents' grave. It turns out that she is the Baroness's other, younger, daughter – the Schuftans were servants at the villa who adopted her – sent away after Melissa's death and now the object of some sort of sacrifice by her mother. To what end? To bring back Melissa? To please her favourite, and possibly jealous, daughter? The plotting is murky in its details, but what is important is that the bad mother is doubly evil – compelling one child to kill, baby, kill, while lining up the other (now an adult) as one of her sacrificial victims. A painting of Melissa portrays her as an already frightening figure, pointing accusingly, sharing the frame with a human skull – might she have been a malignant child in life that the villagers had good reason to leave to die or is this simply the Baroness's preferred image of her as eternally vengeful? That Melissa fades away when Ruth, a youthful but wise witch, strangles the Baroness, suggests the latter. While Dr Eswai is the notional hero of the film, representing a rational perspective that the gothic rarely has much patience with, the real drama plays out between four female characters – the Baroness, Melissa, Monica and Ruth. Like Sdenka in *I wurdalak*, Monica's best chance of survival is to escape the family ties that threaten to destroy her. The 'former home' – the maternal body – is central to Freud's conception of *das unheimlich*, the uncanny, and Villa Graps is a place of plunging staircases and rooms that multiply themselves, dolls that come to life, doubles, and involuntary repetition – Freud recalled the uncanny effect of getting lost in an Italian town and constantly arriving back at the same place (2004: 87), like Eswai finding himself running repeatedly into the same room. The Villa sucks people in and expels them (Eswai, trapped in a spider web, suddenly finds himself outside), and represents death for the returning Monica. If the film never quite found its ideal title, *Operation Uncanny* might have done the job.

The gothic was even more marginal to 1970s Italian genre cinema than that of the 1960s – critical interest tends to shift to the combination of *giallo*, thriller and horror that comprises *il thrilling italiano*. Thus, Bava's 1970s gothics are a more disparate group, disconnected from contemporaneous trends – a film often regarded as nostalgic and backward-looking, a film that was forced to become a completely different film in order to obtain distribution, and a move towards the televisual for a director often seen to epitomize *cinema-cinema*. If the televisual marks a flattening of Bava's gothic aestheticism in *Shock*, *La venere d'Ille*, which was made for the small screen, carries markers of 'quality television' as a period literary adaptation (from Prosper Mérimée's short story) and as part of a prestigious RAI series *I giochi del diavolo – Storie fantastiche dell'Ottocento*. 'Given a castle, what does one do?', asked a review of Georges Franju's 1960 comic murder mystery *Pleins feux sur l'assassin*. 'Everything, replies Franju, that can be done with a castle' (quoted by Ince 2005: 66). Much the same could be said of Bava and the Austrian castle used in *Gli orrori del castello di Norimberga* – Coca Cola machine upstairs, torture chamber downstairs, impaled bodies on the battlements. Roberto Curti expresses a popular view that the film is 'treading water', with Bava reusing old tricks and effects as a 'pragmatic safety net' (2017: 55–6), reminding us of outmoded styles and former glories. Any impression of it recycling the 1960s gothic is reinforced by AIP releasing it with a Les Baxter score. It sits comfortably alongside their early 1970s output, which was still capitalizing on Vincent Price's late stardom in the *Dr Phibes* films – Joseph Cotton's curious performance, starting every line with a chuckle, seems to be aiming for Price's tongue-in-cheek approach to the gothic. But the film's most striking sequence involves the summoning of the witch Elisabeth Hollë, persecuted and executed by the Baron, with the help of a young woman with powerful ESP, Christina Hoffman. Not only are the two women played by the same actress, Rada Rassimov, but they are presented in the same frame through a double exposure effect. Elisabeth-Christina recalls Ruth from *Operazione paura*, not least in the arcane objects that decorate the young medium's apartment, and although she is ostensibly a more marginal presence in the film (Rassimov gets a 'Special Participation' credit), she expresses a more contemporary view – 'Once you killed innocent witches and now you bring murderers back to life'. While Christina falls victim to the Baron, Elisabeth becomes an invisible but audible presence during von Kleist's final gory fate, bringing to mind one of the chants of Italian feminists in the 1970s – 'tremate, tremate, le streghe son tornate' (tremble, tremble, the witches have returned).

Shock was re-titled *Beyond the Door 2* in the United States, again re-packaging a Bava film, if only in name this time, as part of the possession cycle – *Beyond the Door* was the North American title for *Chi sei?*, one of the first Italian exorcism films.[17] Indeed, it is a story of possession to a degree, but not by a devil or demon. Rather, Marco is possessed by his father and – like the children in *Turn of the Screw* (and its stage and film adaptation, *The Innocents*) – adult heterosexuality. The story is largely a claustrophobic three-hander – Dora returns to the house she shared with her dead husband Carlo, a drug addict thought to have committed suicide at sea, with her new partner Bruno and her son Marco, who calls them 'pigs' when he hears them having sex or announces 'Mamma, I have to kill you' with the calm demeanour of a child explaining an imaginary friend. Dora has no recollection of having killed Carlo while under the influence of drugs that he injected her with, and Bruno walled him up, Poe-like, in the cellar before staging his 'missing at sea' suicide. Dora is played by Daria Nicolodi, also the lead in *La venere d'Ille* but most closely associated at the time with Dario Argento for her role in *Profondo rosso* (1975), as co-writer of *Suspiria* and a stormy relationship that was often in the news.

Argento is also invoked in the Goblin-like musical score by the rock group Libra. But if Argento was supposedly influenced by the aestheticism of Bava's early films, *Shock* is likely to disappoint anyone invested in Bava the stylist, notwithstanding a memorable sequence in which Dora's hair takes on a life of its own, like something from a Japanese horror film. *Suspiria* had blown the doors off the Italian gothic, both figuratively and literally, and *Shock* is a more subdued affair. Bava's previous film, the unreleased *Cani arrabbiati*, had used natural light, handheld camera and its enclosed spaces required more from its cast than some of the horror films or thrillers did. *Shock,* flatly lit and unflashy in its camera movement, asks a great deal of Nicolodi, more than Argento ever did, and just as in *La frusta e il corpo,* the focus is on a woman believing her dead lover has returned to punish her – both films end with the central character killing herself, either believing that she has stabbed her tormenter or that she has had her throat cut by him. Demonic children are no strangers to Bava's gothics and thrillers, from the vampire child of *I wurdalak* begging to be let in and Melissa Graps and her bouncing ball to the playful parent-killers of *Ecologia del delitto,* even if their elders are usually the real monsters. This is distilled into the film's most effective shock moment. In a single shot, Marco runs towards his mother, the camera tilts up and it is Carlo that Dora finds in her arms.

C'era una volta... il Western di Bava

Mario was no good at making Westerns, it wasn't his forte.
                              Franco Prosperi. (Gomarasca and Pulici 2004: 8)

If Mario Bava had never made a Western and we had to imagine what a Bava Western might look like, we might envision something like Antonio Margheriti's *Joko invoca Dio... e muori/Vengeance* (1968), with its hero subjected to eye torture in the desert, a pale-skinned villain dressed in cloak, top hat and gloves, and a climax that takes place in an eerily lit sulphur mine. It is, in short, ticking all the boxes that would justify calling it a 'Gothic Western', which is surely the kind of Western that Mario Bava might be expected to make. The Italian Western, after all, with its taste for the eccentric and the grand guignol, its mysterious protagonists and sadistic villains, stylistic quirks and cynical tone, often seemed just a Cinecittà sound stage away from the gothic. The most frequently reproduced still from *La strada per Forte Alamo* shows crucified bodies in a cave, victims of the Ozarks, an image that appears to conform to one's idea of what a Bava Western should look like. But this image is not particularly representative of the film, a much more routine re-hash of serial Western clichés. If we take a less stereotypical view of Bava's output, given that he could turn his hand to an untypical project like *Cani arrabbiati*, which did not rely on his usual repertoire of tricks and effects, there is no intrinsic reason why he should be unsuited to the Western, any more than Margheriti or Fulci were. But then we are presented with his *actual* Westerns, which occupy a particularly awkward position in the Bava canon, not necessarily because they are particularly bad but because neither of the critical frames in which they are most likely to be placed (as Bava films or as Italian Westerns) suggest that they reward close attention. They rarely get more than a passing mention in writing about the Italian Western, usually to make the point that directors associated with other genres also made Westerns during its boom years. Such is the case in the original edition of Christopher Frayling's seminal book, where he refers to *La strada per Forte Alamo* and *Arizona Bill* (its French title) as two different films (1981: 92), suggesting that he either had not seen it or that he had understandably got his Arizona Bills mixed up with his Nebraska Ringos. Bava carries no currency in relation to the Italian Western, whose canon has largely been organized around particular directors (Leone, Corbucci, Sollima, etc.), stars (Eastwood, Van Cleef, Milian, Hill and Spencer) and cycles (the Leone-like Stranger, the political Western, the comic Western). Bava's stars are Ken Clark, Brett Halsey and Charles Southwood, and only *Roy Colt e Winchester Jack* lends itself to being situated in any of the identifiable *filoni* – a comic Western not unlike the 'Trinity' series that began the same year. On the other hand, Bava scholars have rarely been able to work up much enthusiasm for them, often (like his assistant director Franco Prosperi) adding a comment about it being the 'wrong' genre for him. His least successful films, according to Curti, 'are those where the centrality of the story is unavoidable, such as his Westerns' (2015: location 2807), but a film like *Gli invasori* balances narrative (an admittedly derivative one), action and 'Bavaesque' touches effectively, so casting Bava once again as the enemy of narrative is not entirely convincing. It is perhaps truer to say that the Western lends itself less to his visual repertoire. There are inevitable dissenting voices, although not many – Roberto Silvestri (2007: 112) calls *Roy Colt e Winchester Jack* 'a masterpiece of irony and disenchantment' with a 'postmodern and caricatural tone'. But he is playing the iconoclast here by overclaiming for the film, not merely under-appreciated (which is arguable), but an actual masterpiece.[18] Pezzotta is dismissive of the films, and while Lucas writes about them in more detail than anyone else, such is the nature of his book, one senses that he too might have happily skipped them.

Bava is only credited by name on one of the three Westerns now attributed to him (*Roy Colt*), adopts the John M. Old pseudonym on another (*La strada per Forte Alamo*) and is not credited in any capacity on the third (signed by its original director Antonio/Anthony Román). And if his name was not now attached to them, there is every chance that they would not be talked about at all, also-rans of a prolific generic cycle, their expendability leading to either their disappearance or a peripheral afterlife as public domain DVDs or fillers on minor movie channels. In that respect, they test the limits of the Bava cult brand, regardless of their actual quality, which is always open to debate. Is it possible to imagine a blu-ray box set called 'The Mario Bava Western Collection'? I had initially considered starting this section by making a point of how unlikely that would be. But given that *Roy Colt e Winchester Jack* – admittedly the easiest of the three to frame as a cult Italian film and a Bava oddity – has since been released in an HD format, it now seems less unlikely than it once did. The German DVD label Koch Media framed them through the Bava brand, including *Ringo del Nebraska*, which has not always been considered a Bava film.

The three films – I will resist playing the genre game by adding *I coltelli del vendicatore* as a fourth – belong to different production contexts. *La strada per Forte Alamo* earned more than any of the horror films or thrillers Bava had made up to that point at the Italian Box Office. An Italian-French co-production, one of its production companies was owned by Achille Piazzi, who produced a number of peplums, including *Ercole al centro della terra* and therefore knew Bava's ability in raising the production value of a low-budget film. The year 1964 was a turning point for both Italian cinema and the career of someone like Bava. Galatea, supposedly a stable production company and therefore a microcosm of larger crises, ceased production and limped on through film sales until its liquidation – it is at this point that the work-for-hire basis of Bava's labour becomes particularly visible after a period of apparent stability and arguably consistency (Curti 2019: 10). Bava's first Western followed *6 donne per l'assassino,* which was not a Galatea production but had solid production support; its French partner was Georges de Beauregard who had produced films by Melville and Godard. *La strada per Forte Alamo,* the most carefully crafted of Bava's Westerns – its meticulous lighting of its night-time scenes contrasts with the day-for-night shooting of *Ringo del Nebraska* – was the last with the team he had formed at Galatea. Lucas has commented on the replacement of Ubaldo Terzano with Antonio Rinaldi as DP/operator as a perceptible drop in quality. It is the second Bava film to feature the 'John M. Old' byline and anglicized pseudonyms for everyone else – if *La frusta e il corpo* was meant to pass as Hammer or AIP, another John, namely Ford, seems to be invoked this time, most obviously through narrative similarities to *Stagecoach* and *Fort Apache.* Filmed entirely in Rome but trying to pass as an American film – made before the Italian Western started to coalesce into a recognizable brand – *La strada per Forte Alamo* is hugely reliant on Bava's mattes, some of which are particularly ambitious (a canyon flanked by what look like hundreds of Ozarks, for example). As it paints in the American West, it acts as a reminder that Italy's most established Western hero was not Django or Sartana, but Tex Willer, the Texas Ranger who rides through Sergio Bonelli's publication *Tex*, still one of the bestselling *fumetti* at the *edicola*, every bit as iconic as Diabolik or Dylan Dog and older than either. Thanks to its original artist Aurelio Galleppini, Tex Willer rode through an Old West modelled visually on the landscapes of the Dolomites, Trentino and Sardinia, a 'romantic evocation of a mythic America being absorbed into a more parochial representation, and adapted to the local market' (Fisher 2014: 25). If Bava's film seems a bit less certain of its market, it was at least more congenial to it than the other 'foreign' genres tackled by him. Pleasingly familiar without being particularly memorable, it finds Bava in artisan mode, getting the job done. But the nature of that job – the effort to pass as an American film and paint in the Old West – is its main point of historical interest.

Ringo del Nebraska followed *Terrore nello spazio* and was made for the same two production companies, Fulvio Lucisano's Italian International Film and the Spanish Castilla Cooperativa Cinematografica, but this time without the involvement of AIP. If the first film was tailor made for his talents, *Ringo del Nebraska* called for Bava the rescuer, the fast worker. He replaced Román, who had been one of the credited writers on *Terrore nello spazio*. With the Spanish locations by then expected of Italian Westerns, the film is a more visually expansive affair than *La strada per Forte Alamo*. Its score incorporates Morricone-style whistling, its black leather clad villain recalls Jack Palance in *Shane*, and it shares with the earlier Bava Western a fiery redheaded female lead and the same male lead, Ken Clark. While Clark is playing a character called Ringo, there is nothing to suggest that he is the same character played by Giuliano Gemma in two films directed by Duccio Tessari,[19] but the name alone confirms that the various Western *filoni* are now more clearly established. There is no consensus on how much of the film Bava directed, and thus some critical trepidation over who to attribute its strengths or weaknesses to. *Roy Colt e Winchester Jack*, the most interesting of the three, and the one most congenial to cult repackaging, shares its production company (and its writer) with *5 bambole per la luna d'agosto*, Produzione Atlas Cinematografica or PAC, a company that would move into sexploitation in the 1970s (Wood 2014: 306). It also shares the zoom-heavy camera style of later Bava films in other genres. In an interview with Luigi Cozzi, Bava claims to have added the comedy during production of what was originally written as a more serious film (Cozzi 2004: 86), but it seems more likely that it was always designed as comic Western. While *Lo chiamavano Trinità/They Call Me Trinity* was released several months after *Roy Colt*, and the Terence Hill-Bud Spencer partnership had yet to be established as a comic one, Franco and Ciccio had made a number of comic Westerns, largely parodying existing cycles.

If one were to try to find a common factor amongst Bava's Westerns, one might begin with their female characters – Janet, under arrest for killing the soldier who tried to rape her (*La strada per Forte Alamo*), Kay, the disputed 'property' of two thieves who have fallen out (*Ringo del Nebraska*), and above all, Marilù Tolu's Native American Mahila, who offers men a choice of money or marriage in exchange for sex but who ends up with the gold that everyone is searching for, leaving the titular heroes in the dust as she rides off. *Roy Colt e Winchester Jack* is crude and broad in its humour, as close to Franco and Ciccio as Hill and Spencer. A man with a nervous twitch shoots the crutches from under an old man; the front of a house is blown off, leaving it looking like a doll's house, its occupant left exposed in his underwear; a grimacing villain is revealed to be defecating. It was one of the better performing of Bava's later films at the Italian Box Office and was probably the one most in tune with popular taste of the time. It is made with rather less care than the previous two Westerns, however, even if it is a livelier affair. The mattes are much cruder and less convincing than the ones in *La strada per Forte Alamo,* although the knockabout tone makes it less important that they look like what they probably were – pictures cut out of magazines and mounted on sheets of glass. Its play on gender is its main point of interest. The two male leads are sniggering little boys, easily outsmarted by Mahila, and her racial casting notwithstanding, there is a glimmer of a hint that her interest in money qualifies less as gold-digging than reparations.

Bava's Westerns, in their way, tell us as much about his career as a filmmaker and his posthumous celebration as his more celebrated horror films and thrillers. Not only do they draw particular attention to his status as a working filmmaker not always able to choose projects for himself, but they illustrate what can happen to 'ephemeral art' when it passes from one marketplace (the theatrical distribution of Serie B cinema) to another (cult collectability). The disposability of a film like *Roy Colt e Winchester Jack* is still visible – a relatively undistinguished entry in a commercial cycle – but at the same time the cult branding of the director has kept it in the marketplace, albeit on the margins of Italian genre cinema and Bava fandom. This is in contrast with the other film Bava made for PAC, *5 bambole per la luna d'agosto,* which, despite its mixed reputation, has been easier to remediate for cult connoisseurship and easier to rescue from its ephemeral commercial function. *5 bambole* belongs to another group of films closely associated with Bava, the Italian-style thriller. If *La maschera del demonio* has been accorded seminal status for putting in place key aesthetic features associated with *il gotico italiano*, Bava is frequently seen as the initiator of *il giallo italiano,* which, whether seen as a genre, a *filone* or a brand, presents several complications of its own. These are the focus of the next chapter.

Notes

1   As Venturini observes (2014: location 1114), the two strongest points of creative continuity during the gothic cycles were Barbara Steele (nine films) and writer Ernesto Gastaldi (ten films).

2   *Gli invasori* was the most well-resourced and commercially successful of the Galatea films for which he received solo directorial credit.

3   Some of these films could be placed in any number of categories – *La ragazza che sapeva troppo* has elements of the *giallo,* the thriller, comedy, romance and even moments of horror – but I have restricted them to what seem to me to be the two most prominent ones.

4   The most recent Italian DVD of the film classifies it as 'il gotico italiano'.

5   Lee had already capitalized on the success of *Dracula il vampiro,* as it was known in Italy, with a comedy *Tempi duri per il vampiro* (1959) made the year before the Italian gothic *filone* took off.

6   This scene is missing from the UK release version of the film, which is otherwise identical to the Italian cut. Was it because, as Smith (2018: 49) argues, UK distributors aimed peplums at a young audience and wanted to reduce the horror content in the film?

7   Tourneur is the credited director of *La battaglia di Maratona,* after which he would make his final two films for AIP. Bava and Tourneur are not dissimilar figures in some ways – both flourished in a 'B' cinema and are considered masters of atmosphere with a distinct visual touch, both were vulnerable to their preferred genres coming in and out of fashion, and both would be drawn under different circumstances to AIP.

8   This is according to the liner notes accompanying the DVD box set of the series.

9   *Atom Age Vampire* is its English title.

10   They are also absent from Lamberto Bava's 1989 remake, in which the 'masking' of the witch is presented in flashback but little else is taken from the 1960 film.

11   Riccardo Freda claims that he adopted the pseudonym 'Robert Hampton' after witnessing Italian filmgoers deciding not to see *I vampiri* because the poster revealed that it was directed by an Italian.

12   *Dèmoni* was by no means the last Italian horror film – they still appear even now – but arguably the last, apart from Argento's, to make a significant impact on both the local and international market. The circular effect is reinforced by it featuring a mask not unlike the one in *La maschera del demonio.*

13   It is the only one of Bava's 1960s films to still carry an 18 certificate in the UK.

14   We can also add *Horror/The Blancheville Monster* (1963), which claimed to be based on Poe and has some similarities to *The Fall of the House of Usher.*

15   The plastic shrouds are a detail in Pestriniero's original story, but the film makes the resurrection a slow motion setpiece, while it happens offstage in *Una notte di 21 ore.*

16   The same could be said for the title under which it was written, *Le macabre ore della paura* (The Macabre hours of fear; Curti 2015a: location 4354).

17 Both films feature child actor David Colin Jr., but that was hardly a major selling point for the film.
18 While far from a rave review, Leonardo Autera attributed a 'casual verve' to Bava's direction in his *Corriere della sera* review (1970: 15).
19 Although it is not necessarily clear that Gemma is playing the same character in both of those films.

4

Il giallo all'italiana – Bava and the Italian-style thriller

An important part of Bava's cult reputation is that of being a, or even *the*, 'pioneer' of a particular kind of Italian thriller or *giallo*. Both *La ragazza che sapeva troppo* and *6 donne per l'assassino* have been credited with initiating a distinctively Italian approach to the suspense-thriller. But similar claims are also attached to Dario Argento, whose *L'uccello dalle piume di cristallo* is often seen as the commercial spark for the early 1970s peak in the production of 'il thrilling all'italiana', as these films were also sometimes known. Various other films have been credited with being the first, depending on one's definition. As early as 1964, a review of *6 donne per l'assassino* in the film journal *Bianco e Nero* was irritated by it being publicized as 'il primo giallo italiano' (the first Italian *giallo*), citing films by Pietro Germi and Damiano Damiani as stronger candidates for such a claim (E.G.L. 1964: 48), as well as finding too much *grand guignol* in the film for it to even be much of a *giallo* to begin with. Valentina Vitali sums up the confusion succinctly when she suggests that the *giallo* is often presented 'contradictorily, as simultaneously new and pre-existing' (2016: 35). This ties in with a further problem, that of distinguishing between general and more specific uses of the term. As a generic category, the *giallo* derives from a hugely successful exercise in marketing by the Milan publishing house Mondadori, who in 1929 initiated *I libri gialli* as a form of branding for their yellow-jacketed hardback mystery thriller novels, most of them translations of Anglo-American crime novels. The term would soon pervade theatre and cinema, with the formation of the Compagnia Spettacoli Gialli in 1932, while Mario Camerini's 1934 film *Giallo,* more of a comedy than a thriller, was based on a play by the most popular writer in Mondadori's *libri gialli*, Edgar Wallace, and showed one character reading a Mondadori 'Supergiallo' that collected five Wallace novels (Bruni 2017: 52). *Giallo's* theme, the effects of mystery novels on female readers, was a topical one, but one that resurfaces in Bava's *La ragazza che sapeva troppo*, another film that raises the question of whether the *giallo* is Italian or foreign. Several accounts of the *giallo*, such as Koven (2006), acknowledge that the term operates rather differently within Italy to how it has circulated elsewhere – what cult film fans and film studies academics call 'the giallo' is a very particular *type* of *giallo*, frequently characterized by strands of eroticism and/or horror running through it and tending to be weaker in aspects more traditionally associated with the murder mystery (plotting, narrative logic). We could break down the Serie B thriller into three overlapping types – the *giallo-orrore* or *giallo-thrilling,* with its often-graphic serial murders, the *giallo-erotico,* a forerunner of the erotic thriller and the *giallo-poliziesco,* more oriented towards action and organized crime and often seen as a genre in its own right, the *poliziottesco.* But there is no end to the labels we could attach to these films. The lurid, sensational qualities are what, by implication, separate the 'new' from the 'pre-existing', but they are also what connect the films to broader international trends. Lurid thrillers were by no means confined to Italy by the end of the 1960s, even if the Serie B *giallo*-thriller of the 1970s constitutes one of the largest cycles.

The cinematic *giallo* poses certain problems for genre theory (see Kannis 2017 and 2020, for example). Peter Hutchings wonders whether it is:

> a sub-category of the Italian version of the *giallo* that, confusingly, has been given the same name, presumably by English-language critics, as the main category itself? In other words, is it a sub-generic cycle that was recognized by filmmakers and audiences while *gialli* of this type were being produced during the 1960s and 1970s? Or is it a group of films that has been put together by critics (and potentially exploitation fans as well) after that period is over as one of the products of the 'remediation' of Italian cinema?
>
> (2016: 84)

Bava's films illustrate some of the complexities and problems with mapping out the Italian suspense-thriller. His two 'seminal' films were made during a period when *il thrilling all'italiana* had yet to be identified as a recognizable *filone,* their influence something that has been built up in retrospect through the cultification of Serie B cinema.[1] His other three feature-length thrillers were made or released near to or during the peak of *il thrilling all'italiana,*[2] when films now seen as *gialli* were a staple part of the *prima visione* (first run) circuit and often enjoyed extensive publicity campaigns (Ehrenreich 2017). While *Il rosso segno della follia* and *5 bambole per la luna d'agosto* have sometimes been seen as minor Bava films, they both played in *prima visione* cinemas. But Bava's later thrillers do not fit comfortably into the main *giallo/thrilling* cycles of the early 1970s and failed to capitalize on the commercial success many of these films were enjoying. Is there even a consensus about which of Bava's films constitute his *gialli*? In the category's cult-usage, the answer is probably yes – five feature films (*La ragazza che sapeva troppo, 6 donne per l'assassino, Il rosso segno della follia, 5 bambole per la luna d'agosto* and *Ecologia del delitto*) and one episode from another, *Il telefono* from *I tre volti della paura*. There is no great controversy in designating any of these films in this way, even though *Il rosso segno della follia* can also be categorized as a ghost story or gothic horror. It is not the case that they were only referred to as *gialli* later in the way that classic *film noir* were retrospectively classified. But they would also have been classified in other ways as well and were not the only Bava films to be categorized as *gialli* at the time. One press ad described *La ragazza che sapeva troppo* as a 'brivido alla Hitchckoc' (sic) (a Hitchcock-style thrill), even though another characterized it as 'Giallissimo' (full of mystery and thrills). Press ads for *Il rosso segno della follia* also dropped Hitchcock's name, calling it 'Un diabolico "thrilling" alla Hitchcock'. A 1971 review of *Ecologia del delitto* identified it as a *giallo* in its capsule information, but the review itself placed it within '(Bava's) horror *filone*' (E.F. 1971: 13). *La frusta e il corpo*, usually situated amongst Bava's gothics, was dubbed 'un giallo appassionante' (an exciting murder mystery) in initial press ads, while *Terrore nello spazio* was described as an 'interstellar science fiction *giallo*' in an article on Barry Sullivan's starring role in the film (Ceretto 1965: 17). The Italian trailer for *6 donne per l'assassino* promises 'horror that chills the blood', and, like a lot of Italian suspense-thrillers, the film has circulated widely as a horror film outside Italy (and as a *krimi* in Germany), even before it started to be seen as a precursor to the North American slasher film due to its prolific body count and stalking scenes. And what of *Diabolik*, adapted from a comic whose cover has for many years dubbed it 'Il giallo a fumetti' (the comic book thriller), or *Cani arrabbiati*, based on a story found in a Mondadori *giallo*? Why are they not categorized as *gialli* when their sources are? Consensus sometimes counts for more than consistency when it comes to generic classification. And, of course, genres do not always function in the same way across different media. The *giallo* section in a bookshop is one thing, for organizational reasons as much as anything, but as a cult filmic term, the *giallo* is fated to be associated with black-gloved killers, voluptuous women in various states of undress, amateur detectives in tourist hotspots, 1970s fashion and design, gruesome set pieces and wayward plotting.

In seeking to complicate the category of the *giallo*, my aim is not to distinguish the 'right' definitions from the 'wrong' ones here – if anything, it is the opposite of that, to acknowledge its multivalence. I suspect that a common experience of studying the Italian *giallo* over a period of time is to become less, rather than more, certain of what it actually is. As a non-Italian who first encountered the term through thrillers like those of Bava and Argento, I find myself using it in different ways in different contexts (and in different company). After all, for the sake of convenience, we need to call those sexy-violent thrillers *something*. In 2015, I attended a Film Studies conference on the *giallo* in Rome at which most, if not all, of the contributors and attendees probably had a more-or-less shared understanding of what we meant by 'the giallo' in that particular context. But I wondered what might have happened if someone less invested in cult discourses surrounding Italian genre cinema had wandered into a conference on 'the giallo'. Might they wonder why we were talking about trashy thrillers from the 1960s and 1970s, some of them more like horror films or softcore porn, rather than Commissario Montalbano or Giorgio Scerbanenco? That hypothetical 'someone' might even be a scholar of the *giallo*, but in its literary form. Two groups of scholars are particularly invested in the *giallo* as an object of study – one is interested in Italian crime fiction and/or the crime novel in Italy, the other in cult/exploitation cinema. These two groups have different auteur figures – Leonardo Sciascia, Giorgio Scerbanenco and Andrea Camilleri on the one hand, Bava, Argento, Fulci and Sergio Martino on the other. Both are invested in mapping out a canon 'made in Italy' – while the *giallo* originated as a way of branding a notionally foreign genre, the term is now more often used to suggest a certain articulation of Italianness. But for better or worse, there has been relatively little dialogue between these two groups, at least in English, which is why the *giallo*'s biggest mystery remains how its literary and cinematic usage sometimes seem to refer to such markedly different things.

I do not want to suggest, however, that differences in definition are purely determined by national or cultural belonging, that there is a distinct and singular Italian understanding of the term that stands in clear opposition to the understandings of the *giallo* that have formed around the cultification of Italian genre cinema outside Italy. There is, as we shall see, a body of Italian writing – a cult reading formation, invested in the Italy's Serie B cinema on the kinds of thrillers that Bava, Argento and others made that, while it might have to qualify its terms a bit more, seems to have pretty much the same group of films in mind as non-Italian aficionados. My interest here, then, is on how the *giallo* functions discursively, and what this means for Bava's thrillers. What do we mean when we categorize this or that Bava film as a *giallo*? What sort of cult capital is embedded in the English-language usage of the term, or its Italian equivalents?

The 'g' word

It should come as no surprise that '*giallo*' is an unstable term, given that, as David Bordwell observes, there is little agreement on what a genre is to begin with, and how it differs from '*mode, cycle, formula,* or whatever' (1989: 147).

Has anyone ever arrived at a satisfactory definition of the horror genre, for example, which Brigid Cherry argues is actually several genres (2009: 3)? Is *film noir*, Bordwell asks, 'a genre, a style, or a cycle?' (1989: 147) and we might ask similar questions of the *giallo*, also adding *brand* as a mode of categorization, given that that is how it originated and, in some ways, how it currently functions as a cult film category. If we take it as a discursive term, here are some of the things that the *giallo* can be taken to be:

- A form of branding used by Mondadori for crime-mystery novels and subsequently adopted by other Italian publishers.

- Any mystery or crime narrative of any origin that happens to be consumed in Italy – see, for example, the 'Giallo' section in a bookshop or the *Giallo* channel on TV, which heavily features dubbed US Crime shows, or the TV series *Murder, She Wrote*, which is known in Italy as *La Signora in giallo*.

- Italian crime fiction (which tends to be branded in other ways outside Italy – for example, as part of 'Mediterranean Noir').

- An unsolved crime or mystery in the news in Italy.

- A group of low-to-medium budget Italian thrillers made between the 1960s and late 1970s/early 1980s (peaking in the early 1970s) with a sensational approach to sex and violence. This type of *giallo* is associated with certain directors (Bava, Argento, Fulci, Martino, Umberto Lenzi) and stars (Edwige Fenech, George Hilton, Jean Sorel, Carroll Baker, Dagmar Lassander, Nieves Navarro/ Susan Scott) and characterized by certain tropes (black-gloved killers, amateur detectives, travel, the 'jet set'), stylistic qualities (colour, widescreen, flamboyant camerawork, pop/jazz/light-music soundtracks) and an enjoyably kitsch datedness in their production design and fashions.

- A film thriller that is not Italian but is in a similar style to the above. Kannas (2020: 57) cites the inclusion of films on the review site DVD Beaver that are 'mid-identified as giallo', while an article accompanying Arrow's Blu-ray of Brian De Palma's *Dressed to Kill* (1980) calls it an 'American Giallo' (McDonagh 2013).

- Most contentiously, almost any Italian horror film. In this case, 'everyday criticism' (Needham 2003: 144) picks up on the term in a loose association with Italian genre cinema – several English-language reviews of Luca Guadagnino's remake of *Suspiria* (2018) referred to Argento's original film as a 'giallo classic', much to the displeasure of genre purists.[3]

- A contemporary film that knowingly pastiches the visual and musical style and narrative conventions of 1970s Italian thrillers –

the so-called 'neo-giallo'. Given that some of these – *Amer* (2009), for example – are less interested in the murder mystery, there is the strongest sense here of the *giallo* as a *style* of cinema. 'I can take or leave the murder', says Peter Strickland, a British director often seen to be *giallo*-influenced, 'it's the production design, the lighting, the flamboyance and artifice' (Anon. 2019: 49).

Responding to Needham's claim that the cinematic *giallo* defies generic definition (2003: 136), Ian Olney objects that it risks becoming 'all things and nothing' (2013: 105). And indeed, it would not be entirely unreasonable to conclude that a word used in so many different ways is of little analytical use and best confined to organizing one's DVD and Blu-ray collection or marketing 'forgotten' films to completists. But we are way past the point where the *giallo* can be quietly relieved from duty as a generic term. Moreover, there is a danger of Olney shooting the messenger here. Needham is right to see it as a discursive category rather than pursue what Jason Mittell calls 'the textualist assumption' that genres are defined primarily by intrinsic textual features (2004: 7). If the *giallo* does not quite become *all* things, as we can see above, it has been used to refer to a number of things, and if it is the fifth of those categories that sounds most like 'our' *giallo* – the Serie B *thrilling* – it still cannot be so easily separated from the term's other uses. The word functions as a brand, a cycle or *filone* and a genre. The final three definitions above point to the *giallo* as also being determined by matters of style. Discussing the remarkable opening titles of *6 donne per l'assassino*, Alexia Kannis finds 'so much of the *giallo* film's peculiar allure' in 'beguiling compositions that bathe the character's faces in eerie washes of deep rose or moss green' (2017: 174). Before the narrative has begun or a black glove has been put on, Kannis knows that she is in the 'dark world' of the *giallo*. Mary Wood includes Serie B thrillers amongst a range of Italian crime films that could be recategorized as Italian *noir* (2007), but if *giallo* functions partly as a stylistic term, that would be an obstacle to such a renaming, even though the *chiaroscuro* lighting, dark secrets and urban menace of *La ragazza che sapeva troppo* would certainly support the film being seen as a kind of *film noir* or *cinema nero*.

Rick Altman has argued that the generic terminology we use is 'primarily retrospective in nature' and 'fails to capture the variety of needs evinced by previous producers, exhibitors, spectators and other generic users' (1999: 48). At the height of 'il thrilling all'italiana' in the early 1970s, the Rome trade magazine *Intermezzo* applied the following categories to films that now regularly feature in books and articles on the *giallo*:

- Drammatico – *La morte risale a ieri sera/Death Occurred Last Night* (1970), *Una lucertola con la pelle di donna/Lizard in a Woman's Skin* (1971), *La notte che Evelyn uscì dalla tomba/The Night Evelyn*

Came Out of Her Tomb (1971), *Cosa avete fatto a Solange?/What Have You Done to Solange?* (1972).

- Suspense – *Lo strano vizio della Signora Wardh/The Strange Vice of Mrs Wardh* (1971).

- Poliziesco – *Le foto proibite di una signora per bene/Forbidden Photos of a Lady Above Suspicion* (1970), *Il gatto a nove code/ The Cat o' Nine Tails* (1971), *La coda dello scorpione/The Case of the Scorpion's Tail* (1971), *Una farfalla con le ali insanguinate/ Bloodstained Butterfly* (1971), *Sette orchidee macchiate di rosso/ Seven Bloodstained Orchids* (1972).

These categories might strike us as rather arbitrary now. Bava's *5 bambole per la luna d'agosto* was categorized as a *poliziesco,* despite the police being entirely absent from the film, and we could easily swap categories for any of the films named above. Austin Fisher has observed the interchangeability of the terms 'giallo' and 'poliziesco' in Italian film reviews of the 1970s (2019: 156), to which we might add 'thrilling' as a third widely used category for these films. The *giallo* had originally displaced the *poliziesco* as the default generic label for crime fiction following the success of Mondadori's *libri gialli* (Dunnett 2010: 66), but the sense that they were two different names for the same thing never entirely disappeared, even though film-centred accounts tend to differentiate the *giallo* from the more action-oriented *poliziesco* or *poliziottesco* (originally a more derogatory term used by Italian film critics for churned-out cop/gangster films) – the difference between thrillers emphasizing fearful suspense and those emphasizing action and excitement. But what is clear is that the *giallo* was not necessarily the default category for an Italian suspense-thriller. By the early 1970s, the mistranslated term 'il thrilling' was ubiquitous, particularly in publicity – *La morte cammina con i tacchi alti/Death Walks on High Heels* (1971) was characterized in a press-ad as a 'sado-thrilling' in the same style as director Luciano Ercoli's previous hit *Le foto proibite di una signora per bene.*

Altman makes a distinction between what he calls the Critic's Game and the Producer's Game (1999: 38) in the understanding of how genres, and by extension cycles, take shape. The Producer's Game involves identifying a successful formula and seeking to exploit those elements that appeared to make it successful. If we see the Italian suspense-thriller in the light of the Producer's Game, it arguably begins with the producer Luciano Martino, who in 1968 had a hit with a sexed-up variation on *Les Diaboliques* (1955) called *Il dolce corpo di Deborah/The Sweet Body of Deborah* starring the American actress Carroll Baker and written by the prolific screenwriter Ernesto Gastaldi. Martino and others would produce further vehicles for Baker, usually with titillating titles (one of them is called *Orgasmo*), several of them written by Gastaldi, before re-calibrating the formula for younger female stars such as Edwige Fenech in the early 1970s. After the success of *L'uccello dalle piume di cristallo*, elements of the Argento-style thriller could be combined with the Baker *filone* – *Lo strano vizio della Signora Wardh* gains a serial killer in addition to the usual tale of a tormented heroine being driven to near-madness and death by a husband or lover. Bava's thrillers are marginal to the Producer's Game, seemingly having no impact whatsoever, unless we choose to see Dario Argento as having been belatedly influenced by them. The Critic's Game works backwards from having identified a body of films that can be grouped together as belonging to the same genre. It is the Critic's Game that positions Bava as a pioneer and his thrillers as 'seminal', by working backwards from *il thrilling all'italiana* – fully formed and in its violent post-Argento pomp – and identifying its prototype(s). But there is good news and bad news for *La ragazza che sapeva troppo*. On the one hand, a film that previously seemed to lead nowhere becomes the starting point for a 'new' genre or a new style in an existing genre. But this teleological construction of the *giallo* also often casts the film as not yet fully formed, transitional, a 'proto-giallo', as it is sometimes called, or even a *giallo-rosa*.[4] The film is in black and white where the *giallo* is supposed to be colourful, it is semi-comic and even lightly romantic where the *giallo* is meant to be sado-erotic, violent and transgressive, which is why the nastier *6 donne per l'assassino* also enjoys the reputation of being the first of its kind.

There are some similarities between the problems posed by the *giallo* and those posed by *film noir*. In the case of the latter, as James Naremore observes, 'nobody is sure whether the films constitute a period, a cycle, a style, or simply a "phenomenon"' (2008: 6), partly because it was 'largely elaborated after the fact of the films themselves' (ibid.). This would be only partly true of the *giallo* – the question is rather in what sense the term was understood when it was applied to some, if not all, of the films now classified as *gialli*. But like *noir*, it can be approached as a genre, a style, a period and in its cult incarnation, it is certainly a 'phenomenon' of sorts as it is remediated onto high-definition discs and box sets or streamed. Altman suggests that *noir* began 'as a loose, adjectival, add-on mode', settling into a 'noun phase' only after the war, 'adapted by an American culture adept at making dark films but entirely unaware that noir had ever been an adjective' (1999: 60). One might argue that almost the reverse is true of the *giallo*, which began as a noun (a crime-mystery novel) but has also taken on a more adjectival sense in its cult usage.

James Naremore approaches *noir* as a discursive construct that is 'almost entirely a creation of postmodern culture' (2008: 10), attributing its take up as a generic term in no small part to the fact that '"film noir" sounds better than a good many American terms that might be used' and 'has affected the way we view certain mass-produced items' (2008: 2). Much the same can be said of the *giallo*, particularly in its non-Italian usage. It sounds more exotic and cultish than 'thriller' or 'Italian thriller', the image of yellow-jacketed paperbacks suggesting (outside their original context) a lurid quality. Above all, it takes on a canon-building function, and while some of this 'canon' is there for the taking in original production cycles – the *giallo-erotico* shaped by the Carroll Baker cycle, or the Argento-style thriller – it is the linking of the 1970s cycle to the more disparate grouping of films from the 1960s that is particularly suggestive of retrospective canonical surgery. If we only had 1960s Italian thrillers to go on, it is less likely that we would be talking about a distinctive Italian approach to the mystery-thriller, and if we removed Bava's first two thrillers from the 1960s, we might be less likely to see a continuity between the pre- and post-Argento *giallo*. Only the Carroll Baker films look like an actual cycle, and that is because they were often the products of the same people exploiting the same formula and the same star. Bava, then, becomes the key figure in the Critic's Game in organizing 1960s and 1970s thrillers into a single canon.

Jason Mittell, too, argues for seeing genres discursively, rather than being defined solely through their textual features – 'the discourses surrounding and running through a given genre are *themselves* constitutive of that generic category' (2004: 13). While there are many Italian thrillers that share textual features, there are just as many that do not. Even some of the Argento-style thrillers seem linked more by their elaborate titles featuring animals, insects and birds than by actual thematic or narrative connections. The function of genre, according to Mittell (with reference to Foucault's 'author function'), is threefold – as a system of classification, as a site for interpretive consistency and as a marker of cultural value (2004: 15). What is the genre function of the *giallo*? It *Italianizes* the films, and this seems to be true for both Italian and non-Italian aficionados – it is 'entirely ours', claims Davide Pulici in his preface to Claudio Bartolini's *Il Cinema Giallo-Thriller Italiano* (2017: 5), 'it belongs to us completely'. This clearly applies too when others dabble in the form – in an article for horror magazine *Nocturno* on French and Belgian 'neo-giallo' thrillers such as *L'étrange couleur des larmes de ton corps/The Strange Colour of Your Body's Tears* (2013), Bartolini refers to French language filmmakers taking 'our thriller genre' as inspiration (2019: 18).

Unsurprisingly, there is little more agreement over what a *filone* is than there is over what a genre is. Sometimes it is used interchangeably with genre, sometimes it sounds more like a cycle – 'a collection of similar themes or styles, a genre or a subgenre, perhaps also a formula or pattern' (Bondanella and Pacchioni 2017: 433). More suggestive is Ellen Neremberg, who sees it as 'a thick braid of varied film "fibers", as it were, rather than a codifiable genre' (2012: location 1484), something that various genre strands can run through – essentially, if I understand her correctly, a form of hybridity. Thus, she sees Argento mixing 'Italian film noir, the *giallo*, slasher film, and the horror film' (ibid.), and Bava's thrillers could be seen similarly. When the *giallo* is discussed as a cinematic category, it is rarely conceptualized in quite this way, but this seems a particularly productive way of thinking about many of these films, wherein the *giallo* is one of several threads running through them, rather than a genre that they fully inhabit. But whatever kind of category we take a *filone* to be, it usually refers to a very particular kind of industrial product – a film 'that is exploiting already successful thrills and gratifications in a rapid production schedule to maximize profits' (Fisher 2019: 99). These 'gratifications' can also be seen as the threads running through a cycle of films – or linking together a number of cycles (the overlap between the peplum and gothic horror, or between the *giallo* and the more action-oriented *poliziottesco*). In the case of the *giallo all'italiana*, these gratifications include eroticism (perhaps the most consistent linking thread), graphic violence and suspense. The term 'giallo filone' used by Kannis (2017) and Fisher (2019) has the advantage of isolating a group of thrillers that belong to a particular production context, given that the *giallo* (in the broader sense) can also be found in *cinema d'impegno* (the political thrillers of Francesco Rosi, Damiano Damiani and Elio Petri), *cinema d'autore* (Antonioni's *Blow Up* and *The Passenger/Professione: Reporter*) as well as 'Serie A' films such as *La donna della domenica* (1975).[5]

If we take the *filone* as an industrial category, it most closely resembles a cycle. And indeed, there is a danger of the English use of the word suggesting that there is something uniquely Italian about groups of films that follow shorter-term trends and conventions than those of a larger genre. We cannot always be sure, either – especially when determining where a particular film 'belongs' – whether we are discerning the Producer's Game or playing the Critic's Game when identifying a particular *filone* or *sottofilone*. Richard Nowell has used a frontier metaphor to account for how cycles play out (Nowell 2011, cited by Fisher 2019: 183). The cycle is preceded by a 'pioneer' film, or a less innovative 'speculator' that uses an existing but dormant format. The cycle proper begins with a 'trailblazer' hit followed by cash-ins – 'prospective' ones that are made before the cycle's commercial success is confirmed, and 'carpetbagger' ones that are exploiting an established formula (ibid.). *La ragazza che sapeva troppo* and *6 donne per l'assassino* have been cast as the two pioneer films – the formula retrospectively seen to be divided across two separate films. According to Claudio Bartolini (2017: 13), they give us the two branches of 'il nuovo cinema nero italiano' (the new Italian noir cinema). *La ragazza che sapeva troppo* is the 'prototype' for the 'giallo cinematografica all'italiana', with its urban setting, eyewitness protagonist who misses or misreads an important detail, madness as the killer's motive and the use of anonymous phone calls as a source of terror (ibid.: 13). *6 donne per l'assassino*, on the other hand, is a 'pure thriller, confusing, hyper-violent and visually experimental', opening up the 'rivers of blood' to follow in 'il thrilling italiano' of the early 1970s (ibid.). For Bartolini, it is the combination of the *giallo* and the thriller that distinguishes the Italian-style 'thrilling'. Argento's *L'uccello dalle piume di cristallo* has taken on the reputation of being the trailblazer, taking on elements from both of Bava's 'pioneer' films, whether knowingly or not. But *Il dolce corpo di Deborah* would initiate a *filone,* too. In addition to the Baker films, one might also see Lucio Fulci's *Una sull'altra/One of Top of the Other* (1969) as part of this cycle – if a sexed-up reworking of *Les Diaboliques* could be a hit, then why not a sexed-up reworking of *Vertigo*? Of course, we are playing the Critic's Game here, and positioning Bava as pioneer risks obscuring other kinds of belonging those early thrillers might be seen to have had. But this film cycle model adds to the impression of the 1960s *giallo* seemingly failing to find a formula that could generate a *filone* until towards the end of the decade.

Before *thrilling all'italiana:* the *giallo* as brand and genre

In his essay 'Difesa di un colore' (Defence of a colour), Andrea Camilleri, arguably the most internationally successful of all Italian crime writers, notes a degree of uncertainty in the initial line-up of *i libri gialli* published by Mondadori in 1929 (2013/2019: 141). While S. S. Van Dine and, particularly, Edgar Wallace would be a staple part of the series,[6] and Anna Katherine Green's *The Leavenworth Case* (published as *Il mistero delle due cugine*) was generically on topic (if not entirely up to date), Robert Louis Stevenson's *The Suicide Club* (*Il club dei suicidi*) was a less obvious choice. But what was perhaps more important than generic consistency was Mondadori's success in branding. They had colour-coded other genres of literature – *i libri azzurri* (Italian authors, blue), *i libri verdi* (romance, green) and just to confuse generic categories further, *i libri neri* for the French noir of Georges Simenon. But it would be the *giallo* that endured as a category (if not necessarily a coherent one) to this day. Jane Dunnett attributes Mondadori's success to effective advertising, the quality and appearance of their books (the original *gialli* were not cheap products), high editorial standards and the range and quality of their writers (2010: 77). The *giallo* was 'aimed at a new, international middle class' to whom they offered a 'change in pace that could not help but arouse interest' (Mazzei and Valentini 2017: 12). Publicity for the yellow-jacketed hardbacks implied that *giallo* readers were part of an international community of readers (Dunnett 2010: 72), challenging the denigration of detective fiction as an unhealthy foreign invasion. Subsequently, they could be adapted to more affordable formats such as the *Gialli Economici Mondadori* – a large format magazine with two columns of text that reprinted novels from the more expensive hardbacks (ibid.: 64). Furthermore, they were no longer sold solely in bookshops, but also at the *edicola* (news kiosk) and at railway stations, as well as through subscription (ibid.: 68). The 'Supergiallo' seen in the 1934 film *Giallo* was another format, collecting several novels in one volume, published to coincide with the summer holidays (ibid.: 65). When Nora is seen reading a mystery thriller in *La ragazza che sapeva troppo* or invoking the names of her favourite crime writers to help her solve the mystery, it is often interpreted as a self-reflexive move on the film's part. But the worldly (female) *giallo* reader had been announced on the Italian screen nearly thirty years earlier.

When the Mondadori *giallo* returned from its 1941 ban after the war as *Il giallo Mondadori,* the *edicola* would remain one of its permanent homes, and it can still be found there to this day. Not only did it adapt to changing trends in crime fiction – hardboiled, police procedural, the serial-killer novel – but it also interacted with 'the field of visual culture' (Mazzei and Valentini 2017: 12). Another kind of *giallo* would join Mondadori paperbacks and those from other publishers at the *edicola*. The year 1962 saw the publication of the first issue of *Diabolik,* initially a thinly disguised comic book imitation of Fantômas (whose adventures would be republished in a modified form as *gialli* by Mondadori in the early 1960s). When the first adult-oriented *fumetto* took off, it generated a *filone* of its own – a cycle of comics featuring masked criminals in increasingly lurid and violent narratives. They became known in popular discourse as the *fumetti neri* (black comics), but their covers often labelled them as *gialli. Diabolik's* creator Angela Giussani claimed, 'I wanted to make *gialli* for people who could barely read' (quoted by Curti 2016: 97), while *Kriminal* was branded as the 'Supergiallo settimanale' (weekly supergiallo). Often featuring scantily clad women terrorized and killed by masked anti-heroes – the first issue of *Kriminal* has him strangle a woman he has just slept with, using one of her stockings – the *fumetti neri* constituted a type of *giallo* that was closer to the type of sensational Italian thriller emerging, sporadically at first, in the 1960s. The comics were prosecuted in a well-publicized trial, but the *edicola* would be the spawning ground for a new kind of visual culture. Roberto Curti calls the new *edicola* culture of the 1960s a 'marshland' – 'filled with low-price, cheap hybrids that mixed blood, mystery, crime and, most of all, a new and much-awaited ingredient: eroticism' (2015b: 21). The *filone* cinema of the 1960s and 1970s was in many ways a cinema of the *edicola,* where vampires, assassins, spies, cops, Texas Rangers and masked geniuses of crime proliferated. 'Brivido! Avventura! Buon gusto!' promised the back covers of *KKK – I classici dell'orrore,* although the front covers sent the message that there would not be too much 'buon gusto' (good taste). By the end of the 1960s, *il thrilling italiano* was umbilically linked to the erotic *cineromanzi* – magazines such as *Cinesex, Bigfilm, Cinestop* and *Topfilm* featured *fotoromanzo* (photo-comic strip) versions of erotic scenes from current films, with mystery thrillers featured alongside more straightforward sexploitation fare.

Several of Bava's thrillers invite us to make connections with the literary *giallo* of Mondadori and others. There are the in-jokes (to which we shall return) in *La ragazza che sapeva troppo*, which were perhaps not quite as 'new' as we might think. There was the promotional *fotobusta* for *6 donne per l'assassino* that placed the image of the killer inside a red-bordered circle against a yellow background, mimicking the cover designs of Mondadori's books. And *5 bambole per la luna d'agosto* is a thinly disguised reworking of Agatha Christie's *And Then There Were None* (published in Italy as *I dieci piccoli indiani*). *6 donne per l'assassino* is one of several Italian thrillers that were co-produced with West Germany, some of which claimed a connection to Edgar Wallace or his son Bryan Edgar Wallace in the German market (*A doppia faccia/Double Face*, *L'uccello dalle piume di cristallo*, *Cosa avete fatto a Solange?*) and some of which, like Bava's film, did not. Disentangling the German crime film, or *krimi*, from the *giallo* gets harder in co-productions which do not fall back on the London settings favoured in Rialto's Edgar Wallace cycle, particularly as Wallace was a popular reference point in both countries – Mondadori published an average of ten of his novels per year between 1930 and 1941 (Dunnett 2010: 72). In the version of *6 donne per l'assassino* currently circulating on home video, while the entries in Isabella's much-coveted diary are in Italian, the message the killer scribbles in his notebook asking Peggy where she has hidden the diary is in German, one of the enduring traces of its international production. Stylistic differences aside, one might ask whether *giallo* and *krimi* are not ultimately different words for the same thing – both terms raise similar issues around their general and more specific uses, and the *giallo* and *rote krimi* (red crime novel) grew out of similar publishing and branding strategies. Italian thrillers and German cycles such as Rialto's Edgar Wallace series, and CCC's Dr Mabuse and Bryan Edgar Wallace cycles had much in common – 'masked killers and elaborately staged murders, and an excessive style and flamboyant *mise en scene*' (Bergfelder 2005: 160). Both fashioned a 'transnational imaginary' (ibid.: 139), whether it was the fantasy London of the Wallace films or the jet-set Europe of the Serie B *giallo*-thriller. Of Bava's films, *6 donne per l'assassino* feels closest to the German cycle, both as a co-production and (unlike *La ragazza che sapeva*) by downplaying the particularities of its Rome setting. But while *La ragazza che sapeva troppo* capitalizes more obviously on a particular topography of Rome, it too shares certain qualities with the 1960s Wallace films – the mix of suspense, terror and comedy, the *noir*-ish monochrome photography, the use of technology as a means of misdirection (the sinister taped voice in the empty apartment in Piazza Mincio).[7]

Meanwhile, the literary *giallo* was undergoing some significant shifts in the 1960s. While Italians had written *gialli* from early on – fascist quota laws dictated that they should – they had faced constraints in terms of both censorship and popularity, with the public preferring foreign novels. But if the *giallo* began as an Italian name for a foreign genre, the crime thriller 'made in Italy' was seen to have come of age during the 1960s. The literary *gialli* of Leonardo Sciascia were congenial sources for *cinema d'impegno*, using the central mystery as a means to social and political critique – Sciascia was adapted by Petri, Damiani and Rosi. Equally important, if more conventionally generic, Giorgio Scerbanenco situated noir in the new Italy that arose from *il boom*, the economic miracle of the late 1950s/early 1960s, manifesting the 'dark side of progress and urbanization, featuring a dark and threatening "swinging sixties" Milan, where no one was immune from violence' (Ciccioni and Di Ciolla 2008: 3). Adaptations of Scerbanenco belonged more to *filone* cinema and directors such as Duccio Tessari and Fernando di Leo, and his evocation of a threatening urban modernity has some similarities with *il thrilling italiano* of the 1970s (and Argento, in particular). This is one version of what *il giallo all'italiana* looked like if that term is taken to mean a specifically Italian approach to the genre. But for films often dependent on co-production deals with France, West Germany and Spain, and distribution deals with North America and other foreign markets, the *giallo*'s 'made in Italy' status was always going to be more complicated.

Thrilling 'made in Italy'

While Gary Needham wisely opts to characterize it as 'a conceptual category with highly moveable and permeable boundaries that shift around from year to year' (2003: 135), there has been no shortage of definitions of the *giallo* in English. Here are just a few – 'crime-cum-horror films' (Dyer 2015: 204), 'a violent and erotic type of murder mystery that flourished in Italy during the 1960s and 1970s' (Olney 2013: 103–4), 'an exquisitely decorative and vicious thriller... a murder mystery that eroticizes – or at least fetishizes – violence, revelling in the details of titillating murder rather than the details of deduction and police procedure' (Lucas 2008: 170), 'a film form which crossbreeds the murder mystery with horror' (Thrower 1996: 136). While there is an awareness that the *giallo* also exists as a broader category, the '*true* giallo', according to Troy Howarth, is identified by 'the more lurid and sensational aspects of the genre' (2015: 37). There are some recurring patterns here. There is the crossover with horror – as Koven observes, earlier Anglophone histories tended to contextualize the *giallo* as a type of horror cinema (2006: 3). A 1983 article in the British horror magazine *Halls of Horror* describes these 'colourful murder thrillers' as mixing the whodunnit with the slasher film, emphasizing the 'demented killer, usually masked and often wearing leather gloves', murders that are 'incredibly violent, very gory', but shot with 'a great deal of cinematic flair' (Parry 1983: 17).

This is in a piece called 'The Spawn of *Psycho*' that positions the *giallo* in a lineage of slasher cinema starting with Hitchcock's film (itself a more canonical 'pioneer' film). Moreover, the examples given are from only two filmmakers – Bava and Argento. This version of the *giallo* is lurid, erotic, overtly stylized. Both Needham and Howarth suggest that there is a canon of sorts, and Koven may have the same thing in mind when he refers to the 'classic giallo' (2006: 6). Some of these characteristics will be found in Italian accounts, too, even if the terminology is slightly different and the canon harder to isolate. Bruschini and Tentori's 'real Italian thriller' (2013: 25) is, I suspect, very similar to Howarth's '*true* giallo'. Then there are the themes and tropes identified in academic accounts – modernity and travel (Koven, Needham, Kannas), the family (Dyer), troubled investigations into Italy's historical past (Fisher), anxieties about women's emancipation (Bini) – all of which have enriched our understanding of the Italian thriller, while suggesting both that 'the giallo' can also be defined by its thematic preoccupations and that those preoccupations are specifically Italian.

How did the word 'giallo' get taken up in English? And when? I have not found any examples of it being used in Anglophone reviews of the films on their original release (and if it was, such uses were probably relatively isolated). And it was certainly not used in publicity for the films outside Italy, with a number of the films circulating as horror films or even softcore porn in the United States and the UK. But by the early 1980s, the term was starting to circulate more widely. Sometimes, there were signs of confusion over what a *giallo* actually was – a review of Lucio Fulci's zombie film *Paura nella città dei morti viventi/City of the Living Dead* (1980) refers to 'Italian horror films (called "giallo" films, literally translated as "yellow")' (Childs and Jones 1981: 11). I would suggest that three factors were important here. Firstly, while he had enjoyed international success with *L'uccello dalle piume di cristallo*, the cult surrounding Dario Argento intensified after the release of *Suspiria*, and in 1982 he would return to *il thrilling* with *Tenebre/Tenebrae*, a film that seemed to distil all the elements being associated with this still-exotic generic term. Secondly, the prolific cycle of North American slasher films shaped definitions and understandings of the *giallo* – *Ecologia del delitto* has also taken on a 'pioneer' status in the retrospective positioning of it as an embryonic slasher film. Thirdly, the films were starting to circulate on videotape, which made it easier to construct a canon, to play the Critic's Game – a canon initially formed around Dario Argento (and his generic forefather, Bava) and the slasher film. While Raiford Guins identifies 1987 as roughly the time when Italian horror and other *filone* films started to appear in American video stores (2005: 19), this happened slightly earlier in the UK, where several Italian films achieved notoriety as 'Video Nasties', a term coined in 1982. If Anglophone writers are able to acknowledge the existence of the *giallo* as a broader category while still using it to refer to *filone* thrillers, Italian writers qualify their terms rather more. They may even use different terms. Alberto Pezzotta, for example, adheres to the popular view that *La ragazza che sapeva troppo* initiates 'a new genre', but that genre is named 'il thriller italiano', even though 'in France and England it is called "giallo"' (2013: 54). This is a very particular kind of writing on the Italian thriller. Like Anglophone accounts, it is invested in identifying a canon and criteria for inclusion and exclusion. It inhabits a cultish and cinephile sensibility, its writers often attached to specialist magazines such as *Amarcord* or *Nocturno*. It largely shares with English-language accounts a sense of what characterizes and defines these kinds of thrillers, who are its key directors, and which are its more or less 'classic' films. But there is less certainty over what to call them than in English and how inclusive to be when 'giallo' is the generic category in question. In *Profonde Tenebre: Il cinema thrilling italiano 1962-1982*, one of the earliest books on *il thrilling*, Bruschini and Tentori consider a number of generic terms – 'Spaghetti-thriller', 'giallo all'italiana' and 'thrilling alla Dario Argento' (1992: 7), while the 'g' word is conspicuously absent from the book's title. But a later English-language edition is retitled *Italian Giallo Movies* (2013), and adopts the Anglophone usage of the term, at the expense of once again generating some confusion about its beginnings:

> The real Italian thriller was born first with Pietro Germi, then it grew with Bava, while it met with a huge commercial success and popularity with Dario Argento, the filmmaker who invented a new, extraordinary way to visualize the mechanics of suspense and terror.
>
> (2013: 25)

Most commonly, as is the case in the original *Profonde tenebre*, this 'new' Italian genre is a combination of the *giallo* and the thrilling/thriller, allowing it to be separated both from earlier *giallo* films such as the *telefoni neri* films of the 1930s that lack or place less emphasis on suspense and terror, and other innovative cinematic *gialli* such as Pietro Germi's *Un maledetto imbroglio* (1959). Rea (1999), for example, devotes a chapter to *telefoni neri* covering the period 1930–1959 before moving onto year-by-year coverage of what is seen as the era of 'il cinema thrilling italiano' proper, which he takes to be 1960–1979. Bruschini and Piselli's bilingual *Giallo + Thrilling all'Italiana* begins by locating the 'flashes of zoological surrealism' in post-Argento titles in 'i gialli, o meglio i thrilling all'italiana' ('in gialli, or rather the Italian-style thrillers') (2010: 5). The English text omits 'i gialli' and simply opts for 'Italian-styled' thrillers but retains the preferred Italian term 'thrilling all'italiana' for the overall 'cinematographic phenomenon' in question (ibid.: 9). We might consider here the generic functions of 'giallo', 'giallo all'italiana' and 'il thrilling', which I would suggest operate along different registers of 'newness' and 'Italianness'. While 'giallo' both signals something new and distinctly Italian in the cinema of the 1960s and 1970s in a non-Italian context, neither is the case in an Italian one – the *giallo* was both pre-existing and a foreign import. The addition of 'all'italiana' partly addresses this – a specific variation in the *giallo* – although questions remain about how 'Italian style' these films actually were. Aimed at international markets, aligned to a degree with West German *krimi* and permissive French thrillers set in high society such as *La piscine* (1969), they have been seen by Baschiera and Di Chiara to identify less with a nation-state than 'a borderless Europe inhabited by cosmopolitan characters belonging to the high bourgeoisie (representing) an inauthentic, predictable and clichéd transnational identity' (2010: 35). Nevertheless, for an Italian aficionado such as Davide Pulici, the *giallo*-thriller is 'entirely ours' (2017: 5), while the Anglophone usage of the word 'giallo' can also be seen as 'an attempt to seal off Italian production from broader international patterns and cycles of production' (Hutchings 2016: 85). Moreover, might the 'giallo all'italiano' not also extend to *cinema d'impegno* and *cinema di denuncia,* given that they arguably deploy the genre more conspicuously to address an Italian set of concerns? But it is 'il thrilling' that perhaps signals the 'new' most of all. While identifying the 'first' Italian thriller risks opening up a similar set of problems and disagreements, it is easier to argue that there was no significant tradition of suspense-thrillers prior to the 1960s, even though the thriller is such an inclusive category that it encompasses a range of genres and cycles. Moreover, if 'giallo' was an Italian word for a foreign trend, 'thrilling' – a term more widely used in the 1970s – was a foreign word for what is now seen as an Italian trend (sexy-violent thrillers). And by not quite choosing the grammatically correct word, an adjective used as a noun, it also suggests a localized iteration of the thriller akin to the Western all'italiana or 'Spaghetti Western'.

Both Bruschini and Piselli and particularly Bartolini are more inclusive than an English-language account such as Howarth's (2015). But Bartolini's encyclopedic *Cinema Giallo-Thriller Italiano* nevertheless signals that there is a smaller canon within this that is the 'real' Italian giallo-thriller, with 1963 being its starting point and the early 1970s its 'golden age' (2017: 14). His rationale for inclusion is a generic one:

- Suspense – a mystery to be solved and/or sequences built on tension.

- A rational, that is to say non-supernatural, basis.[8]

- Crime, ideally murder, as the narrative fulcrum, and the predominance of these elements over those from other genres (ibid.: 20). Bruschini and Piselli (2010: 98) note that Argento's *Suspiria* and *Inferno* feature 'thrilling-style murders', but neither they or Bartolini include either film, presumably because their supernatural elements are seen to outweigh the mystery or crime.

These criteria support the book's relative inclusiveness, which extends to political thrillers and *cinema d'autore* as well as coming up to date with contemporary Italian thrillers. But the colour stills of black gloves, sharp objects and bare female flesh, as well as Bartolini's introduction, suggest that a more specific *giallo-thriller italiano* enjoys a more privileged position in the book. As if to confirm the impression, unlike Bruschini and Piselli and Rea, Bartolini excludes anything made before 1963. Once again, it all begins with Bava.

Thrilling remade in Italy:
La ragazza che sapeva troppo

Pioneering but somehow incomplete – this has become a recurring judgement of *La ragazza che sapeva troppo* based on its place in the *giallo* canon. Roberto Curti judges it 'uneven, pioneering, tentative' (2019: 17), while Lucas characterizes it as 'a birth pang of the *giallo*, but not the birth itself', and looks ahead to the Italian thriller reaching 'full flower' with 6 *donne per l'assassino* (2007: 471). Those accounts that see the two films as together founding a 'new' genre could be seen to imply that Bava's second feature-length thriller is half-formed, too, but neither Curti nor Lucas present it as such. Given that doubts over whether the *telefoni neri* constituted a type of *giallo* or Italian thriller proper partly hinge on their comic emphasis, the lightness of Bava's film might be inferred to be the most significant sticking point. In any case, this view arises out of the teleological view of *il thrilling*. Of Bava's five feature-length thrillers, only one of them was made after the success of Dario Argento's debut. *5 bambole per la luna d'agosto* was released less than a week before *L'uccello dalle piume di cristallo*, and therefore only *Ecologia del delitto* could have been made with the knowledge that *il thrilling all'Argento* was a formula for commercial success. In any case, it bears little resemblance to Argento's thrillers – more tightly plotted, more ironic and, surprisingly, more violent. In order to situate *La ragazza che sapeva troppo* and perhaps all of Bava's 1960s thrillers (two of which were released in 1970) – we need to look at other kinds of belonging.

La ragazza che sapeva troppo has two foreign reference points – Alfred Hitchcock and Agatha Christie. The Italian title reworks *The Man Who Knew Too Much* (1934 and 1956), but more importantly, Hitchcock was the default point of comparison for any thriller with international potential. Argento would later be described as the 'Italian Hitchcock' and a re-release trailer for *L'uccello dalle piume di cristallo* would make the unlikely claim that Hitchcock saw 'that Italian' as a genuine threat.[9] Peter Hutchings situates Bava's film as part of 'a slew of Hitchcockian or sub-Hitchcockian thrillers' (2016: 84), of which there were two types by the early-to-mid

1960s. One was a lighter comic thriller in the style of *North by Northwest* such as *Charade* (1964), a film about a girl who knows both too much and not enough. These 'light' Hitchcockian thrillers largely came later than Bava's film, but the romantic interplay between Nora and Marcello is not too far from that mode. But the apotheosis of the modern suspense-thriller was *Psycho* (1960), which, along with *Les Diaboliques,* spawned a number of cycles mixing thriller, horror and sometimes some sexual titillation – Hammer's monochrome suspense-thrillers, William Castle's Hitchcock knock-offs, films scripted by Robert Bloch such as *The Psychopath*. Kim Newman calls the 'psycho-thriller' a 'sub-generic grey area' that overlaps the crime film and the horror film (2002: 71). Crime – more specifically, murder – is usually motivated by madness, pushing the crime genre towards the irrationality of horror. 'The pure mystery is uncomfortable with homicidal mania, since a motiveless criminal sabotages the essential puzzle element of a whodunnit' (ibid.). The Italian thriller does not fully embrace madness-as-motivation until after Argento – inheritances and other kinds of financial gain run noirishly through 1960s *giallo* cinema, particularly those that take Clouzot rather than Hitchcock as their model. The murders in *6 donne per l'assassino* are deliberately staged as if by a sex killer, which means that in terms of how the film works, structured around sadistic 'numbers', they effectively *are* sex killings, displaying beautiful dead women for the viewer. In any case, as Richard Dyer observes, there is often a mismatch between motivation and execution 'which exceeds the bounds of expedition' (2015: 182). This might be why *Ecologia del delitto* is sometimes judged to have no plot, whereas if anything Tom Milne's view that it is 'absurdly over-plotted' (1980: 88) is probably closer to the truth. Only two of Bava's killers are motivated by madness. Laura, Valentina Cortese's alphabet killer in *La ragazza che sapeva troppo,* is simultaneously scheming and insane. She killed her sister over an inheritance and the subsequent murders are designed to make her death seem part of a chain of serial killings. But if that makes her sound like a cold and calculated killer, she rants and twitches as she explains her plot to a terrified Nora, insisting that her sister was a monster with evil eyes and relishing how much she suffered in death. John Harrington in *Il rosso segno della follia* clears things up from the start by informing us directly in voiceover that he is 'completely mad', and that his murders all have a psychological motivation. Otherwise, it is 'money, money and more money' as the Contessa puts it in *6 donne per l'assassino*, a plot convention shared with the West German Edgar Wallace films (Bergfelder 2005: 155). While the term 'psycho-thriller' follows Hitchcock's film, inevitably there are examples that precede or coincide with it. Most notably, given the sadism and titillation to come in *il thrilling italiano*, there are the three films produced by the British studio Anglo-Amalgamated that David Pirie dubbed 'Sadian' – *Horrors of the Black Museum* (1959), *Circus of Horrors* (1959) and *Peeping Tom* (1960). 'Their visual inspiration is

1950s pornography, while their central preoccupation is with the British public's insatiable appetite for crimes of violence', according to Pirie (2009: 114). While *Peeping Tom* is usually isolated from the other two films as a misunderstood masterpiece of British cinema, not least because it has an auteur figure (Michael Powell) attached to it, it follows much the same pattern as the other two films – lurid Eastmancolour (as in *6 donne per l'assassino*, if to different effect), titillating murders of less-than-respectable girls punctuated by a pedestrian police investigation (or vice versa). *Horrors of the Black Museum* has much in common with the Italian thrillers to come. Its lead character is a crime writer working on a book called *The Poetry of Murder*, while also committing a series of murders that he can then write about for his insatiable readers. This is not an attempt to identify yet another hypothetical influence, or more 'forgotten *gialli*', but rather to identify some broader trends, particularly in Europe, blurring the crime and horror genres, testing the limits of censorship (as British horror films certainly were) and drawing on a permissive visual culture that was finding its way into popular cinema. At one point in *Peeping Tom*, the killer observes an older man buying pornography in a news agent, the British equivalent of the *edicola*.

Agatha Christie is one of the 'old friends' that (the narrator tells us) Nora appeals to when planning her investigation, along with Mickey Spillane and the ubiquitous Edgar Wallace, whose name was a kind of trans-European 'brand'. As she rigs up Laura's Spanish Steps apartment with talcum powder and string, she is confident that the murder mystery from which she got the idea has yet to be translated into Italian, thus giving her an advantage over the killer. Austin Fisher reads this as a joke about her privileged position as an American reader of crime novels, with first access to the latest bestsellers (2019: 114). But we might surmise that the killer has read at least one translated *giallo* before her – Christie's *The ABC Murders*. Christie's novel supplies the alphabetical chain of killings – whether Nora's name is Davis (Italian version) or Drowson (English version), she is definitely next in line – '"D" come "*delitto*" (D as in murder)?' mocks the killer over the phone. It gives us a killer whose chain of killings is staged to provide a fictitious narrative frame for the one murder they have an actual motive for. A British Agatha Christie adaptation *Murder, She Said* (1961) has sometimes been identified as the possible inspiration for the killer's much-copied attire in *6 donne per l'assassino* (Hutchings 2016: 85). And Bava would return to Christie, less willingly but equally unofficially, in *5 bambole per la luna d'agosto,* a thinly disguised reworking of one of the founding 'subtractive' narratives, to borrow Adam Lowenstein's term (2016: 133). If Christie's insistence on internal logic seems at odds with the sometimes-haphazard narratives of Italian thrillers, it is worth remembering Raymond Chandler's view of the solution to *Murder on the Orient Express* in his essay 'The Simple Art of Murder' (1950/1984: 183) – 'Only a halfwit could guess it'.

FIGURE 6 *Nora's mystery novel in* La ragazza che sapeva troppo.

Christie, the *giallo,* and translated crime fiction bring us to one of the most discussed aspects of the film, namely its apparent self-consciousness about Nora being an avid reader of crime fiction and being initially seen reading a mystery novel at the start of the film. *Evil Eye,* the AIP cut of the film, begins after the credits with a tracking shot along the aisle of the plane as we hear the thoughts of an assortment of travellers. As we reach Nora, we hear her thinking, 'What an idiot! Washing the blood off that knife in a bathtub', before a pan down reveals the book she is reading and reacting to. The Italian version is more eager to get to Nora, skipping her fellow travellers, but instead of her inner voice, we hear the following narration in a male voice:

> This is the story of a vacation – a vacation in Rome, the dream destination of every American between the age of 16 and 70. Nora Davis was 20 years old. Young, full of life, romantic, she satisfied her desire to escape reality by reading *i libri gialli.* But this would be the last one. She had sworn as much to her mother.

Gary Needham takes this scene as evidence of *La ragazza che sapeva troppo* being 'the first "true" starting point of the *giallo*', even going so far as to suggest that the film is saying to the spectator, 'The Italian *giallo* has arrived' (2003: 136). This would require extraordinary foresight on the part of Bava and his writers, but it is an appealing thought nonetheless. Certainly, the film is marked by a sense of *arrival* (at Rome's still-new Fiumicino airport),[10] if not of a new genre, then of something foreign that seeks to blend into an archetypal Italy. Can we, as some do, call Nora's book a *giallo*, given that she is an American (played by an Italian) reading a book in English? The title of the book is usually given as *The Knife*, and those are certainly the words most visible on the cover. But a closer look reveals that the full phrase at the top of the book's cover is 'After he got The Knife', the first three words in smaller type. At the bottom, there are more words, 'Didi's a doll'. Are these the titles of two separate stories, in which case she might be reading a *Supergiallo*-like collection (there is also a 5 on the cover, suggesting a series in the Mondadori style)? Or is *Didi's a Doll* the real title of the book and 'After he got the knife' a teasing promotional tagline? The cover image could be taken to support either interpretation – a huge knife, its hilt shaped like a naked woman modestly covering her groin with her hands, and a woman in black underwear impaled by the knife (it looks like *she*, not he, got the knife). If I am giving this briefly glimpsed prop, probably mocked up as an anglicized version of a Mondadori paperback, rather more attention that it was ever intended to have, I am far from the first person to be drawn back to it. We might interpret its title(s) and cover in any number of ways, but what is clear is that Nora's arrival brings sex and murder to Rome. Travel has been interpreted as one of the defining tropes of the Serie B *giallo*, a *filone* of airports, arrivals and being slightly outside of one's comfort zone even amidst the luxury of tourist hotspots. *La ragazza che sapeva troppo* plays on two kinds of travel – tourism and the importing of foreign mass culture. Is Italy the kind of place where serial killers lurk or do foreigners bring these sensational and morbid fantasies with them? Marcello (an Italian played by an American) poses this question several times in the film:

> Just look around you. Does this seem like a place where a woman gets stabbed? Come, this is the real Rome, where the sun shines bright, and the air is clear. A dream, perhaps, but never a nightmare.

In the 1934 *Giallo*, the heroine believes that her husband is trying to murder her because she has read too many *gialli*, the genre sent up as a bad influence on (particularly female) readers. In *La ragazza che sapeva troppo*, Commissario Facchetti asks Nora – traumatized by having witnessed a murder, having her bag snatched by a nocturnal *scippatore* dressed like one of the Beagle Boys, and seeing her elderly friend succumb to a fatal heart attack – if she reads *i libri gialli*. When she admits that she does, he advises her not to read any more – 'it's very dangerous literature', he tells her, recalling the fascist distaste for crime fiction that *Giallo* seemingly conformed to. Nora is confused by his being referred to as 'Dottore' – a term of respect for someone with a university education or in a position of authority – but he diagnoses her in pseudo-medical terms (and in *Evil Eye*, tells her that he is a 'doctor of homicide'). This is not the only trace of fascism in the world of the film. One of its appeals to the international viewer is its picturesque excursions into tourist Rome – both the Rome of *La dolce vita* (models posing on the Spanish Steps, Nora fantasizing about Marcello Mastroianni in the *Evil Eye* version) and Rome as historical theme park. But this guided tour cannot bypass the traces of fascism. Both versions of the film include a scene at the Foro Italico, with its fascist-era statues, but this is extended in *Evil Eye* to include a thuggish, menacing figure who sexually harasses Nora – she is able to fend him off with a swing of her handbag, but not before a sequence of him stalking her as if intending to kill her. *Evil Eye* also includes a longer version of the *Roman Holiday*-style montage sequence in which Marcello shows her the sights of the Eternal City. At one point, he gestures towards Piazza Venezia and Il Vittoriano (the much-unloved 'typewriter' of Rome that spoils the view of the *centro storico*) and then mimes goose-stepping and a fascist salute before shrugging. The scene is wordless and filmed in extreme long shot, so we have no idea what he might be telling her about the country's political past. And what of that shrug? It has the air of 'What were we thinking?', although Marcello would have been too young to be directly involved in fascist Italy. But it can also be read as a 'shrugging off' of this past, given the relatively light tone of the film. Either way, its exclusion from the Italian version of the film is notable. But as Marcello insists to Nora that Rome is a dream, not a nightmare (*L'incubo* was the film's working title), that murder is something confined to the past (just as fascist-era *gialli* were forbidden to show crimes being committed in Italy), it is the tourist and a foreign generic framework that are able to uncover the darker side of *la dolce vita*. Thus the *noir* and *rosa* aspects of the film can be seen as working through how Rome might be used as setting for a modern thriller, by also working through different images of the city – tourist theme park, *la dolce vita*, fascism, as well as reconfiguring it as a hallucinatory place of terror (Trinità dei Monti inverted and rippling in a puddle, white-painted corridors illuminated by a swinging light bulb, beams of light created by bullet holes in the wall of a darkened room) or a drug-induced *incubo* (Nora's encounter with cigarettes laced with enough marijuana to 'intoxicate *la dolce vita*'). As Curti observes, the Rome of *6 donne per l'assassino* makes little use of Rome as its setting, delaying even confirming it as the setting (2019: 66), a possible result of its ambitions to play as a *krimi* in the West German market. Rome is signified primarily through its association with fashion in the later film – cinema in the years of 'Hollywood on the Tiber' had helped Rome establish itself as fashion capital of Italy over such rivals as Turin, Florence and Milan (Paulicelli 2016: 167). *La ragazza che sapeva troppo* certainly presents archetypal and even clichéd images of Rome, especially in comparison with the urban non-place of Argento's *L'uccello dalle piume di cristallo* (see Siegel 2011), but this plays as part of the film's engagement with situating the *giallo all'italiana* as an urban thriller that is both international and 'made in Italy'.

FIGURE 7 *Mystery and titillation – Nora and the portrait of Bava in the* Evil Eye *version of* La ragazza che sapeva troppo.

Tutti i colori: *Il telefono* and *6 donne per l'assassino*

Il telefono is often seen as the weakest episode in *I tre volti della paura,* particularly in American International's attempt to transform it into a supernatural and entirely heterosexual narrative, easily overshadowed by the familial vampires and hovering spectres of the other two episodes. In the episode film, David Scott Diffrient tells us, the ordering of the stories matters – 'privileged sections tend to come *first* or *last* in the chain of miniature narration' (2014: 75). In this regard, *Il telefono* has changed position in the two versions of the film. It is the opening story in *I tre volti della paura,* although it is hard to imagine that middle episode *I wurdalak* was meant to be seen as less important, given that it is the one that stars Boris Karloff, the film's top-billed star, as well as being the most substantial of the three stories. In *Black Sabbath,* the AIP cut, it is easier to see *The Telephone* as the mid-film filler, both because of AIP's tampering and because the gothic horror of the other two stories was their stock-in-trade in the early 1960s.

However, *Il telefono* has come to enjoy a different reputation in the retrospectively constructed lineage of *il giallo all'italiana.* Lucas describes it as 'an intermediary evolutionary step' between *La ragazza che sapeva troppo* and 'the brilliantly colourful full-blown *giallo*' represented by *6 donne per l'assassino* (2007: 485). Another 'transitional' film, then, except that he also claims it as '(t)echnically… the first colour *giallo*' (ibid.). In some ways,

Il telefono gives us an idea of what *La ragazza che sapeva troppo* might have looked like in colour, with Rosy's apartment similarly decorated to Laura's (it looks like the same set). In the *Evil Eye* cut, there is a longer scene of Nora wearing a baby doll nightie, spied on by the moving eyes of a portrait with Bava's face (wearing a huge moustache that makes him look like Salvador Dali), anticipating the killer's voyeuristic appreciation of Rosy's 'stupendous body' as the camera looks her up and down. If we return to Nora's mystery novel, this is the sequence that enacts the *Didi's a Doll* aspect of its cover. But it also adopts the visual language of the *fumetti neri* and *edicola* culture – *Kriminal*'s artist Magnus (Roberto Raviola) specialized in voluptuous women clad only in lingerie or baby doll nighties, waiting to be strangled, impaled on a spiked gate, or have acid thrown in their faces. *Il telefono* expands the vignette of the young woman being spied on (a voyeuristic gaze we are invited to share) and terrorized by telephone calls from the earlier film. The culprit is again a woman, but Mary's motives are rather different from those of Laura. Mary is Rosy's former lover – she uses the word 'amiche' (the feminine form of 'friends') ironically to describe their relationship – and has been disguising her voice to trick Rosy into thinking that another former lover, Frank, has escaped from prison. The twist comes when Frank arrives just as Mary is confessing her scheme in a letter to a sleeping Rosy, strangling her and then turning on his former lover who manages to stab him with the knife Mary gave her to keep under her pillow (this could easily be the story Nora was reading on the plane – *he* got the knife). This allows Mary to be the threat (holding the knife in a gloved hand and creeping up behind Rosy) but also the one punished by Frank. Is Rosy an expensive call girl and Frank her former pimp or just an ambitious girl with a taste for 'important men', some of whom are dangerous criminals? This is never made very clear, partly perhaps for censorship reasons (even in the Italian version) or perhaps because all we really need to know is that this is a story of money, fashion (Rosy dresses like one of the models in *6 donne per l'assassino*), chic apartments, perversity and retribution. In other words, it bears a streak of Puritanism that brings it closer to the den of vice that is the atelier around which *6 donne per l'assassino* revolves. Titillation and Catholic morality in perpetual tension become one of the driving forces of the Italian thriller – Valentina Vitali notes the pull between Nora's bare thighs and the spectacle of Trinità dei Monti as she lies unconscious after witnessing a murder in *La ragazza che sapeva troppo* (2016: 46). As Paul Ginsborg explains, the ruling Christian Democrat party experienced a tension between its traditional ideology and the values of consumer capitalism as Italy embraced an American-style liberal individualism in the period of *il boom*. They paid lip service to such values as the sanctity of family life, while 'in practice the majority of the party fully espoused the cause of "modernization"' (1990: 153) – the values of individualism and 'the unfettered development of technology and consumer capitalism' (ibid.: 154). The relaxation of censorship, Simone Castaldi argues, 'brought to the surface a large section of the collective imagination that had been deeply repressed' (2010: location 287). Inevitably, not all of this was going to be pretty.

Its title notwithstanding, 6 donne per l'assassino features five murders – the Contessa is the sixth victim, but she is tricked into the injuries that lead to her death, rather than murdered gruesomely like the others. This is a film that encourages us to count (and it will not be the last Bava film of which that is true) – 'Isabella, Nicole, Peggy, and Greta makes four', the Contessa slurs drunkenly before being persuaded by her lover Massimo to despatch the fifth. According to Roberto Curti, the five murders together account for twenty-three minutes of the film's eighty-eight minute running time (2019: 30). In addition to its experiments with colour, lighting and camera movement, 6 donne per l'assassino's reputation as a pioneering film rests on its prioritizing of the setpiece.

> The anticipation of there being another set piece, another number, to thrill to is itself a serial pleasure, it is what we've come for, what we are waiting for. If the killings are not always serial for the killers, they always are for us.
>
> (Dyer 2015: 182)

In the giallo all'italiana, the chain of killings is rarely what it seems, which is why Inspector Silvestri gives up at a certain point and the moral logic of the film intervenes to ensure that the remaining guilty parties destroy each other. In the German Edgar Wallace films, Scotland Yard can usually be relied on to solve the mystery because, as Orwell once observed, Wallace's admiration for the police was a form of 'bully-worship' (1944/1986: 75). Silvestri is certainly a bully, but proves to be an ineffectual one. The murders look like fevered sex killings, but are coldly rational (a Christie-like contrivance with added titillation). Three of them (Isabella, Nicole and Peggy) are motivated by the need for the Contessa and Massimo to silence their blackmailer, who knows that they murdered the Contessa's husband, and then retrieve her incriminating diary while despatching those who have read it. The other two (committed by the Contessa, rather than Massimo) are motivated by the need to provide an alibi (Greta) and a simulation of suicide to frame someone else for the murders (Tao-li). There are differences of opinion over how much weight we should give to the story, or whether we should just lose ourselves in the colours and lurid violence – 'script and acting feeble, but redeemed by marvellous visual sense' was a view not untypical of its original reviews (Hinxman 1966: 5). According to Kim Newman, 'the methodical detection scenes become redundant excuses for stringing together a series of stylishly gruesome murder and suspense sequences which are treated like production numbers in a musical' (1986a: 23). In the giallo more generally, he suggests that the solution to the mystery is 'negligible but has to be gone into' (ibid.: 24). Curti finds the story dusty and formulaic, so that it is Bava's staging of it that matters and has ensured its cult longevity. Ian Olney, on the other hand, argues that it is a 'carefully crafted anti-detective story' akin to modernist developments in 1960s *giallo* fiction, offering its characters as 'masks to be tried on, worn for a time, and exchanged for others as we progress through the movie' (2013: 110–11). I am less convinced that there is much in its narrative that one would not find in one of Agatha Christie's trickier plots, a kind of 'Six Little Mannequins'. Nevertheless, while the detective story is a bit more than 'negligible', it is probably the case that we would not remember it quite so vividly if it was not filmed in such a striking and eccentric manner.

6 donne per l'assassino was made and released in the year that the *fumetti neri* blossomed (if that's the word) into an infamous cycle – *Kriminal, Satanik, Fantax* and *Mister X* made their debuts that year, and more would follow. I have written elsewhere about the relationship between the *fumetti neri* and 1960s *giallo* cinema (Hunt 2016), and Curti (2002) has even suggested that the notorious fifth issue of *Kriminal* set in a girl's reformatory school could almost be taken as an adaptation of Bava's film, published a few months after the film's release. 'They even looked sexy when dead!' is how Carlo Dumontet characterizes the women in *Kriminal* (1998: 9), a dynamic that *6 donne per l'assassino* seems to pursue as Isabella's dead body is dragged away, her skirt hiked up to reveal her thighs, suspenders and underwear, or Greta's breasts heave shortly before she is suffocated with a pillow. While *Diabolik* was always a tamer affair, it made it more explicit that the ur-text of the *fumetti neri* was Fantômas, who had been popular in Italy from the start. Fantômas, too, committed murders whose execution exceeded their motivation, virtually decapitating one victim in order to simply steal her necklace. Curti observes that several reviewers saw the masked killer in *6 donne per l'assassino* as a Fantômas-like figure (the gas station attendant tells the police that he didn't have a face) (2019: 53). The masked criminal aspires to 'a terrifying illegibility', according to Tom Gunning (2008: 26), and Fantômas embodies 'the radical eradication of identity' (ibid.: 26). Ultimately *6 donne per l'assassino* clarifies the identity of the two killer(s) and they explain their plot to each other, much as Diabolik and his accomplice Eva Kant often do at the end of an elaborate heist, but only after extracting maximum chills from its faceless assassin(s).

We know that this 'influential' thriller had no immediate influence whatsoever, at least in the cinema – it pushed an envelope that would not move again for another five or six years. There are other 1960s thrillers and horror films with touches of sado-eroticism, but little sense of a cycle or *filone* taking shape. Antonio Margheriti's *Nude... si muore/Naked... You Die* (1968) is perhaps the closest to Bava's film, which is hardly surprising given that he was initially involved in developing it with future *Diabolik* scriptwriters Tudor Gates and Brian Degas – Lucas includes it as part of Bava's 'Secret Filmography' (2007: 712). It even had a similarly sado-titillating title at one point, *Sette vergini per il diavolo* (Seven Virgins for the Devil). Another title attached to the film was *Cry Nightmare* (traces of which can be heard in the title song), recalling the working title of *La ragazza che sapeva troppo*. That is not its only connection to Bava's first thriller, however – like *La ragazza,* it has also been described as a *giallo-rosa* (Rea 1999: 70) and Lucas notes that both films feature a female character obsessed with mystery novels (2007: 714).[11] Less lurid than its title suggests, at least in its Italian cut,[12] *Nude... si muore* is most interesting for again suggesting a synergy with the *fumetti neri*. The film is set in an all-girls school, a favourite location in *Kriminal.* The notorious fifth issue 'Omicidio al riformatorio' (Murder at the reformatory, 1964) takes place amongst reform schoolgirls who are 'ragazze sulla strada del vizio' (girls on the road of vice), not unlike the models in *6 donne per l'assassino*. The later 'Dramma in collegio' (issue 55, 1965) deals with a schoolgirl prostitution ring, anticipating subsequent Italian thrillers such as *Cosa avete fatto a Solange?* But as its *giallo-rosa* reputation suggests, *Nude... si muore* is lighter in tone than *6 donne per l'assassino*, with a clearly defined and sympathetic heroine and schoolgirls in peril closer to the more engaging and active female characters in *Kriminal,* whose excesses were always presented tongue-in-cheek, than the mannequins marked for death in Bava's previous thriller. But if the *edicola* and *filone* cinema were on the same page in many ways, *6 donne per l'assassino,* for reasons we may never know, failed to capitalize on the popularity of the *fumetti neri,* just as his later thrillers would not manage to ride the wave of *il thrilling all'italiana*. It would be another four years before Bava made another film seen as inhabiting the same generic terrain, even if only in part.

The enchantments of madness:
Il rosso segno della follia

If three of Bava's feature-length thrillers are often accorded seminal status of one sort or another, the other two have less exalted reputations. Lucas reports that *Il rosso segno della follia* was the only film in a Bava retrospective at San Francisco's Roxy Theatre in 1992 not to be given a round of applause when it finished (2007: 793). He attributes this to its 'unsettling but compelling' effect, but it is not difficult to see why it might leave some viewers cold or a little mystified, even in the context of a Bava season. It is one of several films that complicate the generic mapping of Bava's output. It has been described as an 'atypical *giallo*... halfway between thriller and ghost story'

(Bruschini and Tentori 2013: 30) or a 'gothic thriller between Hitchcock (*Psycho*) and Buñuel (*Essayo di un crimen*)' (Bruschini and Piselli 2010: 44). Pezzotta pairs it with *La frusta e il corpo* as films in which a character is either haunted by a former partner or compelled to believe so (2013: 96), to which we could also add *Shock*. The fashion house setting places us back amongst the mannequins (one of the victims stands in an awkward static pose before her murder), suggesting another round of *6 donne per l'assassino*, but the film is considerably less graphic, the murders confined to abstract splashes of blood, distorting lenses, or the one-dimensional image of a victim's face 'torn' in two to reveal the blurred image of the memory that John is trying to recover. In fact, we only witness John Harrington murder two of his bridal wear models, the first in a disorienting sequence on a train where John seemingly glimpses his childhood self in the train corridor, the second amidst eerily lit mannequins. The third murder, that of his wife Mildred (Laura Betti, the film's greatest asset), will transform the film into a marital ghost story. *Il rosso segno della follia* might instead have been a tale of another girl who knew too much, given that Helen – hovering between potential victim and potential love interest – turns out to be helping the police as well as being the sister of an earlier victim, going undercover as another of John's models. But despite being played by Dagmar Lassander, now seen as one of the iconic 'scream queens' of the *giallo all'italiana*, Helen is overshadowed by the figure of Mildred, a ghost who can be seen by everyone *except* the person she is haunting. If we are inclined to play the auteur game, there is another in-joke akin to the portrait of Bava in *Evil Eye*, as John watches *I tre volti della paura* on TV, a film that separates gothic horror and psychological thriller into distinct segments where this film blends them. Then there is the fact that, even more than usual, the film is easier to locate as 'European' film than 'Italian'. *Il rosso segno della follia* was a majority Spanish production, with a Spanish scriptwriter. It was shot mainly in Spain but is set in Paris (with a few location shots of the Eiffel Tower to emphasize the point).

The film's Spanish and English title – *Un hacha para la luna de miel* or *A Hatchet for the Honeymoon* – makes the film sound closer to the body count of *6 donne per l'assassino*, *5 bambole per la luna d'agosto* and *Ecologia del delitto*.[13] But the Italian title, which translates as 'The Red Sign of Madness' brings it closer to the psychological thriller, as John's opening narration confirms:

My name is John Harrington. I'm 30 years old. I am a paranoiac (laughs softly). Paranoiac! An enchanting word – so civilised and full of possibility. The fact is, I'm completely mad, the realisation of which annoyed me at first but is now amusing to me, quite amusing. Nobody suspects that I am a madman, a dangerous murderer – not Mildred, my wife, nor the employees of my fashion centre, nor of course my customers.

While John's mother-fixation could be attributed to the Italian phenomenon of *mammismo*, the prolonged attachment of men to their mothers, its more likely source is *Psycho*, which ends almost as this film begins, with a mocking inner voice that uses a nearby fly to make a point ('Poor little fly', John comments before feeding it to his parrot, 'your insignificant life is a mere biological accident'). Having announced the identity of the killer at the start, if the film is to be taken as a *giallo*, its mystery lies in John unlocking a buried memory that gradually comes into focus with each killing – matricide motivated by possessiveness. His refusal or inability to consummate his marriage is ostensibly explained away as impotence (he claims to rape his victims, but there is nothing in the film to suggest that he actually does) and restaging his mother's murder on her (presumably second) wedding night. But the film is sending out other messages about Mr Harrington. There is his narcissism, evident in his body maintenance routine (a toning belt and sauna), extravagant bouffant hair and a series of outfits that consistently command more attention than anything his models might wear – his printed pyjamas, with a chain-link motif that reminds us of the belt he wears in other scenes, are a particular fashion highlight. When the police come to question him, John is in his hothouse amongst his orchids – 'I'm attracted to everything that is an alteration of nature', the inspector tells him, observing a 'special hybrid' amongst the plants. John is a 'hothouse flower' and mother's boy, and queer killers (and victims) will haunt the Italian thriller throughout the 1970s, not least in the films of Argento – girls raised as boys, boys with overprotective mothers, boys with aberrant chromosomes. 'Did you tell her how much you loved your mother?', Mildred taunts him when he returns from his date with Helen. When she speaks in his mother's voice during a séance, her words reinforce the impression of mother-son intimacy – 'Leave me alone. Don't be naughty... I love you, my baby'. Soon, he cannot perform for the murders either, interrupted during an attempted killing by the police. Missing his usual cue (the sound of footsteps on stairs in his head), he can only kill Mildred by becoming a 'sexually indeterminate bride' himself (Dyer 2015: 196), donning a veil and lipstick as he enters her bedroom with his hatchet on a silver platter. Soon after, Mildred's ghostly appearances frame her as an adult version of the ghostly child in *Operazione paura*. When John is arrested, Mildred reverses her manifestations so that only he can see her, doomed to be haunted by her for the remainder of his (incarcerated) life. In the final scene, he is trapped between two ghosts – his childhood self, who committed matricide, and his cackling dead wife, grabbing handfuls of her own ashes and blowing them through her fingers. A majority Spanish production delayed by two years in release, *Il rosso segno della follia* has little in common with the *gialli* being made contemporaneously (the Carroll Baker *filone*) or the ones it would be released alongside. It is little wonder that it is equally likely to be discussed alongside Bava's gothic horror films as his thrillers. Lucas never refers to it as a *giallo*, and Curti (2015a) includes it in the second volume of his book series on Italian gothic horror (2017). Its investigative scenes are even more cursory – and more carelessly filmed – than those in *6 donne per l'assassino,* and it quickly loses interest in the subtractive narrative that plays a more central role in the next two thrillers.

'Così imparano a fare i cattivi!': 5 bambole per la luna d'agosto and Ecologia del delitto

Ecologia del delitto (Ecology of murder) was released under its original title to little success; it was then screened under the title *Antefatto* (background or backstory) at the Sitges Festival shortly afterwards. When it emerged again as *Reazione a catena* (Chain Reaction) the following year, it also evidently underwent some slight changes to its content. Most notable was the final line of the film. In a complicated plot involving inheritances, land development, legitimate and illegitimate offspring, ecology and capitalist modernity, Alberto and Renata Donati seem to have emerged victorious. They have not committed all the murders in the film – keeping count of who killed who is one of the film's challenges – but they have certainly done their share. But just as they are celebrating the riches to come, they are gunned down in a wilfully bathetic ending by their two small children who have been amusing themselves while their parents are away. In the original version, one of the children delivered the line that was also the title of the original story outline – 'Così imparano a fare i cattivi' ('That will teach them to be naughty'). In *Reazione a catena,* the only version of the film currently available on DVD or Blu-ray, the line is changed to 'Come giocano bene a fare i morti' ('They're really good at playing dead'). A group of bad people being taught a lesson one by one is one of the threads running through the Italian thriller, starting with *6 donne per l'assassino,* but its founding narrative is arguably Agatha Christie's *And Then There Were None* (1939), in which ten characters with dark secrets in their past are lured to an island and killed one by one for their unpunished crimes until no one is left alive. In the final chapter, which might have exasperated Raymond Chandler almost as much as *Murder on the Orient Express,* one of the 'victims' turns out to be the killer, having faked his death before despatching the remaining members of the group and then staging his suicide to look like the final murder. The killer, a terminally ill judge, is both a sadist (by his own admission) who has always wanted to commit murder, and righteous avenger – the perfect archetype for narratives in which the killer is simultaneously a monster and a dispenser of some sort of moral judgement, either their own or that of the story. The most recent BBC version of Christie's story (2015) placed particular emphasis on its misanthropic nastiness, as well as restoring the original ending of the novel. Most film versions depart from this ending, following instead the 1943 Broadway stage adaptation *Ten Little Indians* in having two people survive (and prove to be innocent) and confront the killer at the climax (Aldridge 2016: 80). *5 bambole per la luna d'agosto*, an unofficial adaptation with fewer victims in the title (which only seems to count the women) but almost as many onscreen, clearly intended to imitate the original novel's ending, although that was not what ultimately happened on screen. In any case, all of the versions of Christie's novel (four films in English, an Indian and a Russian version, plus a number of TV adaptations), both of Bava's 1970s thrillers and a number of other *giallo*-thrillers, not to mention slasher films and other horror films, adhere to what Adam Lowenstein calls 'subtractive spectatorship' – 'a desire to subtract or erase human beings from the landscape, to leave it empty' (2016: 133). He continues, 'the desire is for a depopulated or empty landscape, a natural state uncoupled from human life and its attendant tensions' (ibid.: 34). Both *5 bambole per la luna d'agosto* and *Ecologia del delitto* tell essentially the same story. A group of greedy, even murderous, characters all want something, and die one by one as a result. This plays out in a setting that situates modernity (a fashionable villa, a planned luxury resort) in the midst of nature (an island, a bay). As the guilty die, often killing each other off, 'innocents' (who might be shrewder than they seem) inherit whatever is left – Isabelle, now rich, on her swing, the Donati children playing in the unspoiled bay.[14]

5 bambole per la luna d'agosto was made in between two official versions of Christie's story, one in 1965 and another in 1974, both by the same producer, Harry Alan Towers, who would go on to make a third version in 1989. The first two Towers films used virtually the same script but changed the setting – the 1965 version takes place on a snow-covered mountain reached by cable car, and the 1974 version in a mansion in the desert – so that the *where* of the story becomes in some ways more important than the *what,* which might already be familiar to the audience. Bava shot *5 bambole* at Tor Caldara, which functions as an equivalent to the island in Christie's novel. But the film is at its least visually interesting when it ventures outside, often seemingly assembled from indifferent coverage, slow zooms and shots of Edy Galliani's character Isabelle watching from behind a rock that appear to have been inserted almost randomly at various points. It is George Stark's modernist beach house that brings the film to life – Bartolini aptly sums up the film as 'the victory of decor over characters' (2017: 80). As a *giallo,* it is certainly a disaster – an overfamiliar story made incomprehensible, drained of all suspense and lacking the star power that keeps most official adaptations of the story going. And while narrative incoherence is by no means unusual for 1970s Italian *gialli,* it is their set pieces that are often seen to redeem them for their admirers. However, the murders in *5 bambole* largely happen off-screen and are discovered after the fact. If *6 donne per l'assassino* makes a spectacle of death in two ways – the murders as violent set pieces, and the arrangement of bodies into a deathly tableau – *5 bambole* skips straight to the latter, one of the victims even going directly to the freezer where the corpses accumulate without any indication of how he was killed. The film features the female star now most closely associated with *il thrilling all'italiana*, Edwige Fenech, but, apart from a go-go dance in the film's opening scene, she is just one interchangeable *bambola* amongst the others, her (relatively early) death revealed by a sudden whip-pan to her body tied to a tree, a knife in her left breast. It is as a film about sunken baths, spiral staircases and revolving beds that *5 bambole* is probably now more likely to be enjoyed. And here is the key to the film's increasing rehabilitation, as the cultification of the Italian *giallo* also extends to its time-bound fashions and production design – although even at the time there were reviewers who enjoyed its 'atmosphere of opulent vulgarity and decadence' (Bilbow 1971: 12). This is the Italian *thrilling* boiled down to its retro-kitsch elements, rather than its generic ones – 'lounge' music, outrageous fashions (an episode involving a stolen gold lamé shawl comes to nothing, as if it only exists to show off another flamboyant item of clothing), louche interior design, glamorous but dull people. It is one of the Bava films that support the critical view that he was not interested in people, at least until they could be turned into objects, here wrapped in plastic. When Mark Aldridge complains that Bruno Nicolai's score for the 1974 *And Then There Were None* 'occasionally veers into easy-listening music' (2016: 132), one wonders how he might respond to Piero Umiliani's score for *5 bambole per la luna d'agosto*. While its most memorable cue is a darkly comic waltz accompanying the swinging of polythene-wrapped bodies in the freezer, much of the soundtrack veers between pop and easy listening – it is a soundtrack for luxurious interior design and bedroom arrangement. Sometimes the characters can be organized into interesting compositions around the interior design – the men grouped around the spiral staircase, or the glass balls that roll towards the sunken bath where Jill is found dead. But at one point, the (interior) landscape is literally depopulated when the drugged inhabitants are removed and hidden before the authorities arrive to search the house, then replaced to the exact positions where they lost consciousness as they leave. This depopulated landscape has less in common with the embryonic slasher countdown of *Ecologia del delitto* than it does with the climax of a more canonical Italian film, Antonioni's *L'eclisse* (1962), set in the EUR district of Rome built during the fascist era and emptied of human life, 'leaving us with details of buildings and objects and, of course, with the uncertainty of suspended time, waiting for something to happen or appear' (Paulicelli 2016: 143). The *giallo*, unlike *cinema d'autore*, can only suspend time and empty space for so long, but this scene is entirely consistent with the camera's interest in interior space over human life.

A word that recurs in more sympathetic accounts of *5 bambole* – a film that carries the distinction of being the one Bava regarded as his worst – is

FIGURE 8 *And then there were none – the empty luxurious villa in* 5 bambole per la luna d'agosto.

'sabotage'.[15] Pezzotta (2013: 103) and Acerbo (2007: 183) both use the word to describe Bava's approach to the film, and a review as early as 1970 seemed to have something similar in mind (Cappabianca 1970: 194–5). Lucas calls it an 'anti-thriller' (2007: 813) and recounts the story of Riccardo Freda and Bava's daughter Elena being shocked when they first saw the film (ibid.: 823), not on this occasion by its violence but by how carelessly made it appeared to be. 'Sabotage' carries with it the implication of agency – instead of it being a film that Bava perhaps was defeated by (a bad script, insufficient preparation time when he replaced another director at short notice), it becomes a project that he acted on, subverted and rebelled against, bending it to his creative will in the only way that he could. Admittedly, if it is true that he was responsible for changing the identity of the killer, as he claimed (Pezzotta 2013: 103), then he can be credited with sabotaging the film's narrative (or at least with making it worse than it already was). All logic points to the killer being Professor Fritz Larson (or Gerry Farrell, as he is called in the English version), who refuses to sell his secret formula to the venal industrialists and their wives gathered at Stark's house and is positioned in judgement of their cynicism and venality. When he fakes his own death, with the aid of Isabelle, he seems doubly set up to follow Christie's righteously cruel judge in emptying the landscape of the unpunished. But instead, the Professor has only killed his colleague, before the events shown onscreen, in order to steal his formula (for what purpose? He turns down all offers of money) and has blurted out everything to the police because Isabelle used sodium pentothal to drug him when staging his death. The killer turns out to be Howard Ross' Jack, not only an arbitrary choice from a group of indistinguishably avaricious men, but one that literally makes no sense. Jack could not possibly have killed his wife, who was on the balcony of their bedroom while he was still in bed. He finds her shot through the head – a shot clearly fired from the opposite direction as Jack was behind her (and has no reason to pretend to be shocked by her death when there is no one else there to witness his performance). If Bava tinkered to make a dull project more interesting and less predictable, he might have made it visually more interesting, but killed off what was left of the narrative. 'L'assassino uccide sempre lentamente ma con crudeltà' (the murderer always kills slowly but cruelly), claimed the *locandina* for the film, suggesting the kind of sado-thrilling that would come to characterize 1970s Serie B thrillers, but one of Trudi's lines is often cited to sum up the narrative more succinctly – 'It feels like everybody's waiting for something that's never going to happen'. *5 bambole* makes us wait for things to happen and when they do, it refuses to show them to us – *something exciting happened*, it tells us, *but it happened somewhere else.* Chris Fujiwara has called Italian *filone* cinema a 'tidal wave of boredom' (2007: 244), not the artful boredom of auteur cinema, but boredom arising from 'an exhaustive approach to standardized, sensation-mongering genres'. This is less of a dismissal than it probably sounds – Fujiwara is probing the dynamics of cinematic boredom, a 'state of freedom' that places excitement at arm's length (ibid.: 243–4). We are amongst bored (and boring) people – the trans-European jet-set of late 1960s thrillers, alternating their time between outrageous parties, arch backbiting and studied cynical *ennui* in cool modernist surroundings. 'Instead of taking part in a narrative', Fujiwara says of the characters in Umberto Lenzi's *Spasmo* (1974), 'they are hiding from it' (ibid.: 248). Or hidden from it, one might say of *5 bambole per la luna d'agosto*. To be bored by a film, argues Fujiwara, 'is to reject the offer, or to collude with the film's failure to offer, a distraction from one's own condition and one's own duration' (ibid.: 241). But if we entertain the notion of self-sabotage, if that is a realistic thing to believe that a jobbing filmmaker might do, *5 bambole* almost seems to invite us to collude not with its failure but with its own narrative boredom.

No one could accuse *Ecologia del delitto* of making us wait for something to happen. Two characters are violently killed in the opening minutes, the second of them having only just murdered the first, his wife. Most of these killings are motivated by the desire to possess the bay owned by Isa Miranda's Countess, the film's first victim, and turn it into a luxury resort, contaminating a 'paradise on earth' (as one character calls it) with *modernismo*, a word spat out by the Countess as unscrupulous property developer Franco Ventura tries to tempt her with money in a flashback. But not all the murders are financially motivated, at least not directly. The final two killings – of the parents by their children – are both a game and a punishment (of *i cattivi*), returning the bay to a state of paradise and saving it from becoming 'a sea of cement'. But even more loosely motivated are the film's four most spectacular murders, including a billhook splitting one character's face, and the spearing of a copulating couple whose shared death rattle is decidedly orgasmic. As if that was not enough, they are then 'arranged' in a bathtub like some horrendous conjoining of dead limbs for Renata to discover later in the film. The motivation for these murders claimed by their killer – object lessons in execution exceeding motivation – derives from a preceding murder, of the fourth person in the group, who was skinny dipping in the bay when she unwittingly discovered the corpse of the Countess' husband, his hand touching her naked posterior in a parody of his debauched former lifestyle. The Count had been killed in the opening scene by the Countess' illegitimate son Simone, described as 'part watchman, part woodsman, part petty thief', and easily the most prolific killer in the film. The four unlucky victims are just in the wrong place at the wrong time, Ventura's temporarily abandoned cottage, where they stop off for some sex, drugs and music. Simone later tells Ventura that he killed them because of the discovery of Count Donati's corpse. But we have already seen him spying on them at the cottage – Bava was understandably proud of a shot of what initially looks like the sun setting but a focus pull reveals to be Simone's eye – so we might infer that he has an appetite for this kind of thing. *Ecologia del delitto* is sometimes mistakenly taken as virtually plotless, perhaps because the sheer number of murders and their ferocity threaten to overwhelm the narrative (and because high body counts are now associated with the more simplistic narratives of slasher films). But certainly, this episode's main function is to increase the film's body count, and it is here that the film most resembles the future North American slasher film, where a voyeuristic killer and horny teenagers are all that is required to paint the screen red. The film's influence on one slasher franchise, the *Friday the 13th* series, has been discussed many times – Bava once again fated to influence more commercially successful (and usually American) films. The film's many titles – more than any other Bava film – are indicative of its shifting sense of belonging.[16] The project had initially attracted the interest of Dino De Laurentiis, clearly recognizing the commercial power of *il thrilling all'Argento,* and this is the first thriller Bava made after the younger director's breakthrough. Bruschini and Tentori suggest that it 'deconstructs the mechanics of Argento's films' (2013: 8), while Lowenstein sees it as 'a critical dialogue with *giallo* conventions by the man who all but invented the form' (2016: 130). We have no way of knowing if Bava thought of himself as having invented anything, and some of the film's ideas originated in any case with writer Dardano Sacchetti (who had worked with Argento on his second film *Il gatto a nove code*). Fisher (2019: 136) sees it as the 'pioneer' of a *sottofilone* of 'rural *gialli*' exploring the tension between cosmopolitanism and provincialism that would include Lucio Fulci's *Non si sevizia un paperino/Don't Torture a Ducking* (1972) and Sergio Martino's *I corpi presentano tracce di violenza carnale/Torso* (1973). But Bava's film did not achieve the kind of commercial success, at least in

Italy, to suggest a profitable *filone* and Fisher acknowledges that this is a very small cycle, with up to a year passing between each film. Nevertheless, this would be arguably Bava's most influential film on American genre cinema, especially as, unlike his earlier gothics, it was not re-working a successful formula established elsewhere. In some ways, it is easier to see *Ecologia del delitto* as a 'pioneering' film than Bava's first two thrillers. Made at the height of Argento fever, it does not follow any of the conventions that were popular at the time, for whatever reason. Might it have been more successful at home if it had, or are the reasons for its failure more banal, a casualty of poor distribution? Perhaps the original Italian audience for *il thrilling* was less interested in the size of its body count than later cult audiences would be – Argento's films had relatively engaging central characters, a youthful outlook and a recognizable urban milieu. But the violence and mean-spiritedness of Bava's film would travel well, even if some of the nuances now discerned in the film were probably of less importance when *Carnage*, *Twitch of the Death Nerve* or *Last House – Part 2* turned up at the drive-in or Grindhouse.[17] Nevertheless, for better or worse, that would be where the film initially earned its reputation.

Separating out a director's films that belong to a single genre is, of course, an artificial exercise, even when we can agree on what the genre is or whether it even is a genre. But from a rhetorical point of view, both the *giallo* (or *thrilling*) and the 'Bava *giallo*' exist – they are categories that continue and will continue to be analysed, argued over, subjected to new readings and interpretations. But considering his pioneering reputation, Bava's thrillers do not fit neatly into the way the Italian thriller is mapped out, even in comparison with those of other directors associated with the *giallo*, who either assert a strong auteurist identity (Argento) or conform more visibly to industrial trends (Lenzi, Martino).[18] Whether this makes him an outsider-maverick figure – inventing genres, sabotaging films – or someone who was out of step with changing trends and tastes is a matter for debate. In some ways, casting Bava as a founding figure does not always do his films any favours, as in the case of *La ragazza che sapeva troppo*, so often judged on the basis of what had yet to come. But above all, Bava's thrillers illustrate the complexities of the *giallo* as a category as well as some of its limitations in making sense of the unpredictable flows and fortunes of *filone* cinema.

Notes

1   See Kannas (2020: 39–63) on the cultification of the *giallo*.
2   *Il rosso segno della follia* was made in 1968–69, but not released in Italy until 1970 a few months after *5 bambole per la luna d'agosto*, which had been made in 1969. While it could just as easily be categorized as gothic horror, its delayed release arguably pulled it into the emerging *filone* of *il thrilling*.

3   Although, while it is often seen as Argento's move into outright horror, *Suspiria* was also referred to as a *giallo* in some of its original Italian reviews.

4   A 'pink' *giallo,* suggesting the feminization of an ostensibly 'masculine' genre, often through romance, as with the more widely used critical term 'neorealismo rosa' (pink neorealism) for the cycle of films in the 1950s that retained the working-class realism of the more critically respectable genre but pushed it in a lighter, usually comic, direction.

5   On paper, *La donna della domenica* has all the makings of a *filone giallo* – its murders, after all, are committed with a phallic sculpture. But it has too many markers of quality and prestige – the wrong director (Luigi Comencini, rather than Lenzi or Martino), the wrong stars (Marcello Mastroianni and Jacqueline Bissett, rather than George Hilton and Edwige Fenech) and a basis in a bestselling novel (by the Turin-based *giallisti* Carlo Fruttero and Franco Lucentini).

6   With, respectively, *The Benson Murder Case* (published as *La strana morte di signor Benson*) and *Captain of Souls* (*L'uomo dai due corpi*).

7   A not dissimilar scene appears in *Die toten augen von London/Dead Eyes of London* (1961).

8   Concessions are made for paranormal 'frills', such as the ESP in *Profondo rosso,* while *Il rosso segno della follia* is included on the basis that Mildred's ghost could be interpreted as psychological projection (Bartolini 2017: 243).

9   Hitchcock seems to have viewed a different Italian – Antonioni – as someone he needed to try and catch up with.

10   Fiumicino opened in 1961, giving the film another sense of the 'new'.

11   And, in this case, also Marvel comics, which had yet to arrive in Italy.

12   Unclothed versions of some scenes were evidently shot for foreign markets.

13   Strictly speaking, the Spanish title qualifies as the 'original' one, but the film was released in Italy a few months earlier than in Spain and so was first exhibited under its Italian title.

14   The original closing line of *Ecologia del delitto* suggests that the children knowingly 'punish' their parents, while *Reazione a catena* has them unwittingly kill them as part of their play.

15   If we were looking for actual evidence of sabotage, or some bored filmmakers amusing themselves, we might consider what happens to Jack after his death, falling amongst some fruit and vegetables in the walk-in freezer. When the camera returns to him, a carrot has been placed between his legs and he has his hand on one of a pair of grapefruits. This vulgar gag seemed to have largely gone unnoticed by reviewers and critics, although Tim Lucas draws attention to it in his Blu-ray commentary.

16   It has circulated as *Ecologia del delitto, Antefatto, Reazione a catena, Carnage, Twitch of the Death Nerve, Last House – Part Two, Bloodbath* and *Bay of Blood.*

17   See Lowenstein for an interesting discussion of the film's location, Sabaudia, a former swamp drained during the fascist era, a 'landscape built by fascism and inherited by capitalist Italy' (2016: 136–7). Bava, he suggests, 'restores death and impurity to a landscape Mussolini had "redeemed" from death for agricultural fertility and purified fascist productivity' (ibid.: 133).

18   Closer to Bava is Fulci, whose earlier thrillers are interesting and accomplished but do not seem to form a coherent group.

5

The poetics of 'Serie B' – Bava and film style

'Bava was not a great storyteller', concedes Martin Scorsese in his Foreword to Lucas's book (2007: 13), expressing a view commonly held even by admirers of the director, before quickly adding that 'he didn't have to be and he wasn't trying to be'. Instead, he claims, he was good at using 'light, shadow, colour, sound... movement and texture to lead his viewers down uncharted paths into a kind of collective dream' (ibid.). Lucas is more interested in narrative, but nevertheless presents Bava as an 'inarticulate' orchestrator of 'macabre atmospheres' (ibid.: 21). A recent box set from Arrow Films characterized Bava in similar terms, titling the collection 'Macabre Visions'. Bava, then, is popularly seen as a stylist, 'the brand name for a desperate kind of worst-case beauty' (O'Brien 1993: 168), crafting a dream-like cinema of atmosphere and sensation more than (if not necessarily rather than) substance. Any evaluation of Bava as a filmmaker might depend in part on whether one thinks such things as atmosphere compensate for, or might even be more important than, any perceived narrative deficiencies. As Robert Spadoni suggests, 'atmosphere can not only make up for a weak narrative but thrive in the vacuum created by its diminished force' (2014a: 110), or alternatively it can be seen as 'a kind of aesthetic leftover' (Spadoni 2014b: 155), a side dish rather than a main course.

While the narrative deficiencies of Bava's films are sometimes overstated, there are probably reasons why the attention turns more to style and atmosphere. Serie B cinema was oriented towards what Vitali calls 'generic sales points' (2016: 46), which Wagstaff characterizes as the 'physiological responses' produced by 'items or moments in films' that he likens to peaks on an electrocardiogram (1992: 253). Wagstaff is talking specifically about films tailored for the hypothetical distracted *terza visione* viewer, an idea taken up by other scholars. Mikel Koven sees *Ecologia del delitto*, for example, as 'an ideal type of film text for the *terza visione* audience', with its high body count and titillating episodes of nudity and sex, while its less eventful passages give viewers 'the space they require to move around and socialize within the cinema space' (2006: 27–8). Like most of Bava's films, *Ecologia del delitto* opened initially in *prima visione* cinemas, but that need not invalidate Koven's argument entirely. *Le fatiche di Ercole* had set a precedent by opening in first run cinemas but making most of its money in *seconde* and *terze visioni*. As we have seen, there is no shortage of plot in *Ecologia del delitto* and its characters are more well-drawn than those in the comparable *5 bambole per la luna d'agosto,* or at least a cast of quality character actors that includes Laura Betti, Luigi Pistilli, and Leopoldo Trieste makes them seem so. But that need not negate Koven's point either. Rather, it might suggest different points of entry into the film as it passed through different exhibition sites, including those that could not have been foreseen – its digital remediation still allows it to be enjoyed as breathless splatter or something with a bit more substance. At least one Italian critic was already picking up on its ironic tone and ecological themes during its original release, and if Italian audiences did not respond to its electrocardiogram peaks for whatever reason, it seems that the American drive-in crowd did. And therein lies another characteristic of Serie B cinema, namely that genres such as horror, the thriller and the Western were designed to travel and sometimes even expected to perform better in foreign markets.

Bava was in many respects typical of Serie B cinema, a cinema that sought to engage its audience in very particular ways. *Filone* films such as horror films, thrillers and Science Fiction fantasy are organized more around sensations than emotions. Murray Smith's work on character engagement in cinema makes a distinction between alignment and allegiance. The former refers to 'those aspects of textual structure that pertain to our access to the actions, thoughts, and feelings of characters' (1999: 220), while the latter covers 'those aspects of the text that pertain to our evaluation and emotional response to characters' (ibid.), in other words, those that make us sympathize with or 'identify with' a character. To use a current popular term, allegiance is partly about relatability. As Julian Hanich argues, films that seek to elicit fear or more intense forms of suspense can afford to bypass allegiance and character engagement by making us experience these emotions or sensations directly (2010: 98). Moullet describes the majority of Bava's characters (and actors) as 'nonentities', insisting that 'one cannot worry about the destiny, or life, of flimsy characters, who render identification impossible, and who one doesn't always end up distinguishing one from another' (1997: 51). When Nicole is stalked in Franco's antique shop by the faceless killer in *6 donne per l'assassino,* we may not be entirely clear as to what distinguishes her from the other five women in the film, but it is easy enough to identify with the sensation of being pursued through an unusual environment, made stranger by the pulsating coloured lighting, and catching glimpses of a masked and gloved figure seemingly appearing and disappearing at will. The horror genre has often been populated by thinly drawn, interchangeable and disposable characters, with little noticeable loss of audience interest. A greater emphasis on character engagement in the horror genre or thriller can be a marker of quality, however – one of the ways in which Argento set himself apart from the flood of 'thrillings' was to have more engaging leads, even if characters became more disposable further down the cast list. Quite a few films within the 'thrilling' *filone* – including several of Bava's – make a point of a disinterested cynicism towards their characters, with victims scarcely more sympathetic than their killers. If you are looking for someone to 'root for', you will have a long wait while watching *6 donne per l'assassino, 5 bambole per la luna d'agosto* or *Ecologia del delitto*, none of which have a clear central protagonist. This disinterestedness and paucity of emotional cues is shared with certain forms of art cinema, and they often take place in a similar world of the bored rich competing for the spectator's attention with their beautiful surroundings, but the films are too eventful to be otherwise mistaken for serious auteur cinema. If they are ambivalent about modernity, as several scholars have argued, that is partly because a large part of Italian cinema from Antonioni to Totò seemed to be ambivalent about it in the years following *il boom*, the country's economic miracle. The gothic usually gives us more clearly defined central characters because its moral structures, like those of the peplum, are more consistent and conventional than those of *il thrilling*. But the heroes of Bava's gothic films are rarely memorable. Dr Eswai in *Operazione paura* is only interesting insofar as interesting things happen to him, a stock 'man of science' who must learn to take the supernatural seriously. The mysterious Ruth, often filmed as if she were a figure to be feared, is an infinitely more imposing presence, ultimately heroic but confirming that it is the more mysterious characters that we are likely to remember. Katia is a striking figure in *La maschera del demonio* simply because she is played by Barbara Steele (who in any case is visibly having more fun playing Asa) and because of her resemblance to the witch-vampire. Her first appearance at the ruined crypt with two Great Danes, looking like Persephone at the entrance to the Underworld, capitalizes on this before she is largely consigned to screaming and fainting. None of this is unusual for the genre – Hammer's romantic leads are rarely much more compelling, although the Corman-Poe films are notable for some strong female characters and performances from the likes of Steele, Hazel Court and Elizabeth Shepherd.

Dubbing can register with varying degrees of intensity – the villains and 'Bond Girls' of the 1960s Bond films were often dubbed, and the dubbing and English dialogue of Leone's films and other more upmarket Westerns were accomplished enough to not only avoid adverse comment but even become quotable. But dubbing can distance and disengage the viewer, the voices 'vacuous, colourless, vague' and 'uncommitted' to the bodies and faces onscreen, as Chris Fujiwara puts it (2007: 252–3). Those familiar with Christopher Lee's voice may find the English dubbing of him in *Ercole al centro della terra* and *La frusta e il corpo* more jarring than in the Italian versions because it is even more evident that it is not the actor's voice (the voice actor has an American accent in both films). Dubbing also has the potential to intensify the uncanniness of a horror film, inadvertently adding an additional layer of 'free-floating cosmic dread' (O'Brien 1993: 163). But at worst, it can generate laughter through the incongruity and exacerbation of awkwardly translated dialogue. Moreover, we are sometimes looking at Italian films seeking to pass as British or American, giving them a 'placelessness' that adds to their aesthetic fascination, even if this is likely to be a distanced fascination. Only in recent years have Bava's films circulated, primarily on home media, in subtitled versions – their theatrical life was marked by a multiplicity of voices and languages.

Hanich makes a distinction between two forms of aesthetic engagement – *enthrallment,* a heightened aesthetic appreciation, and *immersion,* a heightened aesthetic involvement, a feeling of being 'in the film' (2010: 64). Italian horror films and thrillers tend to be only intermittently immersive, usually in their setpieces, with too many things pulling the viewer 'out of the film' for sustained immersion to take place, from dubbing and variable performances to unconvincing effects, narrative longueurs, or flat dialogue. But they seem to have lost little of their enthrallment for the cult connoisseur. The emphasis on enthrallment over immersion might explain why Bava's populist genre films seem to have been appreciated more by aesthetes than the wider film audiences they were ostensibly designed for – according to Lamberto Bava, his father's admirers in Italy were mainly intellectuals.[1] There are exceptions, of course. The pressure-cooker tension created by *Cani arrabbiati* is immersive in a somatic as well as diegetic way, like being shut in a car on an exceptionally hot day with several volatile personalities. For its brutal twist to be felt at the end, we need to have felt some degree of allegiance with Riccardo. A more complex case is presented by *La frusta e il corpo* and our engagement with the character of Nevenka. Slow-moving and likely to bore some viewers, and if Gastaldi intended it as a *giallo,* not up to much as a murder mystery, it requires both alignment and a degree of allegiance with the central character, whose experiences we share. This is enhanced by Daliah Lavi's performance and Bava allowing her face to be the centre of attention in key scenes – there is little chance of the camera wandering off to look at some roses when she is onscreen. There is little attempt to build allegiance with Cristiano/Christian or Katia, the notionally 'good' couple that the camera *does* wander away from at one point. As in *Cani arrabbiati*, we have been partly deceived into whatever allegiance we might have with Nevenka – we might have guessed that she killed Kurt, her sadistic tormentor/lover, but probably felt that he deserved it, but we are not meant to have worked out that he has only 'returned' in her own mind and through her own perverse desires – which, amongst other things, hold heterosexual monogamy at bay. When Murray Smith refers to 'perverse allegiance', it is taken to mean 'responses of sympathy to characters on the basis of their embodiment of socially or morally *undesirable* traits' (1999: 222). He also suggests that such allegiances are rare and that most films that appear to elicit perverse allegiance 'do so only temporarily or strategically, ultimately eliciting morally approbatory emotional responses' (ibid.). The modern viewer is less likely to see Nevenka's masochism as 'undesirable' – the film's censorship problems give us some idea of how it was more likely to have been perceived in its original context – and the film, knowingly or otherwise, creates a space for an allegiance that is perverse in a more specific sense, and therefore less likely to be broken by the film's denouement.

With exceptions noted, some of the factors outlined above might encourage us to focus more on style and atmosphere than narrative and character, particularly when trying to make some sort of critical case for Bava and finding ways of negotiating the films' perceived weaknesses. But Bava the film stylist cannot be separated from the contexts that shaped his filmmaking practices. Again, a good deal of this is typical for the type of filmmaking that flourished under the *filone* mode of production, where artisans with high levels of technical skill but modest resources and short schedules added value – and probably kept themselves interested – by adding stylistic flourishes to freshen up formulaic, often imitative, scenarios churned out and sometimes re-written during production. Adopting David Bordwell's poetics approach to film analysis, Gary Bettinson characterizes it as an approach less concerned with interpretation than being 'alert to the filmmaker's practical constraints and choices, which are conceptualised on a problem-solving model' (2015: location 1232). Bettinson is writing about the Hong Kong arthouse director Wong Kar-wai, but in some ways the problem-solving model is even better suited to someone like Bava, who would always be facing greater practical constraints than the notoriously profligate and, for some, self-indulgent Wong. For one thing, it accords with how Bava seems to have seen (and enjoyed) filmmaking himself, as a series of technical challenges. He reportedly approached *Diabolik* as though it was made on a lower budget than it was, resisting De Laurentiis's greater resources in favour of artisanal challenges. For the invested viewer, Bava's problem-solving may enliven an otherwise undistinguished film – reproducing the Old West in Rome or generating an army of Ozarks massed on either side of a canyon makes *La strada per Forte Alamo* more interesting than it might otherwise be. But the poetics approach, as Bettinson points out, also extends to considering how far 'the solutions are anchored in story, form, and theme' (ibid.). The lengthy tracking shot through the atelier during the final scene of *6 donne per l'assassino* is a case in point. It is one of Bava's notable stylistic flourishes, made possible partly by the input of his most capable camera operator, Ubaldo Terzano. It invites us to read it as subjective, particularly when 'it' (the camera? the person whose viewpoint it represents?) bumps into and almost knocks over one of the many mannequins populating the fashion house. The shot lasts one minute and twenty-two seconds and ends on the view through the doorway of Morlachi's study, framing him within a narrow vertical gap as he tries to open a green box. A closer shot from inside the room finds him hurriedly taking pens, paper, a gun, and a letter-opener from his desk, before using the knife to force the box open, removing the Contessa's jewellery. He hears a noise and goes to look, walking into a pool of fuchsia light, knocking over a mannequin himself when he hears a noise. Rushing back to his study, he finds the box empty and the gun missing (a zoom from his POV, accompanied by a musical 'stab', underlines his shock). The Contessa, badly injured from a fall orchestrated by Morlachi, emerges from a secret door behind a bookcase, the jewellery in her hand. By seemingly giving her two entrances from two different directions, the film briefly generates some spatial disorientation. It certainly disorients Roberto Curti, who notes that it was already in the script (and so may or may not have been Bava's idea) but calls it an inconsistency, where it seems to be the Contessa but *cannot* be because of her entrance from behind the bookcase (2019: 95). In fact, it is entirely possible for it to be her, allowing for it to be an extraordinarily convoluted and contrived way for her distract him so that she can get into the study, grab the jewellery and gun without him seeing her and then take him by surprise, particularly as she is mortally injured after a fall from her balcony. The mannequin that nearly falls suggests a physical presence, the wounded Contessa unsteady on her feet. Might whoever's idea it was have seen it partly as an opportunity for Bava and Terzano to generate some bravura mystery and suspense and a bit of value-added cinematographic virtuosity? As it stands, it is both a livening up of a contrived piece of plotting – how to give the injured Contessa the element of surprise – and an eye-catching sequence that exceeds its narrative function and probably provided some amusement for Bava and his cameraman. It could be taken as an example of what Pezzotta sees as Bava putting maximum emphasis on the 'wrong' sequences, and it evidently irritated reviewer Peter John Dyer for that reason, taking the film 'beyond the point of exhaustion' (1966: 18). But it is not extraneous to plot or theme – it gets its characters to where they need to be, even if it does so in a manner that prioritizes spectacle and suspense over spatial logic. The circular tracking shot in *La frusta e il corpo* that follows a shot-reverse-shot dialogue exchange between Christian and Katia, leaving them to their exposition and ending on a vase of red roses, performs a less obvious narrative purpose, even if the roses can be seen as a thematic motif in the film – there is a red rose in the glass jar containing the dagger with which Kurt's earlier lover killed herself. As a result, there is more of a sense that its primary purpose is to keep a talky scene visually interesting, even while the roses provide some tenuous thematic relevance.

The aesthetics of problem-solving and changes in working contexts mean that Bava's output as a director lends itself to a degree of periodization. For the sake of convenience, I am calling 1957–64 the Galatea period, even though he was not tied exclusively to the company and made his last film for them in 1963. It represents a period of relative stability, with recurring collaborators and a degree of genre specialization made possible by the first gothic cycles and the tail end of the peplum. Bava's films during this period display high levels of traditional filmic craft and fewer examples of the short cuts taken in some of the later films, and the 'Bava touch' emerges as a combination of trademark visual signatures (coloured gels, spot lighting, mobile camera, glass mattes and other *trucchi*) alongside practices used more widely in low-budget European genre cinema, such as the zoom. As Lucas notes, the camerawork is particularly fluid in the films made with Terzano as camera operator, whether due to his particular skills or a more congenial working context. In *La maschera del demonio,* a mobile continuous shot travels from Katia playing the piano, past her brother Constantine cleaning a rifle, to the back of Prince Vajda's high-backed chair before circling to a frontal view of him staring gloomily into space. The cut is prompted by one of the piano notes producing an eerie moaning sound – the camera now looks down on Katya before descending to a more level framing of her. This is not one of the film's more famous sequences – it does not involve masks, eye sockets, tombs, or resurrections – but is made with particular care and is indicative of Galatea's investment in the film.[2] There is nothing comparable in the other Italian horror films of the same year, although *Il mulino delle donne di pietra* is by no means visually undistinguished. The sequence stands in contrast to Bava's highly productive peer Antonio Margheriti, who would have been more likely to shoot the same sequence with a more static three-camera set-up. But it also stands in contrast with the use of the zoom as a time and labour-saving device in some of Bava's later films. This is, significantly, the period during which Bava was identified as a filmmaker to watch, even if he was not always seen to deliver. The colour films add further decorative layers, first seen in his peplum work (as both director and DP) and culminating in the film that perhaps most foregrounds an expressive and eye-catching emphasis on visual style, *6 donne per l'assassino*. For evidence of this, we need look no further than its title sequence.

We first see an indistinct, out-of-focus field of what look like stars or glistening lights – as they come into focus, they are revealed as sparkles on a lamé dress. The camera tilts up to reveal its wearer, a red mannequin in a black wig. As the camera closes in, the shot goes out of focus again. As we shall see, shots that begin by coming into focus and end by going out of focus will become a recurring feature of Bava's later films, alongside greater use of the zoom. We are then introduced to each member of the cast, often via a short track to the right that finds them posed, usually alongside a mannequin. Cameron Mitchell, framed and lit from below, bathed in

FIGURE 9 *Eva Bartok as the Contessa in the title sequence of* 6 donne per l'assassino.

violent fuchsia light. Eva Bartok holds a cigarette to the right of the frame, while her mirror reflection appears to look warily at mannequins lit in blues and purples to the left. Tracking past several wicker mannequins, we find Thomas Reiner – both the blue light on the right side of his face and a furtive glance at the camera make him look more sinister than the stern but ultimately inept police inspector we encounter in the film. When the camera comes to rest on Arianna Gorini, only just in shot, we can see a nude statue behind her. Dante Di Paolo shares the frame with a wicker mannequin, while Mary Arden is placed between roses and a mannequin in a sparkly dress that seemingly reaches for her. Franco Ressel shares the frame with a mannequin and, like Reiner, looks directly into the camera. Claude Dantes, tinged slightly green, is positioned behind some roses while a red mannequin lurks behind her shoulder. Luciano Pigozzi, framed from below, face partly in shadow, shares the frame with a wicker mannequin lit with a fuchsia light, in contrast with the green lit wall behind him. Lea Krugher, positioned to the right, and a red mannequin centrally positioned, each smell a rose. Massimo Righi shares the frame with a fuchsia-bathed mannequin before a static shot finds Francesca Ungaro fending off an attempted strangling by a red mannequin. Finally, Giuliano Raffaelli and Harriet White Medin each share static frames with mannequins. The remaining technical credits play over what looks like a reversal of the opening shot, ending with the same out-of-focus shot with which it began.

The previous year, Bava had ended *I tre volti della paura* with Karloff's comic signing off and a literal pull-back-and-reveal to show the artisan's *trucchi* and perhaps also the limited resources available to *cinema del risparmio*. This title sequence is similarly playful, self-conscious and attention-getting, but the effect is different. One might even argue that it is sufficiently elaborate to qualify as a setpiece, rather than a throwaway gag. Taken out of the context of Bava's career as a working filmmaker, and away from stories of his self-deprecating modesty, it feels like the kind of scene a young tyro auteur might use to announce his or her arrival. The closest Argento got to this were the 'interrupted' credits for *Profondo rosso*, which pause at midpoint for a murder played out in silhouette on a wall, and *Suspiria*'s mid-credits narration, delivered by Argento himself in the Italian version. The titles for *6 donne per l'assassino* could be seen as another example of maximum effort going into the 'wrong' sequence, although elaborate title sequences are by no means unusual. Curti reads the sequence as a nod to the Mondadori *gialli,* which (as with other pulp novels sold at the *edicola*) presented their cast of characters before the story began (2019: 43), and he may be right in thinking that this was the association recalled for the film's original Italian audience. Alexia Kannis, on the other hand, likens the figures to *Cluedo* playing cards (2020: 10), which seems even more appropriate to the narrative that follows. But at the same time, it exceeds in presentation its function as a scorecard for its *dramatis personae*. English-speaking audiences would not get to see this sequence until the film's revival on VHS and then DVD, the Woolner Brothers version replacing it with a newly shot title sequence (also featuring mannequins but no cast members) and alternative music cues from Carlo Rustichelli's score to the samba used in the European cut, one of the first times that incongruously 'light' music featured prominently in a violent Italian suspense-thriller. By posing its cast in ironic and largely static fashion, it identifies them as types (shifty, 'exotic', seductive, mysterious, imperilled) rather than characters, barely more rounded than the mannequins trying to upstage them in the frame. But ironic amusement is in tension with those lurid colours, suggestive of a film that is overheated, unafraid of bad taste and even kitsch – as Kannis puts it, 'it's as if the film's style is leaking out, staining the surface of the film' (2020: 10). The title sequence only holds back one of the film's aesthetic cards – its astounding and almost unprecedented sadism – although the static poses could be seen to anticipate the staging of the bodies subsequent to their slaughter. Above all, it establishes a visual system for the film, albeit one that can partly be found in other colour Bava films from this period, one that is neither naturalistic nor necessarily connotative – dolly shots, mannequins and human bodies standing in for one another, wild colours, a cast one could easily lose track of without this introduction to its range of types. But it also emerges out of distinct circumstances in the problem-solving scenario – how to make a mechanically plotted suspense-thriller stand out at a time when many films were seeking to emulate Hitchcock or channel Edgar Wallace.

From *La strada per Forte Alamo* to *Diabolik*, the second 'period', there is less stylistic consistency and Bava's work-for-hire status is more evident. Sometimes evidently employed primarily for his facility with special effects, sometimes able to play to his strengths (most evidently in *Operazione paura*), he also came close to Serie A with his work for De Laurentiis on *Diabolik* and *Odissea*. As the budgets get lower, the camerawork is less fluid, the lighting less expressive and the problem-solving more visible. This sometimes looks like a virtue of the films, as in *Terrore nello spazio*, which attempts more on a smaller budget than *Diabolik* does on a relatively larger one – it is often celebrated as a triumph of *l'arte del risparmio*, with its miniatures, double exposures, alien skies fashioned from coloured liquids in aquariums, dry ice and plastic rocks, and leather space suits with skull caps. Some of the effects might generate some amusement now and perhaps always did, like the communication monitors that are clearly windows with actors huddled together on the other side (although wrist monitors are more seamlessly incorporated later in the film). With an even more interchangeable cast of characters than in some of Bava's thrillers – one minor character is played by two different actors at different points in the film – the effects and design work have a lot of work to do. Most noticeably, the characters are constantly dwarfed by their surroundings, whether in the sparsely furnished sound stage that is the Argos interior, the alien ship containing the remains of huge skeletons, or confined to tiny corners of composite shots created by Bava's *trucchi*. While an early tracking shot moves eerily through a virtually silent control room, the camera is more likely to zoom than physically move. As Captain Markery and his crew investigate the planet and their sister ship, the Galliot, a crash zoom first punctuates the discovery of two corpses who have evidently killed each other. When they look through the window of the ship, there is another zoom into another body, followed by a pan along a line of corpses to that of Markery's brother, whereupon a zoom out is followed immediately by a zoom into Markery's shocked reaction. Bava's increasing use of the zoom, particularly the crash zoom or *zoom a schiaffo* (slap zoom), will be discussed in greater detail later.

After the retreat from De Laurentiis and potentially more prestigious productions, Bava entered what has been identified as a decadent (Acerbo 2007: 183) or even 'embarrassing' (Wood 2014: 308) final phase of his career, recycling old effects and tricks, or lapsing into 'facile, mechanical effect-seeking with a lazy reliance on the zoom lens' (Hardy *et al.* 1985: 183). While sometimes photographed by Bava himself, they generally look less like the work of a cinematographer, and while they are stylistically diverse, they have more in common with techniques used by a younger generation of *filone* directors. Formally, they range from the retro-gothic of *Gli orrori del castello di Norimberga*, the pop-kitsch of *Quante volte... quella notte* and *5 bambole per la luna d'agosto*, to the claustrophobic real time of *Cani arrabbiati*, as far away from the decorativeness of the colour gothics as one could get. There are signs of both exhaustion and attempts as reinvention, and several of the films were dogged by distribution problems or delays in their release. *Lisa e il diavolo* has a more ambitious storyline than usual, in addition to its reputation as a 'personal' film, but it is less visually inventive than the more traditional *Gli orrori del castello di Norimberga* – at one point, a beautiful sequence showing the shadows of the moving pieces on a music box across Elke Sommer's unconscious face gives way to the bathos of a soft-focus flashback. The film has nothing to match the pursuit of Sommer in the earlier film through an environment backlit to the point that light overwhelms and almost eliminates physical space.

The first film in this notional 'period' is telling in mixing the visually inspired, the disorienting and the playful (or even experimental) with the visibly rushed and a clumsiness that conveys boredom with some of the scenes of exposition. *Il rosso segno della follia* opens with one of Bava's most disorienting sequences, marked by shifts between uncertain points of view and flashbacks to fragmented memories. A sequence of seven shots alternates between John Harrington's moving point of view as he walks along a train corridor towards a young boy (who we will later learn is his younger self) and a static shot from behind Harrington that almost suggests that he too is being watched, but, in any case, violates the thirty-degree continuity rule jarringly. The reverse shot of John is initially withheld, and when we do see his face for the first time, a brief flash of light projects its reflection onto the door. A fragmented memory represented as a POV shot climbing

FIGURE 10 *Spatial disorientation in* Il rosso segno della follia.

some stairs and the sound of echoing footsteps is followed by the boy in the train corridor (the boy from the flashback, displaced in time) examining his own reflection, which the camera slowly zooms into. The memory that returns in increments is a recurring trope in Italian genre cinema (Leone and Argento, for example) and while it lends itself to being read in the light of Italy's own troubled memory about its past, I will take it here more as a generic mechanism that also facilitates the kind of formal flourishes that can make a Serie B film stand out. As the boy looks at his own reflection, John is essentially looking at himself, and possibly also watching both versions of himself from a third vantage point – a personality not so much split as shattered. By comparison, what we might expect to be more obvious meat for Bava, the murder of a bride in her compartment, is handled in a more prosaic fashion – distorted images, flashbacks of a stole being dragged across the floor as a woman's voice calls his name and a comparatively circumspect approach to the actual violence from the director of 6 *donne per l'assassino*, confined to splashes of blood. A sound bridge both smooths a cut from an exterior shot of the train to one of a model train and briefly fools us into laughing at what looks like an exceptionally unconvincing model effect as opposed to a literal model train. From this elliptical opening, the film then becomes *overcommunicative,* with John's internal monologue announcing his madness to us alongside some preliminary exposition. This is not the film's last formal flourish – a bravura circular pan later in the film executes a temporal and spatial transition from John in his chamber of mannequins and dead brides to his participation in his wife Mildred's séance in a single shot. The mannequins and the participants in the séance are lit from below with the same sinister light – the interchangeability of human and inanimate figures is one of Bava's recurring visual conceits. Opinions will vary on how much thematic weight to give to this 'Bavaesque' trope, but the problem-solving artisan knows that a good and eye-catching trick is worth repeating. Later in the film, by contrast, we sometimes seem to witness the bored cameraman, determined to do *something* with dialogue scenes involving the police inspector, a Columbo-like figure with a propensity for making revealing observations just as he is about to depart an interrogation. Hitchcock spoke disparagingly of 'photographs of people talking', and Bava's slow and repetitive zooms seem to express a particular distaste for them, where once a fluid camera movement might inject some life into them (or leave them behind to look at a vase of roses). This is a cinema of intermittent engagement, where the dull bits are enlivened by visual embellishments where possible but sometimes allowed to coagulate into full boredom.

From here, I want to focus on three aspects of Bava's filmmaking – its decorative and atmospheric dimensions; the use of the zoom, a contentious technique, particularly in his later films; and finally, a more recent way of viewing certain Bava films, as exhibiting a 'pop' aesthetic.

'Macabre Visions': The atmospheric and the pretty

Atmosphere, as Julian Hanich observes, poses certain difficulties for film studies, existing as 'diffuse emotive colourations of the lived-body without concrete object' (2010: 170). The term originated as a meteorological concept but from the eighteenth century it also became a way of describing 'a certain mood hanging in the air' (Böhme 2017: 2). It is both spatial and emotional – Böhme calls it *'tuned space'* and characterizes it as 'quasi-objective' insofar as atmospheres exist and can be deliberately created but at the same time they are 'nothing without a subject feeling them' (ibid.: 1–2). Nor will they necessarily be felt in the same way by different people. Analysing atmosphere always runs the risk of either descending into banality – a film is simply 'atmospheric', as Bava's films are often said to be – or confining the discussion to atmosphere's more tangible components. Hanich's own discussion of atmosphere, entirely understandably, becomes largely a discussion of setting – in the case of the horror film or suspense-thriller, the cut-off place, the labyrinth, the descent, and endless space. In the case of Bava, we might equally easily shift the discussion to genre, given that one of the defining features of the gothic – the most consistent generic thread in the films that Bava directed – is that of atmosphere, and horror more generally is one of the more obviously 'atmospheric' genres (Spadoni 2014b: 151). And the prevailing atmospheres of the gothic bring us back in turn to where we started, with setting. Bava's films, particularly the earlier ones, abound in gothic settings: castles and graveyards, thunderstorms, both the wild and mountainous regions of the eighteenth-century gothic, and the 'dark, labyrinthine streets' of later variants (Botting 1996: 2) that are particularly evident in the locations in Faleria, the abandoned and partly ruined town to the north of Rome that are used in *Operazione paura*. The Bava gothic, as is true of the gothic more generally, refuses to stay in its own graveyard, trespassing on the ancient world of the peplum (most evidently in *Ercole al centro della terra* but also in certain parts of in *Gli invasori*) and the urban terrors of *il thrilling* (thunderstorms underpin key scenes in *La ragazza che sapeva troppo* and *6 donne per l'assassino*). All films have atmospheres of some sort, but there is wide agreement that 'some are more atmospheric than others' (Spadoni 2020: 61). The 'Bavaesque' or 'Bavian' seems first and foremost to describe an atmosphere, something that sets Bava apart even from other Italian horror directors. This is not to say that all Bava films share the same atmosphere; thus, the 'Bavaesque' is arguably found in the gothics and those other films tinged by the gothic. According to Tom Milne, *Operazione paura* is a film in which 'atmosphere is everything' (1967: 104), and therefore one that bypasses Bava's supposed weaknesses as a storyteller. If atmosphere is *everything*, what are the implications for narrative? Spadoni cautions against assuming too dramatic a divide between narrative and atmosphere – atmosphere is diffuse, it is everywhere (2020: 53). But he also suggests that narrative and atmosphere often play out a push–pull dance in the horror genre –'less of one can mean more of the other' (2014a: 109) at different points in the film. It is easy to find atmosphere in *Operazione paura*'s ruined town and its labyrinthine streets, the Baroness' vast cobweb-shrouded bedroom, windows from which ghostly figures look out or look in, candleholders that look like human arms, ruined dolls and sinister paintings. Spadoni likens atmosphere to a coating or a skin (ibid.: 58), seemingly tactile, and this is a film where a character can be trapped in a huge cobweb, feel the cold touch of a ghost's hand or the grip of a leech vine. However, while the narrative of *Operazione paura* is simple enough to hang a series of striking images and sequences on, it is also itself laced with doom and decay and played out amongst witches, mediums, tangible and intangible phantoms, coins placed in the hearts of the recently dead. Moreover, the film offers none of the light relief that tempers the gloom in other gothic horror films of the period – laughter is confined to Melissa Graps' malign giggle. Milne's comment draws attention to something else identified by Spadoni – the isolation of atmosphere as a distinct component in a film is always implicitly *evaluative* (2020: 52), whether it is regarded as compensation or whether it is perceived to be 'everything'.

The monochrome and colour films allow different atmospheric variations. The scene in *La ragazza che sapeva troppo* where Nora hears Ethel cry out in the night and rushes in vain to give her the medicine by her bed has at its disposal roughly the same elements that are used in *La goccia d'acqua* – a corpse in a bed, a thunderstorm that causes lights to flicker on and off, a frightened woman, a cat. Bava uses relatively conventional film language in both films – a whip-pan to the breathless Ethel is the most dramatic camera movement in *La ragazza*, while *La goccia d'acqua* uses zooms to underline its scares. A point-of-view shot from Nora's perspective shows Ethel's corpse rocking back and forth on her bed, but this is revealed to be caused by her cat clambering up the bedding – a spooky false scare in a resolutely non-supernatural film. In *La goccia d'acqua*, two pulsing colours compete in Nurse Chester's apartment after she returns with the dead medium's stolen ring – a green light attributed to a flashing sign outside the building shown in the episode's opening shot and a fuchsia light that has no diegetic source, but which is associated with the medium's spacious house (where it also has no diegetic source but merely adds a sinister layer to an already-unnerving location, with its high ceilings, dolls scattered on the floor and Tarot cards scattered on a table). Bava's use of vibrant colours does not always have this kind of associative dimension, which here suggests the invasion of Nurse Chester's home with the uncanny presence of the medium (just as the buzzing fly and dripping water have followed her). Often colour has a spatial function, enhancing the depth of the frame, as in the long corridor with high ceilings in the medium's house, marked by splashes of green and magenta light. Doorways are sometimes framed in dramatic colours, suggestive of an uncanny or threatening space beyond. Sometimes there is a token light source – 6 *donne per l'assassino* also uses the flashing neon sign outside the building in the sequence where Peggy is stalked and murdered in the antique showroom. Sometimes a blue or green light, usually from below, underlines the deathly pallor of a vampiric countenance, a more common use of colour in the genre. But just as frequently, there is no referent beyond an atmospheric one.

Bava's use of coloured gels in his lighting is one of the most recognizable marks of the 'Bavaesque', and yet it is far from unique to him, particularly in genres dealing with the fantastic. In Mario Camerini's *Ulisse* (1954), cinematographer Harold Rosson used a green gel to light Silvana Mangano as Circe, both distinguishing her from her other role as Penelope and suggesting her powers of sorcery.[3] The Corman-Poe films photographed by Floyd Crosby used colour filters in dream sequences and flashbacks, while Nicolas Roeg used coloured gels in certain sequences in *Masque of the Red Death*. But a more obvious point of comparison is Jack Asher, the cinematographer on eight of Hammer's formative gothic horror films, who used gels to add greens, purples, and other colours to sections of the film's sets. In *The Mummy* (1959), part of the tomb of Princess Ananka is bathed in a green light that has no literal source but has an obvious atmospheric function, a colour that often signals the sinister and the supernatural. Our first view of the swamp from which Christopher Lee's titular Karris will rise finds it in red hues attributed to the dawn light but also transforming it into a diabolical cauldron – it will take on a greenish aspect for the film's nocturnal sequences. Perfectly in keeping with the Hammer style, Asher's use of colour somehow manages to balance the flamboyant with the restrained – splashes of non-naturalistic colour within an otherwise more or less naturalistic *mise-en-scene*. Rather than trying to determine who might have influenced who out of these two great cameramen, it might be more productive to see this as a period in which artisans were able to experiment with colour in modestly budgeted genre films – Bava initially in the peplum, Asher in the gothic. Both were attracted to a similar range of colours, but Bava arguably amplified what Asher did with colour, making its presence more aggressively felt in both frequency and intensity.[4]

Bava's use of pinks, purples (also an Asher favourite), magenta and fuchsia register as particular stylistic quirks. This colour range has been used in two more recent horror films. *Mandy* (2018) uses them to hallucinogenic effect, associated with the semi-psychedelic rituals practised by the film's Manson-like villains, while Richard Stanley uses them to suggest H.P. Lovecraft's *Colour Out of Space* (2019), a colour supposedly so alien in the original story that it has no referent in our own spectrum. In Bava's films, whether gothic or thriller, they suggest a *colour out of place*, colour as an unsettling presence. Perhaps most important of all, Bava's colour enhances the production value of Serie B films, something that did not go unnoticed by film distributors or the more sympathetic reviewers. But they were also sometimes seen as vulgar or kitsch, which might also be why they appeal to contemporary cult tastes.

An understandable emphasis on Bava's colour films risks downplaying his achievements in monochrome. One of *La ragazza che sapeva troppo*'s most effective sequences is a case in point. Nora is lured to a deserted apartment at Piazza Mincio in the Coppedè district of Rome, a location that now has strong cinematic associations with *il thrilling italiano* and gothic horror because of its later use in Francesco Barilli's *Il profumo della signora in nero/Perfume of the Lady in Black* (1974) and Argento's *Inferno*, where it is drenched in Bava-like colours. *La ragazza che sapeva troppo* is unusual amongst Bava films in its use of recognizable, and even iconic, locations, most notably Trinità dei Monti and the Foro Italico. But the exterior, with its baroque fountain and an architectural style that can pass as gothic, misleads us about the interior that Nora will ultimately encounter – the entrance is that of Palazzo del Ragno (the Palace of the Spider), where Bava surprisingly does not capitalize on the spider web motif above the door, indistinct in long shot. Initially, the interior meets our expectations – a cage elevator (much loved by 1970s Italian thrillers), with Nora's reflection giving her the appearance of a disembodied head floating in the darkness. Then there is a *noir*-like staircase for her to ascend, heavy shadows thrown by the high contrast lighting. These scenes are intercut with the arrival of a second taxi in front of the fountain, and a slow zoom accompanied by footsteps representing the point of view of what ultimately turns out to be a false threat (Marcello has followed her, fearing for her safety). But Nora's eventual destination is a freshly decorated but unfurnished apartment, harshly lit with bare white walls and swinging lightbulbs. The bare apartment produces one of the film's most frequently reproduced images – Nora filmed from a low angle in tight close-up, occupying the lower right of an unbalanced frame with only the top half of her head in shot, her eyes spot lit, a bulb swinging above her head and throwing shadows across her face. Bava and Terzano make this bare space seem both constrictive, through the tight close-ups of Nora or framing her in the doorway of a darkened room, and potentially labyrinthine, as in the shot of a white corridor, unpopulated and completely empty except for its swinging bulbs and an incongruously placed wooden chair. This is one of Bava's most meticulously constructed sequences, and one dependent on particular lighting effects, but there is no place here for the pulsating colours of the gothic films that immediately follow it.

We might hesitate to call Bava's films pretty – sometimes pretty violent, admittedly – but some of them are sufficiently decorative to invite some consideration of Rosalind Galt's use of the word as a filmic aesthetic. 'By the standards of realism, the pretty image is "too much", but it is also not

FIGURE 11 La ragazza che sapeva troppo – *unbalanced composition and* noir *lighting.*

enough to be redeemed as radical excess. Not quite beautiful or sublime, it is also not camp or countercultural' (2011: 11). This ultimately seems to exclude Bava and also Argento, another horror-thriller director with an eye for the pictorial and aestheticized. Bava's films are often seen to be excessive, both stylistically and in their violence. However, although his use of colour is more excessive than that of Jack Asher, it is less so than that of Henri Georges Clouzot's abandoned *L'infer* (1964 – uncompleted), which was being shot around the same time as Bava's most colourful films, or even Argento's *Suspiria,* which had the resources to make a more assaultive use of non-naturalistic lighting. Nevertheless, Bava's films, especially the earlier ones, display some of the qualities associated with the pretty – 'colourful, carefully composed, balanced, richly textured, or ornamental… deep colours, arabesque camera movements' (ibid.) – even if this must be qualified by their modest resources. Moreover, as Galt explains, the word 'pretty' derives from 'prœtt', meaning 'a trick, a wile or a craft' with there even being an 'implication of witchery' (ibid.: 7). The decorative side of Bava sometimes seems to have been a source of suspicion, with the *Monthly Film Bulletin* review of *Ercole al centro della terra* seeing its 'enjoyable marvels' as a 'limited box of tricks' (Anon. 1963a: 21) or *Cahiers du Cinéma* recoiling from the 'debauchery of hideous lighting' in *6 donne per l'assassino* (Anon. 1965c: 90) – prettiness is 'what goes wrong with aesthetics' (Galt 2011: 7), a surface appeal that goes nowhere, the more deceitful twin of vulgarity. The prettiness of Bava, if that is the correct term, also acts as a disguise of sorts. It has made the films look as though they were designed for longevity and aesthetic appreciation, as opposed to ephemeral art with short-term commercial ambitions – if the scripts sometimes suggest the latter, the Galatea-era films and some of the mid-period films often suggest the former. Digital remediation has enhanced this aspect of the films, even though high definition has not always been kind to low-budget genre cinema, including some of Corman's, pulling its aesthetic limitations into an unforgiving light.

Prettiness, suggests Galt, has a strong affiliation with art cinema (ibid.: 12), and Bava admirers have often made much of the similarities between *Operazione paura* and Fellini's *Toby Dammit,* even if they use similar imagery to rather different ends. Cocteau was another reference point in reviews of this Bava film in particular – the candleholders shaped like human arms that line the corridors of Villa Graps most obviously invite comparison with the living human arms that perform the same function in *La belle et la bête* (1948). Cocteau, a canonical artistic figure and poet, used artisanal *trucchi* not unlike those used by the problem-solving artisan Bava to create the fantastic.

Operazione paura is one of Bava's more impoverished productions, but also now perhaps the most well-regarded of his mid-period films.[5] Its low-key distribution did not prevent it from catching the eye of several reviewers who saw it (some of whom went out of their way to do so), and Lamberto Bava claims that it was the film that brought his father to Dino De Laurentiis' attention. The camerawork is less fluid than in the Galatea-period films; with a smaller number of dolly shots and a larger number of zooms, the coloured gels are more subdued, so that atmosphere is more reliant on its settings (a mixture of sound stages and locations) and a series of 'poetic' images. Villa Graps consists of frescoed corridors, a plunging spiral staircase filmed from above, an underground crypt that somehow also manages to be on a precipice, a macabre painting of Melissa, an abandoned bedroom filled with dolls (amongst which Melissa materializes), and above all, the Baroness' spacious bedroom where she resides Miss Haversham-like amidst cobwebbed bric-a-brac, a huge four poster bed with black drapes, a distorting mirror, and the habitual imposing fireplace that is only missing a secret passageway but will frame the final confrontation between Ruth and the Baroness. Already the quintessential gothic 'bad place', Villa Graps also becomes a labyrinth through camera and editing – the staircase an abyss, a room that traps its occupant in a loop, multiplying both itself and doubling whoever passes through it, a cobwebbed painting that mysteriously transports its captive outside. Ruth's home is almost equally striking, equating her with birds of prey, animal skulls, and what look like instruments of torture (matching her seemingly cruel treatments for Melissa's intended victims that include leech vines and birch twig floggings). Ruth could easily be another Asa, holding her cloak closed around her body as if concealing a similarly decaying torso, and the film consistently frames her as a threatening and ambiguous figure – appearing and disappearing in the narrow streets of the town, glimpsed

FIGURE 12 *Ruth and birds of prey* – Operazione paura.

through a gap between the panels of a door as she cooks up a proverbial witch's brew. It is often observed that the film reverses conventional images of good and evil – a blonde child and a raven-haired sorceress – but the Baroness is exactly the evil mother that she appears to be, lit ominously from below or gazing at her twisted reflection, perhaps what the medium in *La goccia d'acqua*, another recluse communing with the dead, might have looked like in life. The film has produced several uncanny images before it reaches its first interior – a slow zoom into faces staring from a window, as if frozen into the dirty glass, red-hooded pallbearers seen on the horizon like some sort of multi-limbed insect or creature. Given that Bava's evocation of the fantastic arises out of a problem-solving aesthetic, the deserted town of Faleria is one of the film's advantages, like a crumbling film set with its narrow streets, archways and backlit alleyways.

Bava and the zoom

During the first post-credits scene in *Gli orrori del castello di Norimberga*, Peter von Kleist meets his Uncle Karl at the airport. They shake hands and there is a cut to a close-up of their hands on the direct opposite side of the 180-degree continuity line. We zoom out, and each character is now facing in the opposite direction to the previous shot. This is far from the most elegant sequence in a Bava film, and to be fair, it is probably quickly forgotten as the film moves onto to more lurid events. But what has happened in this throwaway moment? One can easily picture a smoother, continuity-friendly, and institutionally more 'correct', version of this scene that chooses its reverse shots more carefully. Does the cut conceal a lack of coverage by crossing the continuity line and zooming out from a close-up of a handshake? Or is this an attempt to add a tiny spark of visual interest to a perfunctory scene? Either way, the zoom is central to this unusual, but not necessarily untypical, pair of shots. Where the zoom had quickly taken on a role in the horror genre as a means of underlining shock moments or registering the shock of a character – 'reacting' with, or even *for*, them – by the late 1960s it was proliferating in even the most banal sequences of European genre films.

Luc Moullet calls the zoom, more specifically its 'abuse', Bava's trademark, even more than his choice of genre (1997: 52), and it was something that critics commented on, usually negatively, even in his earlier, less zoom-heavy, films. If the zoom was a natural fit for the horror film as a means of punctuating shock, the most emotionally charged camera movement in *La maschera del demonio* is the vertical spin on its axis that the camera performs on the face of Prince Vajda as his corpse is discovered, bringing his initially inverted scarred features into close-up. Similar in effect to a crash zoom, it brings the horror into unanticipated proximity to the viewer. Moullet acknowledges that Bava's use of the zoom is a matter of escalation from his mid-period onwards – 'The more we go on... the more of them there are, and the more they work', he insists (ibid.). The extent to which they 'work' has been a matter of debate, and I would make two suggestions here. Firstly, if the zoom is a trademark mainly of Bava's later films, then that is more a matter of following trends in low-budget genre filmmaking than a question of 'personal style', even if Bava made striking use of it in certain instances. Secondly, if we were to identify a filmmaker for whom the zoom is a trademark of sorts throughout their career, we might suggest that Jess Franco is a more likely candidate. 'He was a jazz musician who played the trombone until he discovered the zoom lens', complained maverick producer Harry Alan Towers, 'he's still got that annoying habit of zooming in and out with the camera for no discernible reason' (Bryce 1991: 87). Often enervating in effect, despite the zoom's association with excitability, Franco's use of the zoom is central to why he is often dismissed as a bad filmmaker, lacking even Bava's technical proficiency, or core to defences of what is arguably a distinctive cinematic style, whether 'good' or 'bad'. Given the ubiquity of the zoom in this kind of cinema, doing all it can to grab our attention, why is it a particular issue for critics of Bava? I would argue that Bava's use of the zoom is contentious because, as a cameraman (and a very good one), he was by implication expected to be better than that after having displayed the mobility of the camera in films like *La maschera del demonio* and *6 donne per l'assassino*. In this view of events, the visible care evident in Bava's earlier films is replaced by laziness and technical shortcuts,

camera mobility replaced by the zoom and the pan, the tight editing of Mario
Serandrei by the use of focus pulls or whip-pans in shot transitions. But just
as Franco has his enthusiastic champions, Moullet is just one defender of
Bava's 'abuse' of the zoom. While professing to 'detest' the zoom, he insists
that this proliferation works, preferring it to the more selective use in the
mid-1960s:

> It is the in-between, the happy (the unhappy) medium which does
> not work. We reach a delirium, an orgy, a gratuitous vertigo... which
> transports us, linked to which a whole arsenal of formal devices, aimed at
> confounding the true and the false, the actor and the puppet, dream and
> reality. A calling into question of cinema, and at the same time its lyrical
> affirmation by the importance of *movement* which animates the film.
>
> (1997: 52)

Pezzotta seems to be making a similar claim when he argues that a 'mediocre
director' who uses the zoom 'badly' does so with a particular aim in mind,
whereas Bava in *5 bambole per la luna d'agosto* uses it without a purpose
and thus, the 'ugly' becomes 'waste, gratuitous arabesque, pop flourish:
in a word, it becomes beautiful' (2013: 103). There is more than a touch
of iconoclasm here, a display of cultural capital and counter-aestheticism
in order to convert 'bad' taste into a kind of *cinema-cinema*. The artisan
can no longer be defended along the lines of craft, and perhaps not even
atmosphere, given that the prevailing atmosphere of *5 bambole* is boredom,
the 'pall of vacation idleness' that often hangs over Italian jet-set thrillers
(Fujiwara 2007: 248).

   How did the zoom get such a bad – or, alternatively, paracinematic –
reputation? Between the 1950s and 1960s, various versions of the zoom –
the Pan Cinor, the Zoomar and the Angénieux – passed into wider usage
in a range of cinemas. Far from automatically being a sign of low quality,
such esteemed auteur figures as Roberto Rossellini, Claude Chabrol and
Robert Altman have been credited with its creative use. John Belton claims
that Altman's zooms function like jazz improvizations (1980/1981: 25), an
analogy sometimes mobilized in defence of Jess Franco, while Robin Wood
sees them as both an authorial presence and a means of 'dissolving space and
undermining our sense of physical reality' (1986: 35). By not using the zoom
'tactfully', invisibly – as a pseudo-tracking shot – Altman's 'obtrusiveness'
made a virtue of the zoom's unique properties (ibid.). Hitchcock famously
combined the zoom with a dolly shot to create the effect of James Stewart's
eponymous condition in *Vertigo* (1958) but made a more contentious use of
it during a climactic scene in *Marnie* (1964). As Tippi Hedren attempts to
steal money from an open safe, a series of zooms in and out represent her
conflicted point of view as she realizes that she is no longer capable of stealing.
This was one of a several effects in the film originally seen as evidence of

Hitchcock's declining powers (or fiercely defended by auteurist critics), a use of the zoom that now seems closer to the hyperbolic zooms of low-budget European genre cinema than his innovative and much-copied *Vertigo*-effect. As the 1960s progressed, the zoom could also convey a youthful energy, the rhythm of pop music. Bob Fosse uses the zoom extensively in the musical numbers in *Sweet Charity* (1969), sometimes in support of the numbers' rhythmic qualities, sometimes to give greater emphasis to the sheer variety of camera set-ups, sometimes – as in the Hong Kong martial arts cinema of the 1970s – to pick out detail shots without cutting, and above all to add to the film's air of hipster jazziness. The zoom in and out was a popular way of filming pop music on TV or discotheque and party scenes in films, such as the one in *Diabolik,* which begins with zooms roughly coordinated with the beat of Ennio Morricone's pastiche of acid rock. In other words, a certain *grooviness* was indicated by the rhythmic zoom by the end of the 1960s. This seems to be what the opening scene of *5 bambole per la luna d'agosto* is aiming for (or mocking?), as the camera zooms in and out of the gyrating body of Edwige Fenech.

Massimo Locatelli suggests that the zoom was particularly well suited to forms of cinema 'united in their "impassioned" use of film language' (2017: 104). Horror provided a particularly congenial home for it. Even Stanley Kubrick, hardly the most 'impassioned' of filmmakers, used crash-zooms in his frosty art-horror adaptation of *The Shining* (1980). Curti sees the zoom as 'the visual counterpart of that tendency to hyperbole and violent exclamation' in the gothic (2019: 69), and that certainly accords with Bava's early use of it. But it was taken up more broadly by Italian Serie B cinema, not only because of its suitability for a sensationalist genre cinema but because of its capacity for saving time, labour and money (Willemen 2013: 106), which

FIGURES 13 and 14 *The 'dysfunctional' zoom in 5* bambole per la luna d'agosto.

had made it popular in the television industry in the 1950s before being used more extensively in cinema. From *Il rosso segno della follia* onwards, zooms and pans are used in certain sequences as a substitute for editing, breaking continuous shots into establishing shots, medium shots, and close-ups, or providing an equivalent to shot/reverse shot sequences without cutting. Such scenes are sometimes ingenious, but clearly also motivated by pragmatism or haste. Locatelli argues that at a certain point, the zoom underwent a shift from a 'comprehensible' use of the device (a murder victim found in a cupboard, a terrifying figure at a window) to being 'dysfunctional, incoherent, indistinct, cruel, i.e. the sign of an "impassioned" or euphoric semiotic style' (2017: 108), a tail wagging a particularly overexcited dog. Umberto Lenzi's *Orgasmo/Paranoia* (1968), the second of Carroll Baker's *gialli-erotici*, has a pre-credits sequence consisting of eighteen shots, six of which include a zoom of some sort. Four of the six shots zoom in, one zooms out, while the other shot includes zooms both outward and inward. As the opening credits roll, cue the film's seventh zoom. What has prompted such cinematographic excitability? A murder? A chase or stalking scene? The scene depicts the arrival of Baker, a wealthy widow, at Fiumicino Airport, where she is met by photographers and her lawyer, and is watched by a mysterious figure with binoculars (one of the zooms picks him out). The zooms, like the handshake sequence in *Gli orrori del castello di Norimberga,* give a functional scene a shot of energy (jarringly in the Bava film). *Orgasmo* will settle narratively into slow-burn psychological suspense but conveys restless energy and movement in its pre-credits scene. In the B cinema of several European film industries, the zoom is rarely far away. In *Diabolik* – more of a B+ film –

one of Valmont's henchmen arrives on his yacht via three zoom shots that provide a jittery ellipsis (zoom into the approaching speedboat/zoom into Valmont's yacht/zoom out from Valmont and his henchman already in mid-conversation on the yacht). Writing about a later Lenzi thriller, *Spasmo*, Chris Fujiwara contrasts the movement of the zoom with the 'static visual patterns' of the film's characters – 'exterior movement is held in abeyance while the movement of consciousness is performed by the zoom' (2007: 248), an observation that would apply particularly to *5 bambole per la luna d'agosto*. If the zoom often suggests excitability and impassioned film language, it can also generate enervation and boredom, as happens in parts of *Il rosso segno della follia* and particularly *5 bambole per la luna d'agosto*. An early scene in *5 bambole* finds three of the wives in the kitchen discussing Jill's 'beast' of a husband, George, before they are joined by Isabelle, who has been picking daisies on the island. The scene consists of nine shots that use five different camera set-ups:

1. The camera moves past a long counter covered in food, coming to rest on Trudi and Peggy (who is putting the dressing on a salad). It tilts up to frame them in a two-shot, then moves to bring Jill into shot; she is painting a picture on the right-hand side of the frame. A slight zoom in re-frames Trudi, Jill and her painting as they talk about George, excluding Peggy from the shot.

2. Detail shot – Jill adds some paint to her picture.

3. Return to the previous set-up.

4. Medium close-up of Trudi as she asks Jill how she could marry someone like George.

5. Detail shot of Jill painting, as in shot 2.

6. Reaction shot of Peggy as Jill's answer to Trudi confirms that she married George for money.

7. Establishing shot of the group that almost immediately zooms in on Isabelle as she enters the room.

8. Peggy in the same set-up as 6.

9. Return to set-up from previous shot – Isabelle is flanked by Trudi and Jill with her painting. Zoom out as Isabelle gives daisies to each of them, then zoom back into a closer shot of Isabelle, who declines the invitation to help in the kitchen. Zoom out again until all four are in shot, then zoom back into Isabelle as she is asked whether she is afraid of being alone on the island.

I have deliberately chosen a rather boring scene, the kind of functional linking scene that offers few opportunities (apart from that mountain of food) to fashion anything of visual interest. There is some attempt at a conventional scene breakdown up to the point of Isabelle's entrance, at which point the zoom largely takes over the function of editing – significantly, Bava himself is credited as editor on the film. All four characters are in place and Isabelle is the only one who moves out of position, the zoom re-framing the action or alternating between an establishing shot of the group and closer shots of Isabelle whenever she speaks. Even for admirers of Bava's use of the zoom, this probably qualifies as a 'bad' or uninteresting use. Its function is clear – keep the characters and action in shot by as economical a means as possible – but without either the kinetic quality of the shock zoom or the inferred perversity of the 'unmotivated' zoom. The zoom 'functions as an intrusive, emphatically overt sign of the narrator's performance of the narrative', claims Willemen (2013: 106), whether that is taken as 'the crassly commercial filmmaker's way of drawing attention to himself' or the 'arty' way in which the auteur signals 'the presence of the narrator'. But the former, even when promoted to cult auteur status, as with someone like Bava (or Franco), cannot be easily disentangled from the zoom's economic functions. While the zoom proliferated in horror films, thrillers and action films in 1970s Italian cinema, the more aspirational Argento placed increasing emphasis on the full mobility of his camera and the technology at his disposal as a marker of distinction and comparative affluence, gliding and creeping, taking flight, climbing walls and rooftops.

Riccardo Freda was critical of Bava's use of the zoom in *La maschera del demonio* (Curti 2019: 70) as a substitute for tracking, a familiar objection to its usage – Belton finds an example of this kind of suspicion of the zoom as early as a 1957 edition of *American Cinematographer* (1980/1981: 21). But Bava and Terzano use both to different effect. The zoom is consistently used to underline moments of shock and never to simulate camera mobility – the appearance of Javutich in Prince Wajda's bedroom, the Prince's repelling of the vampire with the cross (a zoom out), the discovery of a dead servant, Kruvajan's decaying face in his coffin. The zoom as gothic interrobang was by no means taken up by all of the contemporaneous horror cycles. With some exceptions Hammer made little use of it in their more sober approach to the genre – when Christopher Lee's ruined face is brought startlingly into close-up in *The Curse of Frankenstein* (1957), it is by means of a fast dolly shot. And Roger Corman made sparing use of the zoom in the Poe cycle, mainly to underline shocks. *La ragazza che sapeva troppo*, more oriented towards suspense and comedy than shocks, makes less use of the zoom than the gothics or subsequent thrillers, so that it stands out rather more in a shot that fills the frame with nurses' wimples, their heads then lifting to reveal Nora in her hospital bed, before a zoom re-frames her in close-up. In *I tre volti della paura*, the zoom is again allied to shock moments – Karloff's Gorka at the door or window, the medium in her rocking chair, dripping taps, a ghostly hand. *La frusta e il corpo* uses shock zooms for some of Kurt's nocturnal appearances, but also deploys the Pan Cinor to create a 'swooning' effect as Nevenka follows the sound of a whip to a room populated only by furniture covered by dustsheets. The zoom first becomes more conspicuous and insistent in *Terrore nello spazio*, as in the sequence discussed earlier, seemingly supporting Tim Lucas' claim that the replacement of Terzano with Antonio Rinaldi marked a move away from the fluidity of the earlier films. But this might also have been a sign of changing production circumstances – where Galatea were willing to extend both the budget and the shooting schedule to incorporate mobile camerawork into *La maschera del demonio*, the impression of mid-1960s Bava films is sometimes that he was valued more for his speed than anything else.

Operazione paura still uses the zoom to underline shock moments, particularly the various appearances of Melissa Graps, such as the moment when Karl the morose burgomeister encounters her inside a large cabinet as he searches for some documents. Zooms are also used to introduce characters for the first time – even a nameless extra gets a zoom as she leaves her house as coffin bearers pass in the post-credits scene. Ruth is first introduced – materializing in a misty street as Dr Eswai is attacked – by a zoom in, followed by an immediate zoom out. Re-framing her in long shot before cutting sets up the subsequent cut back to her, or at least where she ought to be – she has disappeared as mysteriously as she first appeared. When the Aurum Encyclopedia complains of the 'lazy reliance on the zoom lens' in Bava's later films, it is clearly identified as a bad habit that develops subsequent to *Operazione paura*, praised as 'one of his – and therefore one of the genre's – best pictures' (Hardy *et al.* 1985: 183). When does the use of a cinematic technique become its *over*use, something that is deployed 'lazily'? *Operazione paura* has many more zoom shots than *La maschera del demonio*, and given its small budget, one of the reasons for this may have been expediency. With its constant eye for a striking image or imaginative setpiece, and at least enough resources to make Villa Graps a memorably sinister locale, is it a question of the film 'earning' its zoom shots? Locatelli's notion of *coherent* and *incoherent* uses of the zoom might provide a key here. While zooming into ghostly children, hands at the window and mysterious witches might be a visual cliché, it is still in alignment with the hyperbole of the gothic. Moreover, the zoom is central to two of the film's most striking sequences. In the first, the zoom combined with a tilt simulates Melissa's point of view from her swing, or so it seems – the camera then seems to 'step off' the swing and pull back to reveal a clear, static shot of Melissa on the swing.[6] Later, a slow zoom as the camera rotates helps to create the effect of an endlessly spiralling staircase in Villa Graps. The zoom's bending and stretching of space is well suited to a film in which space is never what it seems to be.

5 bambole per la luna d'agosto, like *Operazione paura*, introduces its larger cast of characters with a series of zooms. The effect, however, is rather different. The over-excited zooms in and out of Fenech's body are one thing –

Quante volte… quella notte also uses the zoom to signal sexual arousal, its first use in the film being a zoom into Tina's posterior from Gianni's point of view as she bends over. Fenech/Mary, initially framed in medium close-up, is upside down in the frame, bent backwards over a sofa, her hands moving in time to the music. The camera zooms out to a long shot of the whole group and then quickly back into medium close-up, and repeats the same sequence two more times. It is then followed by seven zoom shots in succession:

1. A slow zoom into Trudi, ending on a close-up of her eyes.

2. Close-up of Jack's eyes, zoom out to a medium shot as he glances around furtively.

3. Slow zoom into Peggy, Jack's wife – as with Trudi, ending on an extreme close-up of her eyes.

4. Slow zoom into George, whose lips are moving inaudibly – he is clicking his fingers, so he might be either singing or speaking.

5. Slow zoom into the eyes of Jill, George's wife.

6. Master shot of the group, zoom into Mary and the Professor. She rolls over onto her stomach and takes his drink from him.

7. Exterior shot – extreme close-up of Isabelle, who has been watching from outside. Fast zoom out so that we can see the group, including Mary now dancing on her feet, through the glass door.

There then follows a few static shots of individual characters watching Mary dance, including Nick, her husband, the only character not to get an introductory zoom. The scene introduces the characters, and yet at the same time, it does not – we are none the wiser about any of them, and the film is in no rush to rectify that. The zooms do not function like the ones in *Operazione paura,* and, if anything, the sequence is closer to the title sequence of *6 donne per l'assassino*. But not only is it cruder in effect, with its seemingly pointless zooms in or out of people's eyes, but if it is introducing a series of *types*, even those types are largely indistinguishable from one another. We might come to some conclusions about Mary (especially as she is played by Fenech), George, Jack and the Professor (the only one evidently not enjoying himself), but several other characters remain blanks until the end of the film or their death, whichever comes first. The slow zooms add to the impression of a scene taking far longer than it needs to – which is true of some of Bava's more conventionally bravura sequences, too – and, Fenech apart, not having done much to earn it. It vaguely signals mystery and intrigue, but in a way that dissipates into virtually nothing. Moreover, all diegetic sound is absent apart from the music, which varies in volume whether heard by Isabelle from outside or by 'us' inside the villa. It is first heard faintly in the distance, then louder as a needle (in an initially out-of-focus shot) is shown on a record on a turntable. This is the same blurring of diegetic and non-diegetic sound that

Argento would later deploy in a murder setpiece in *Tenebre* (1982) – why can we not hear George 'drumming' on a table as he dances with Mary? Willemen argues that the zoom 'acknowledges the presence of the audience in a way that transforms the performance space into a public space rather than a privatised diegetic space' (2013: 108), but the interest of this scene lies partly in the difficulty in determining what kind of space – public and performative or privatized and diegetic – we are being presented with.

The 'abuse' of the camera extends also to whip-pans for scene transitions and another technique that is ubiquitous in later Bava films – shots that begin by coming into focus and/or end by going out of focus. Possibly another time-saving device, allowing for in-camera editing, it finds its most interesting uses in *Ecologia del delitto*, including the shot of Simone's eye that initially looks like a sunset on the horizon and the final revelation of the killers of the Donatis. The most violent episode of the film, the murders at Ventura's summer cottage, presents four successive shots at one point that use focus as a means of shot transition.

1. Exterior. The shot comes into focus on the slashed throat of Brigitte Skay's character,[7] murdered after swimming in the bay. The camera finds a window, zooms in and the shot goes out of focus.

2. Interior. Roberto/Bobby is reading. Zoom in, shot goes out of focus.

3. Shot comes into focus on couple in bed together (where they will soon be impaled). The camera zooms in slightly and the shot goes out of focus.

4. Moving out-of-focus shot (probably intended to look like a continuation of the previous shot) comes into focus on the killer's eyes looking through a narrow gap in the venetian blinds.

A similar pattern follows the killing of Roberto with a billhook through his face.

1. Roberto/Bobby, billhook embedded in his face, falls to the ground. Zoom into his face, image goes out of focus.

2. Close-up – the billhook is removed from his face, slight zoom out as the killer rolls him over so that he is face down.

3. Brief shot of a dark screen.

4. The shot comes into focus on the body. The camera, evidently handheld, moves and zooms, seemingly representing the killer's point of view as he walks through the cottage, going out of focus as it closes in on a glass panel.

5. The shot comes into focus and surveys the room. It finds a large spear and the image goes out of focus again, reddening as the image loses definition.

6. A door handle comes into focus as the camera continues its movement, turning 180 degrees to look through the gap through a slightly opened door at the next two victims having sex.

Going in or out of focus to mark a shot transition (or occasionally disguise a cut) can add a similar languor and enervation as the slow zoom, but the effect is different here. Going out of focus can signal an eliding of time, as in flashbacks. A much more respectable film, Claude Chabrol's *Les noces Rouges* (1973) uses shots that go out of focus as a transitional device, but only between scenes (including a flashback), never within a scene. Using it *within* a scene is more unusual and creates an uncertainty about time. We rarely know where we are as a shot begins, and we could easily find ourselves in the midst of a killing already taking place. In a scene whose action anticipates the routine slasher films that came later, we might expect either a tighter edit or a more continuous mobile shot from the killer's point of view, as opposed to one that appears to zone out as it surveys the cottage, refusing to provide a clear view of interior space.

Perhaps the apotheosis of the 'dysfunctional' – and yet, strangely expressive and affective – use of the zoom is the multiple-zoom, the repeat printing of the same zoom shot three or four times in succession. This kind of technique was not exclusive to Bava – as an approach to repetitive editing, we can even trace the principle back to Soviet Montage, while Hong Kong action cinema later made use of 'action replays' to sell a particularly exciting stunt or fight move. To borrow a phrase Bordwell uses in relation to Hong Kong cinema, it is a kind of 'expressive amplification', giving an emotional quality to a particular action (2001: 86). The multiple-zoom escalates the shock-zoom, already an affective technique – if one objection to the zoom is that it is a poor substitute for the dolly, one could imagine a similar complaint to the effect that sometimes it does an actor's emoting for them, registering shock on their behalf. There are examples of the multiple-zoom in both *Ecologia del delitto* and *Gli orrori del castello di Norimberga*. In the first film, we might experience the delirium that Moullet talks about as Renata Donati finds the bodies of the murdered youths in Ventura's cottage, piled up in a bathtub. She turns on the light in the bathroom in order to splash water on her face and reacts to something she has seen in the mirror that is not yet visible to the viewer. A zoom out reveals what she has seen in the mirror, the four bodies horribly entangled in the bathtub, and the same zoom is repeated three more times before zooming back into a tighter shot of her reaction in the mirror. The rapid repeat-zoom intensifies the zoom's capacity for registering shock – a somatic analogue to not-being-able-to-believe-your-eyes – and has the effect of suspending or extending time, trapping the gaze in that affective moment, like a stylus caught in the groove of a record or Dr Eswai running repeatedly through the same room. For the horror film or the *giallo*-thriller, it might be the zoom's highest technical contribution, Serie B's more affordable equivalent to Hitchcock's *Vertigo*- shot. Eva and the viewer will have a similar reverberation of fear when she runs away from Baron von Kleist in *Gli orrori del castello di Norimberga*, initially introduced by a single crash zoom into his mutilated face. She races up some stairs only to find him waiting for her (best not to ask how), and the moment is amplified by four repeated zooms, each punctuated by a musical sting.

Pop Bava

If I have to think about him as an artist, then I think of him as a pop artist.

Roy Bava (*Mario Bava: Maestro of the Macabre*)

Both *Diabolik* and *5 bambole per la luna d'agosto* feature the most modishly luxurious item of furniture in 1960s/1970s cinema – a revolving circular bed. In 1966, Hugh Hefner was photographed working on a circular bed that not only revolved but also apparently (and perhaps, inevitably) vibrated. This is the kind of bed on which Diabolik and Eva make out amidst their stolen cash, and Edwige Fenech reclines in her red underwear, perhaps with a cheque for a million dollars still concealed in her bra where the Professor left it. Sex, money, the meeting of technology and modern home furnishing – just what is it that makes today's homes so different, so appealing, as Richard Hamilton's famous collage asked? The revolving bed is where we first find Monica Vitti in the title role of Joseph Losey's *Modesty Blaise* (1966), and the ironic tone of pop art was a shaping force in all the 1960s films adapted from comics, *Diabolik* included. If we are looking to link Bava to pop art, however indirectly, *Diabolik* is the obvious place to start – Pezzotta calls it 'truly Warholian' (2013: 92), even though he goes on to suggest that *5 bambole per la luna d'agosto* represents a more fully developed comic book aesthetic, regardless of it not being adapted from one. The most unusual sequence in *Diabolik* features an identikit device that the villains use to track and capture Eva. A selection of mouths, eyes and hairstyles materialize and mutate on its screen, some of them growing into fully formed faces, with added colours that themselves shift and transform into Warhol-style screenprints. One face looks initially like a Lichtenstein rendition of Barbarella before the face collapses in on itself, her blonde hair transforming into one of his abstract 'comic book' paint swirls. The same face appears again soon afterwards, only to have its features erased. Another looks exactly like Twiggy, its natural colours giving way to deepest crimson, then a monochrome outline, then disappearing altogether. Finally, a drawing of Eva takes shape that looks less like Marisa Mell than the *fumetto* version of the character.

Tim Lucas has coined the term 'Continental Op' to account for those 1960s European films that are 'characterized, first and foremost, by dominant design', showcasing 'abstract worlds where art screams from every frame in which all the traditional elements of nature are denied, replaced by chic, eye-boggling colours, gels and mouè patterns' (2012: 18). But the trickle through of 'pop' is also a shaping force, not least in the ironic and knowingly superficial treatment of films inspired directly or otherwise by the aesthetics of comics. According to David Buxton, the 'pop gaze established a new regime of truth... no longer based... on the "outside world" but on the higher reality of design', which involved 'learning to concentrate one's gaze on surfaces in a world in which fetishism had been extended to almost all objects (and to people themselves)' (1990: 99). While the secret agent genre was arguably the paradigmatic vehicle for 'the new world of total design' (ibid.: 72), *il thrilling all'italiana* also exhibits an aspirational aesthetic of luxury and affluence, where our gaze is as likely to be directed to what Edwige Fenech is wearing or to the interior design of her apartment as to whatever might befall her in a tale we have probably been told several times before. In its evacuation of any other point of interest, *5 bambole per la luna d'agosto* places this gaze front and centre. Compare and contrast two successive scenes. In the first, Mary has just found the body of houseboy Jacques and runs, not especially quickly, first along a beach and then past some trees (she seems to be running in a circle at one point), Piero Umiliani's Hammond organ adding to the sense that nothing of any great import is happening in a scene that one might otherwise expect to have some dramatic impact. This is immediately followed by a swaying wide-angle mobile shot that finds some of the other characters lazing on sofas in the spacious living room, its spiral staircase a constant compositional bonus – drinking, smoking, gazing languidly into space. Now literally nothing is happening, but the camera is giving us a great deal more to look at. Whenever there is a well-composed shot in *5 bambole,* it usually either involves the interior design of the villa or arranges its characters as static objects, whether lounging on sofas or hanging in a meat locker. In its eccentric way and more so than the more obviously 'stylish' earlier films, this is the closest a Bava film gets to the parametric narration that David Bordwell talks about, where style is 'promoted to the level of shaping force in the film' (1985: 279) and organized '*across the film* according to distinct principles' (ibid.: 281).

Alloway divided the development of pop art into three phases. The first was more of a critical discourse than an actual art practice, arguing for a more inclusive understanding of art that extended its borders to include the industrial and the ephemeral. In its second phase, artists such as Lichtenstein and Warhol produced work that incorporated mass media into exhibited art. In the final phase, these notions of pop fed back into mass culture, including cinema and comics (1975: 121). If Bava, and other filmmakers like him, can in any way be connected to pop, it is in this third, more diffuse, trickle-down sense.

FIGURE 15 *'Pop' Bava – the nightclub in* Quante volte… quella notte.

When Alloway initially identified pop as both an aesthetic and a mode of appreciation, he set out some of what Buxton (1990) later called the 'pop gaze'. In popular cinema, 'the drama of possessions' took priority over actions and psychology in defining characters (Alloway 1969: 42). Films were 'lessons in the acquisition of objects, models for luxury, diagrams of bedroom arrangement', above all, 'lessons in style (of clothes, of bearing)' (ibid.). Alloway directs our gaze away from narrative and characterization and towards *design* – what kind of environment the characters inhabit and, equally importantly, *how* they inhabit it. *Quante volte… quella notte* is less interesting for its adolescent sex comedy take on *Rashomon* than two extraordinary interiors. Gianni's bachelor pad is furnished not only with raised floors, plants and the kind of metallic *objets d'arte* that sometimes prove lethal in Dario Argento films, but an actual swing – here is a bachelor who swings in every sense. Even more memorable is a nightclub that outdoes the one in *Diabolik,* with inflatable furniture and women in suspended cages wearing Paco Rabanne-like dresses. One of the reasons why these films are still popular with cult film lovers – and *5 bambole* is no longer seen as one of Bava's worst films – is because a 'pop gaze' that was probably opportunistic and 'thoroughly devalued by over-usage' (Hebdige 1988: 121) in its original context has become a retro-gaze. Bava as unlikely pop auteur is a more recent way of seeing him, and his later films more specifically – Acerbo and Pisoni's 2007 Bava anthology devotes an entire subsection to 'Il pop' as a distinct phase in Bava's career. But if *5 bambole per la luna d'agosto* has probably never made anyone sit on the edge of their seat in suspense, there is nothing new about sitting further forward to take in the 'opulent vulgarity and decadence' that one reviewer found to be the film's saving grace (Bilbow 1971: 12).

'In entertainment film', writes Bordwell, 'the artisan's imagination goes to work upon well-defined norms' (2000: 13), and a filmmaker like Bava illustrates the point. His 1960s films work more or less within classical norms. 'Hollywood' had, after all, taken up residence in Rome during a significant transitional point in his career and a good deal of Serie B cinema sought to be the cinematic equivalent to Dr Eswai's doppelgänger. Those norms were freshened up with stylistic quirks or amplified, as with Bava's coloured lighting, eccentric camera movements, and experiments with the zoom, while the films capitalized on new approaches to cinematic violence that Hollywood would take longer to adopt. But as those norms broke down, film language became more 'dysfunctional' in low-budget genre films from Europe and other 'exploitation' industries, while at the same time new, more localized norms emerged – greater use of the zoom being one of the most noticeable. In some ways, the zoom – or at least a particular (over) use of it – draws a line between Bava the artisan-auteur (the triumph of technical skill and traditional craft) and Bava the cult-auteur (bad taste appreciated as aesthetic beauty). It is questionable whether he would have gained a reputation as a stylist on the basis of the films made after *Diabolik*, but in many ways they are the films that have most to tell us about how intensified film styles adapted to changing production circumstances and generic norms – the 'Bavaesque' had had its moment, but the artisan was still at work.

Notes

1   In the 2007 featurette *Kill, Bava, Kill!* included on Arrow's 2017 blu-ray of the film. A *Corriere della sera* review of *Diabolik* included 'snobbish intellectuals' amongst its likely audience (G. Gr. 1968: 13).

2   The film had a six-week schedule, which gave Bava and his team the time for such aesthetic indulgences.

3   Lucas adds the film to Bava's 'Secret Filmography' purely on the basis of its resemblance to his later use of coloured gels, but there is no other evidence to connect him to the film. It is 'Bavaesque' before such a thing existed.

4   If Asher added considerable production value to early Hammer, it was evidently more than the company thought they could afford or needed in the longer term, and he was replaced by DPs who worked more quickly. Coloured gels did not, however, completely disappear from the Hammer style.

5   Lucas makes one of his most extravagant claims for the film, likening its place in the horror genre to that of *2001: A Space Odyssey* (1968) in Science Fiction – 'a point of embarkation, when these genres began to venture away from

traditional linear narratives towards literally new dimensions in storytelling that dared penetrate into areas ambiguous, abstract, and intuitive' (2007: 673).

6 *Quante volte… quella notte* also uses the zoom to create the view from a swing.

7 Brünnhilde in the English version, unnamed in the Italian version.

6

'Grandi stronzate'? Critical reception and reputation

Interviewer: Why do you think the Americans and the French appreciated your films more than the Italians?
Bava: Because they're more gullible than us.

(Lippi and Codelli 1976: 153)

According to Peter Hutchings, Bava's status as a major figure in the horror genre was bestowed 'entirely retrospectively, for during his directorial career... (he) received little critical attention and was not generally known to the film-going public, either in his native Italy or elsewhere' (2016: 79). This is largely true, but the aim of this chapter is to probe more deeply into the question of Bava's reputation, often represented as a journey from obscurity and critical disdain to long overdue critical adulation. Bourdieu characterizes the field of cultural production as an 'economic world reversed' (1993: 29). The field of restricted production – the world of high art – prioritizes symbolic over economic value, playing a game in which 'loser wins' by the criteria of ordinary economies (ibid.: 39). Bava's films generally underperformed in the field of large-scale production, aggressively commercial films that would be better received over time by a more restricted audience. It might be going too far to say that they have accrued greater symbolic than economic value over time, but that would not be an inappropriate claim to make for their current status as cult-art objects. A particular version of cult – the 'forgotten' or neglected film or filmmaker re-evaluated by connoisseurs – plays out a restricted, and most likely unintended, game of 'loser wins'. In the case of someone like Bava, the films become 'quasi-legitimate', as David Andrews puts it, acquiring a 'more sustainable, albeit still ambivalent, cult-art identity' and winning acclaim in both 'illegitimate *and* legitimate circles' (2013: 108). Nebulous

but eminently marketable, cult cinephilia is nothing if not what Bourdieu
would call a universe of belief.

With all this in mind, it is worth both offering some qualifications and
to unpack some of the claims about Bava's re-evaluation and to trace
the fluctuations of 'belief' in the value of his films. Firstly, while I would
agree that Bava's status grew after his death, he had always had his critical
admirers, even in Italy – in 1964, his name appeared on the front cover of
Vittorio Spinazzola's annual curated collection of critical essays, *Film 1964*,
in an issue dedicated to 'film di massa e cinema d'avanguardia' (popular
film and avant-garde cinema) and Spinazzola had already praised *Ercole
al centro della terra* and the 'antico operatore' (veteran cinematographer)
the previous year in an essay on the peplum (Spinazzola 1963). Secondly,
becoming a 'major figure' in the horror genre – let alone Italian horror
more specifically – comes with the same circumscribed status as that of
'cult filmmaker'. Canonical filmmakers (Hitchcock, Polanski, Kubrick) may
dabble in the horror genre, but the likes of John Carpenter, Lucio Fulci and
George Romero maintain their reputations as 'masters' in more specialized,
and often fannish, circles. Moreover, depending on how one defines 'the
film-going public', Bava is still not generally known outside of cult and
cinephile appreciation, even if that cult is perhaps larger than it was due
to readier access to the full range of his films.[1] Has Bava's reputation, then,
substantially changed – and if so, how? – or simply been consolidated by the
remediation of his films and books such as Tim Lucas's heavyweight volume?
An earlier cinephile appreciation of Bava found him equally thrilling and
frustrating. Why was such an obvious talent so inconsistent? Why did he not
take the same care with the narrative as his setpieces? Sometimes a cursory
acknowledgement of the circumstances under which Bava worked answered
these questions, but one might also ask: why are we no longer concerned by
the unevenness of individual Bava films, let alone his output as a whole? To
borrow Stanley Fish's term, there have been some shifts in the interpretive
communities that critique Bava. An interpretive community is 'a bundle of
interests, of particular purposes and goals, its perspective is interested rather
than neutral' (Fish 1980: 14). Bava's films have passed through a number of
interpretive communities, shaped by, for example, neorealism, auteur cinema
and *cinema d'impegno* (by which standards, Bava's *cinema d'evasione* or
cinema-cinema was bound to found lacking), surrealism and the sado-erotic,
cult's predilection for the 'transgressive', the marginal and the excessive
(with the well-made 'mainstream' film its conformist Other) or alternatively
the kitsch and the retro (which allowed the rehabilitation of previously 'bad'
or 'decadent' Bava films). They have also passed through different national
sites of reception, which have framed 'Mario Bava' in different ways – the
artisan/auteur divide being the most noticeable. I have focused here on Italy,
where Bava's critical neglect was supposedly at its most egregious, France,
where cinephile appreciation of films from other industries is often seen to

transform their status (as in the auteurist approach to Hollywood cinema), and his English-language reception in the United States and the UK. There are doubtless other important and interesting contexts for the reception of Bava and Italian genre cinema more generally – Germany particularly comes to mind, given the overlap between Italian and German crime-mystery-suspense films – but not only do linguistic constraints play a part here, but there is also a particular synergy between the examples I have chosen. As is evident in the quote at the top of this chapter, Bava's reputation outside Italy (and particularly in France) became a recurring reference point in domestic discussions of his films – 'this director so loved by French critics and the "alternative" circuit and so undervalued by the local industry and general public', as his obituary in *Corriere della sera* put it (Po 1980: 20). If we take Bava's own pronouncements at face value – and we should probably be cautious about doing so – it was also a source of amusement, if not embarrassment, to him.

When evaluating the critical standing of a filmmaker like Bava through reference to reviews of his films, some qualifications need to be borne in mind. Firstly, the critical evaluation of an individual Bava film is not necessarily the same thing as an evaluation of Bava the director. The most obvious example is *La maschera del demonio,* which has long enjoyed a certain privileged status as a genre 'classic' of sorts – even Carlos Clarens, so dismissive of Bava otherwise, thought it had 'the best black-and-white photography to enhance a horror movie in the past two decades' (1971: 229). Sometimes its reputation even appeared to compromise that of Bava more generally – the film that he never lived up to. Secondly, Bava often represented, even for his early admirers, not so much an individual oeuvre as a particular kind of Italian genre cinema, encompassing horror, fantasy and the more flamboyant end of the peplum. We might call it the cinema of 'Bava-Freda-Cottafavi', given that these three directors were often critical reference points for one another, particularly outside Italy.[2] These were filmmakers that, as Christopher Frayling observed of Duccio Tessari, 'nameless critics in *The Monthly Film Bulletin* did not feel too ashamed to admire' (1981: 263).

The cult-cinephile triumvirate Bava-Freda-Cottafavi – an unholy trinity if ever there was one – is symptomatic of how artistic reputations change. Bava has arguably eclipsed the other two in visibility and reputation, but if anything, he was once regarded as the lesser of the three by those who favoured this type of cinema. In the early 1960s, an argument broke out between French critics at *Cahiers du Cinéma* and *Présence du cinema* and those at Italian journals such as *Bianco e nero* over the merits of Vittorio Cottafavi – some French critics were putting him on the same level as Mizoguchi and Preminger. When Spinazzola, himself an admirer of Cottafavi, recounts this row, even he feels that critics across the alps had got carried away (1963: 98–9). If less extravagant claims were made elsewhere,

prior to Leone, Cottafavi was the most critically praised Italian director of
genre films. A dismissive review of Bava's *Ercole al centro della terra* in the
British *Monthly Film Bulletin* concludes, 'At the moment, Cottafavi reigns
supreme' (Anon. 1963a: 21). Michel Caen, reviewing the same film, made
the same unflattering comparison in *Midi-Minuit Fantastique* (1962: 62),
even though he judged Cottafavi to be 'overly adored'. Reviewing the UK
VHS release of Cottafavi's *Ercole all conquista all'Atlantide*, Tom Milne –
also one of Bava's most sympathetic UK critics – wrote:

> It is easy to overrate Cottafavi, since he so obviously had the instincts of
> a film-maker… and so effortlessly outdistanced such rivals as Freda and
> Bava. Equally easy, though, to underrate him, since most of his film work
> was confined to the lower, and invariably atrociously dubbed, reaches of
> fantasy, adventure, horror and historical adventure.
>
> (Milne 1986: 19)

In 'Ercole alla conquista degli schermi' (Hercules conquers the screens),
Vittorio Spinazzola singles out Cottafavi as the only director of the peplum
with sufficient artistic personality to rise above the level of 'good artisanal
products' fashioned by Francisci, Freda and, presumably, Bava (1963:
106). Luc Moullet's film *Les Sièges de l'Alcazar* (1989) features extracts
from Cottafavi's films and a film critic protagonist – like Moullet, a writer
for *Cahiers du Cinéma* – obsessed with the director. Cottafavi was the
fully formed filmmaker – the word 'auteur' is not used but seems to be
implied by Spinazzola – Freda the capable journeyman, Bava the brilliant
cinematographer but rather less convincing director. When Cottafavi died
in December 1998, the obituary in the UK broadsheet *The Guardian*
acknowledged that he was 'later to be acclaimed, particularly by French
critics, as a cult figure', but judged that he was 'probably too much of a
self-conscious intellectual to become a good director of commercial film'
(Lane 1998), even though his ability to range from Brecht to Reg Park
had probably once been seen as one of his strengths. His TV work in
particular stressed his literary and theatrical background. I would venture
that Cottafavi would have been a fairly obscure figure for most *Guardian*
readers – even more so than Bava, who had enjoyed a full season at the
National Film Theatre in August of that year. The obituary in *Corriere
della sera* was rather different in tone – 'Goodbye, Cottafavi, a "father" of
our mythological cinema' was the headline (Porro 1998: 38). Again, the
French critics were credited with elevating his reputation, but the obituary
concluded that 'he lived his final years with the respect he was owed as an
author who could turn his hand to anything, capable of uniting the highs
and lows of entertainment' (ibid.). It would be an exaggeration to say that
this 'father' of the peplum is a forgotten figure – there was a retrospective
devoted to him at the Cinémathèque as recently as 2017, and there are two
Italian language books on the director (the most recent from 2010) – but

he has largely disappeared from English-language cinephilia. *The Guardian* called him the 'lost hero of Italian cinema', where Bava tends to be framed as a rediscovered one, and one now relatively easy to seek out. Digital remediation has not served Cottafavi well – his work is spottily available on DVD – largely because the peplum has not enjoyed the same degree of attention and care as other *filoni*, as though never shedding the aura of ephemerality. Cottafavi fell not so much out of critical favour as partly out of view, while Bava became ever more visible – and vividly so. But might this also be because Cottafavi's reputation was partly that of a cultured man parachuted in to elevate lowly genres, whereas Bava – the artisan belatedly elevated to auteur – makes for a more appealing cult narrative? Cottafavi appealed to cinephiles in France and the UK but has not been taken up by the cult cinephilia situated in the home film cultures where Bava's films have flourished. Freda, meanwhile, finds his reputation closely tied to that of his former cinematographer, his cultification largely focused on a small number of his films – in particular, his gothic horror films of the early 1960s and later thrillers such as *L'iguana dalla lingua di fuoco* that can be pulled into the canon of *il giallo italiano*.

How do artistic reputations and canons take shape, particularly when they travel through different national and critical contexts? A reputation is 'pluralistic, collective, pervasive, and multisourced', dispersed through a set of interconnected networks (Craik 2009: 91). The reputation of an author, artist or artisan is not solely that of a person – it might even be at odds with the biographical individual – but a body of work and a creative identity extrapolated (or invented), often in conflicting versions, from that work. Artistic reputations develop 'through a process of consensus building in the relevant art world. Like all forms of consensus, the consensus on reputations, at every level, changes from time to time' (Becker, quoted by Kapsis 1992: 5). Robert Kapsis (1992) traces the remaking of Alfred Hitchcock's reputation from master entertainer to serious artist, helped in no small part by critical shifts in the valuing of popular cinema. Hitchcock's reputation networks were particularly strong, encompassing industry, peers, influential critics and public fame, and have only grown stronger since his death, as posthumous reputations often do, even as biographies have filled in the 'dark side' of his personality. Such shifts in reputation are driven by critical gatekeepers as much as (if not more than) inherent qualities in the work itself – 'the art-world orientation expects change in an artists' reputation also to reflect changes in the aesthetic judgements and standards of critics, aestheticians, and other key art-world members' (Kapsis 1992: 7). Examining this requires us to take a step back from the idea that Bava was once undervalued and misunderstood, but now has at least some of the recognition he deserves. 'Any instance of canonization', writes David Church (2015: 1), is a process of 'asserting the worth of certain objects over others, retrospectively ascribing ahistorical and transcendent values to selected texts as a means of defensively disavowing the historically constructed nature of both these valuations and the canonizers' assumed authority'. But do cult reputations, often seen to move from neglect to re-evaluation, operate in the same way? The gatekeepers engaged in building the reputation in question may have more limited influence, an influence confined to a niche audience in the larger 'hierarchy of consecration', to borrow Bourdieu's phrase (1993: 136). It is likely that consensus will be more localized, even unstable, the reputation never fully settling. It might even be a requirement of a cult reputation that it is not more widely recognized and therefore maintains its 'outsider' status. But when Bava seasons appear at the Cinémathèque Française or the British Film Institute, we are evidently talking about a reputation that, if not quite canonical, has achieved a degree of 'quasi-legitimate' validation that complicates the boundaries between cult and the 'legitimate' canon.

Kapsis sets out a number of factors that can affect the progress of reputation-building. In the case of Hitchcock, the 'Master of Suspense' participated in and actively encouraged the critical shift from seeing him as 'merely' an entertainer to being a serious artist and auteur – agreeing to a book-length interview with Francois Truffaut, studying selected European auteur films by the likes of Antonioni, Godard and Bergman and considering how he could incorporate elements of 'art cinema' into suspense thrillers (Kapsis 1992: 2). Argento – the 'Italian Hitchcock', let us not forget – exercised a similar managing of his public artistic profile, with the nods to Antonioni in his early films and insistence in interviews that he was exploring his own fears and nightmares in his films, just as Truffaut once claimed that Hitchcock had 'in his head dreams, obsessions and preoccupations which are not those of the masses' (quoted by Kapsis 1989: 24). Of course, Bava, who presented himself as a nervous and easily frightened man, also claimed to put his fears onscreen – collaborators recount tales of him trembling in terror at some of the ideas in his scripts. But he was as far as one could be from the self-promotion of Argento or Hitchcock – there is a self-effacement bordering on a self-sabotaging of his own reputation. While this sometimes seems to have depended on the mood he was in – there are rare instances of affection for some of his own films – he famously told L'Espresso that he had only ever made 'grandi stronzate', roughly translated, a load of bullshit (quoted by Pezzotta 2013: 8). Connected to, and perhaps more important than self-promotion, is 'sponsorship by prominent members of the film community' (Kapsis 1992: 2). Hitchcock had half the future nouvelle vague batting for him, but it is here particularly that Bava's acclaim has been posthumous – Scorsese et al. have been more recent sponsors. Joe Dante wrote about Bava's films in the US horror magazine Castle of Frankenstein, actively seeking them out in grindhouse cinemas, but that was before he had any kind of standing as a filmmaker himself. The closest Bava had to a Truffaut was Luigi Cozzi, who interviewed him both for Italy's first horror magazine Horror, edited by Alfredo Castelli (who also interviewed him for the magazine), and in his capacity as Italian correspondent for

Famous Monsters of Filmland, but there is something of a gulf between the relative esteem enjoyed by Cozzi and Truffaut. Surviving family members can also act as reputational gatekeepers (Stollery 2019: 57). Lamberto Bava has played an active role in reputation-maintenance for his father, referencing his films in his own (the metallic mask in *Dèmoni*), remaking them (*La maschera del demonio*) and 'completing' them (*Kidnapped*). But his own reputation plays a rather complex role in sustaining Mario Bava's status. Lamberto Bava's career overlaps with his father's, co-directing his final two projects (and directing parts of *Lisa e il diavolo* before that) – his official debut, *Macabro* (1980), made the year of Mario's death, involved another well-regarded figure, Pupi Avati. Overall, Lamberto Bava's career tells us less about his talent as a filmmaker than the problems – greater even than those that his father faced – confronting a genre filmmaker in Italy during the 1980s and 1990s, as deregulated TV decimated popular cinema and the already precarious international market for Italian horror films disappeared. Lamberto Bava has made well-regarded films (*Macabro*), popular films (*Dèmoni* and *Dèmoni 2*) and a hugely popular fantasy TV series (*Fantaghirò*, 1991–6), but there is a lot of routine TV work and thrillers that look like pale imitations of the era of *il thrilling*. In some ways this is to the benefit of Mario Bava's reputation – Lamberto neither eclipses him nor embarrasses him, just enough of a cult name in his own right to act as reputational ambassador, at least for genre fans.

A second factor is changing aesthetic standards and critical discourse. Bava as the embodiment of *cinema-cinema*, or less flatteringly the cinematographer in the director's chair, was not always seen as a positive. The display of technique seemingly for its own sake was sometimes seen as a limitation, where now these exercises in cinematic style are 'the object of formalist concerns on the part of maverick critics' with Bava 'the master of a popular form of surrealism, modernism or, at any rate, aestheticism' (Vitali 2016: 73). The following review of *Ercole al centro della terra* reads initially like a celebration of Bava's film style:

> Employing the same camera technique as in his earlier *Mask of the Demon,* Mario Bava here conjures up several enjoyable marvels as he follows Hercules into a vividly filtered Hades... the film also provides designers and special effects men with a field day – horrid, bubbly lava, several natty transformations, turbulent seascapes, brooding clouds and a gaggle of misshapen monsters are included in the mixture.
>
> (Anon. 1963a: 21)

So far, so good – this sounds a lot like praise. But these 'eye-catching moments' are then dismissed as 'a limited box of tricks' and Bava's direction seen as betraying 'the absence of a real style'. One particular shift played out around Bava's use of colour, sometimes originally seen as merely decorative or even vulgar, but now often cited as one of the reasons why 6 *donne per l'assassino* is more fully developed than the monochrome *La ragazza che sapeva troppo*. Bava is now not only the maestro of horror, but 'a first-rate colourist' according to a retrospective review of *Ercole al centro della terra* in *The Village Voice* (Stein 1989: 71). Bava's gels and non-naturalistic colours are now central to the aesthetic appreciation of his films, as is evident in the subtitle of Tim Lucas's book (taken from a Sergio Martino film). But here is what two French critics – the cinephile culture that supposedly worshipped him – thought of Bava's colour cinematography in, respectively, *Ercole al centro della terra* and 6 *donne per l'assassino*.

> To suggest the fantastic, Bava, like Corman, plays the photographic effects card. It's all there: Ziegfeld lighting, filters, false perspective etc. We also need to talk about the overuse of the zoom.
>
> (Caen 1962: 62)

> Every crime is a pretext for the debauchery of hideous lighting and gross effects: all in a muddle of objects that Ophüls, Sternberg or even Albicocco would never have dared.
>
> (Anon. 1965c: 90)

Another French critic, writing about *La frusta e il corpo* in *Midi-Minuit Fantastique*, thought that one of Bava's pseudonyms, (John) 'Foam', was apt in the face of '"zooms" into door handles, close-ups in red, green, random tracking shots' and accused the director of having 'the bad taste of a colourist' (Eisenschitz 1964: 62). An Italian review of 6 *donne per l'assassino* made a similar complaint about its 'desperate chromatic experiment, mainly leaning on a range of reds' (E.G.L. 1964: 48). Spinazzola was a rare dissenting voice, calling Bava 'a master in the use of the zoom lens, of filters and coloured gels' (1963: 105).

A third factor is what Kapsis calls 'genre meaning systems' (1989: 17), shifts in our ways of talking about genre. In the case of Hitchcock, the suspense thriller was elevated along with the director's reputation – from the 1970s, it became more common for critics and filmmakers to take the genre more seriously. As we have seen, Bava's reputation is partly bound up with his 'pioneer' status with regards to the *giallo all'italiana* and a particular cult framing of 'Italian horror' as transgressive, stylistically excessive and erotically charged, but this is of course a niche reputation. A type of criticism that emerged in the 1970s that stressed the politics of the new American horror of that decade did not particularly translate across to Italian horror, less clearly 'about' its immediate socio-political context (if perhaps latently symptomatic of it in some way) and difficult to present as in any way politically progressive. But it did signal a move away from an earlier criticism that valued subtle, suggestive horror and the artistry of classic 1930s/1940s horror over the more graphic variant that began to appear in the late 1950s. More important still was the de-centring of the Anglo-American tradition of horror cinema, whereby Italy would take on particular prominence, and Bava, along with Argento, would reign as a crowning auteur figure. The English-language *Aurum Film Encyclopedia* is representative of the foregrounding of Bava as an important figure in European horror, even if it held to the view that his later work was a zoom-heavy disappointment (Hardy *et al.* 1985). 'Late works' are often subject to re-evaluation, and this would happen over time to what Acerbo calls Bava's 'decadent' period (2007: 183), although such 'mechanical' and 'lazy' films as *5 bambole per la luna d'agosto* would have their defenders earlier than one might expect. As we shall see, Bava's critical reputation did not follow a straightforward trajectory in any of the places where it is usually seen to have either taken shape or been held back.

'This director so loved by the French and the "alternative" circuit': Bava's Italian critical reception

Second class cinema, escapism at a cheap price, films to be used and thrown away; so many labels, some even vicious, were attached to the films of Mario Bava, Riccardo Freda, Antonio Margheriti. But they are also part of Italian film history, capable artisans in the factory of dreams at Cinecittà, the Hollywood beyond the Tiber.

(G.T. 1992: 41)

The above comments appeared in an article in *Corriere della sera* covering a season of Italian horror films in Milan, 'Horror all'italiana', that included *La maschera del demonio* and *I tre volti della paura*. The re-discovery of 'Italian horror' as an entity in its home country is often linked to the 1976 Festival Internazionale del Film di Fantascienza and the publication of the accompanying catalogue *Fant'Italia* (Lippi and Codelli 1976), 'a point of reference for fans of Italian horror' (Noto 2016: 209), which included an interview with Bava (the one in which he unhelpfully characterized his French admirers as 'more gullible than us'). Two years later, in the second volume of his seminal *Storia del cinema dell'orrore* (1978), Teo Mora – Professor of Algebra by day, horror afficionado by night – acknowledged the importance of *Fant'Italia* and the 1976 festival at Trieste and devoted a chapter to the 1957–66 period of Italian horror alongside studies of Fisher, Corman and others. The third volume would take it up to 1978. A canon was forming, and, importantly, forming in the country perceived to have been neglectful of its own fantasy cinema. One might argue that Italian audiences had been more neglectful than critics, the latter often obliged to review films that were opening in *prime visioni* even if they felt little enthusiasm for them and often assigned them to an anonymous *vice* (deputy) reviewer – box office figures testify to a general indifference towards homegrown horror until Dario Argento's brand of terror broke through. Both *Fant'Italia's* writers and Mora speak of critical neglect and the need for re-evaluation, with the former adopting an adversarial tone towards an 'asphyxial and provincial non-culture' still attached to 'a neo-deceased realism that is eternally theorised, prophetised, banalised' (Lippi and Codelli 1976: 11). As early as 1963, Spinazzola had cited the 'irresistible canon' of neorealism as one of the reasons for the critical neglect of the peplum (1963: 95), an example of the 'crude wielding of neorealism as a truncheon to thrash forms of cinema that cannot be so described' (O'Leary and O'Rawe 2011: 108). But if the rehabilitation of horror, fantasy and adventure cinema was initially a niche and cultish intervention, it would gain some mainstream traction not long after Bava's death. In 1981, the TV channel Rete 1 announced a season of Italian horror for the following year. 'But does Italian horror really exist?' asked *La stampa* rhetorically, 'Is it worth the trouble to recuperate it?' (U. bz 1981: 21). Clearly the answer was yes. When the season was shown the following summer, the same writer expressed surprise at one of the films included – surely *La ragazza che sapeva troppo* was a *giallo* and not strictly part of 'Horror all'italiana' – but took the opportunity to praise Bava and his film, now evidently a 'classic giallo' with a 'strong atmosphere' and 'certain violent contrasts of light and shadow' that anticipated the early films of Dario Argento (U.bz 1982: 23). Bava was now a 'maestro' of the genre (even if it was not clear which genre), the headline pronouncing it 'a thriller everyone should see (but it isn't a horror film at all)'. This more mainstream rehabilitation was making more modest claims for 'horror all'italiana' than genre enthusiasts were starting to do – it was still a cinema of artisans (which is not, after all, an unreasonable view), promoted to the level of 'prodotto medio' (G.T. 1992: 41). *Film medio* was a term that surfaced in some critical debates around Italian cinema in the 1960s and 1970s, 'the average or run-of-the-mill film', the 'highest peaks of commercial cinema and the lowest ends of authorial cinema' is how Vitali (2016: 62) interprets it. This probably does not sound particularly flattering now, and maybe more than a little condescending. But there was a tacit acknowledgement by some critics that an economically stable film industry needed such films – solid, well-made, if artistically unadventurous, films. According to critic Lino Miccichè (1975: 106) this type of film did not exist in Italy prior to the 1960s, whereupon it assumed a greater importance. In an interesting but hostile review of *6 donne per l'assassino* in *Bianco e nero,* a journal that at the time normally only provided credits for Bava's films and showed little interest in reviewing them, the writer called Bava 'a reliable artisan', an ideal candidate – and the *giallo* a perfect genre – to produce *film medi,* 'not the production of art but well made (popular film)' (E.G.L 1964: 48). How regrettable, then – 'we don't know if it's his fault or the producer's' – that he should squander his talent on 'sadism beyond the pale' and 'bad taste' (ibid.). By way of perspective, Hitchcock was cited as a positive example of *film medio* – 'Why don't we also try it here, leaving the horrific to the "Grand Guignol", which after all no longer exists, and for good reason' (ibid.). While the critic loathed the film, this is one of the earlier examples of Bava's talent being grudgingly acknowledged in Italy – someone who had the ability, if not the inclination, to escape Serie B and progress to *il film medio* (around the time of *Diabolik* and *Odissea,* that door was certainly open). By the early 1990s, a good deal of Serie B cinema was seemingly being retrospectively promoted to *film medi,* and some would go further than that.

If we are looking for evidence of Italy lagging behind France, the UK and the United States in the appreciation of Bava, *La maschera del demonio*'s reception would certainly support that narrative. It was something of a sensation in foreign markets – a 'spine-chilling "gasser"', as New York trade paper *The Daily Film* put it (H.M. 1961: 8) – even if some of its admirers (especially in France) later felt that Bava had flattered to deceive. In Italy, it landed with as dull a thud as the more routine vampire films of the same year, such as *L'amante del vampiro* and *L'ultima preda del vampiro. Corriere della sera* at least acknowledged its technical qualities, particularly Bava and Terzano's cinematography, and that it was strong stuff, an 'encyclopedia of fright and disgust' – 'Even the viewer well acquainted with the Mabuses, the Jekylls and the Frankensteins will find a higher dosage of shivers than normal' (Ian. 1960: 6). But the review concluded that 'everything is too "grand guignol" not to look ridiculous' (ibid.). The tone here is a familiar one from the kind of reviews Hammer films were receiving in the UK once their initial shock value had faded – chills punctured by amusement. Trade paper *Intermezzo* called it 'a film of very little value', awarding it one star for artistic quality (Mediocre) and two for its commercial prospects (Anon. 1960: 13). 'Horror and disgust are the basis of this not very credible story told by Mario Bava with the help of Italian and foreign actors' (ibid.). Lest we put this down to critical snobbery, the same magazine complained that *Rocco e i suoi fratelli* (1960) was too long and *L'avventura* (1960) too intellectual. Morando Morandini in *La notte,* one of the most distinguished Italian critics of the time, was one of the first to object to Bava's 'technicist delirium':

Tracking to and fro, moving with the crane, using the zoom (optical dolly), not denying himself any forbidden blow to shake the autonomic nervous system of the spectator. This is the first great reservation we must make about the film; the second regards the script in which there accumulates, with no regard for logic or verisimilitude… actions, misdeeds, macabre details, horrifying details that sometimes arouse the laughter often provoked by disgust. Therefore let's allow ourselves to say that these are the films… that should never go into circulation.

(13 August 1960, quoted by Acerbo and Pisoni 2007a: 271)

Violence, 'grand guignol' and other notional transgressions in Bava's films were not necessarily a particular point of controversy, notwithstanding Morandini's plea for this type of film to not be released. One would never guess the censorship problems *La frusta e il corpo* had faced from some of its reviews, even though *Segnalazioni cinematografiche* called it a 'mediocre and twisted storyline pivoting on perversion and seasoned with macabre elements' (1963, quoted by Acerbo and Pisoni 2007a: 276). 'Architecture, sets and music do their best to frighten the spectator, which comes off for a while', wrote *Corriere della sera*'s reviewer, 'but it's then countered by a timid smile and with good reason' (V. 1963: 8). Despite an earlier report identifying Bava as director, the review named John M. Old as *regista*, although *Il giorno*'s anonymous film critic suspected that 'it was made by an Italian, expert in matters of the genre' (30 August 1963, quoted by Acerbo and Pisoni 2007a: 276). Reviewing *6 donne per l'assassino* in communist daily *L'unità*, Ugo Casiraghi observed wryly, 'We cannot deny that, as a butcher, he has a pulse' (26 June 1964, quoted by Curti 2019: 36). The same review was one of the first to observe that Bava was gaining a reputation elsewhere, albeit a reputation that I would suggest was exaggerated by Italian critics – 'Mario Bava, whom those crazy French critics extol and adore as a genre founder, is a fellow who has lots of fun playing with macabre ornaments, intermittent lighting and changing colours' (ibid.: 67). Exaggerated or not, the French enthusiasm for Bava – or Bava-Freda-Cottafavi – became a point of reference for Italian reviewers, particularly around the release of *Diabolik*.

But it wasn't just 'those crazy French critics' who were warming to Bava and Italian horror-thrilling cinema. He had a small group of admirers closer to home, those Pezzotta calls 'the happy few' (2013: 14). There were Spinazzola and Goffredo Fofi amongst film critics, although the latter first wrote about Bava in his seminal article 'Terreur en Italie' for *Midi-Minuit Fantastique* – 'one always recognises the signature of Bava', an 'excellent director', he wrote, while acknowledging his struggles in less congenial genres (1963: 82). There was the writer Bernadino Zapponi, who had planned to devote an issue of his journal *Il delatore* to Bava before it ceased publication (Pezzotta 2013: 13), but as the writer of Fellini's *Toby Dammit* found other ways of paying tribute by representing the devil as a little blonde girl with a bouncing ball familiar from *Operazione paura*. Then there was comic book writer Luciano Secchi, better known as Max Bunker, a man of similar artistic temperament to Bava in combining the macabre with dark humour. The similarity between one of the stories in *Kriminal* and *6 donne per l'assassino* (both appeared in 1964) may be a coincidence, but it seems less of a coincidence that a vampire story in *Satanik* featured a character called Count Wurdalak. By the turn of the decade, some of this enthusiasm could be discerned in some of the more mainstream reviews of Bava's films. Here, for example, is Leonardo Autera's review of *Ecologia del delitto* in *Corriere della sera*:

> Mario Bava is perhaps the only homegrown director who knows how to transfer to the screen with conviction, but also a pinch or irony that serves him *in extremis*, all the most macabre and truculent repertoire of Grand Guignol.
>
> (1971: 13)

Because of its failure at the Italian box office,[3] *Ecologia del delitto* has taken on the reputation of a misunderstood film that had to relocate to the American grindhouse to find its audience (there is some truth in that) and wait many years to be fully appreciated. But while I do not want to position Autera as either typical in his opinion of Bava or in some way 'ahead of his time', it is of no small interest that it was an Italian critic who saw the film in a manner very similar to the way it is seen now. Autera's review picked up on the film's ecological theme, admittedly flagged up in its original release title – 'The final turning point of the film (which we obviously don't anticipate) can be read in that sense, which seeds the story with a last touch of lighthearted cynicism' (ibid.). Bava the ironist has also become a popular way of seeing his films – 'A game in short, this film of Bava's that, taken in the right spirit, is rather amusing' (ibid.). Finally, while the film belongs to the zoom-and-focus-heavy, less traditionally crafted period of Bava's films, Autera praised the 'excellent technical skills of the director (and operator at the same time), unbridled above all in his cutting and the livid and bloody tonalities of the images' (ibid.).[4] It was not unusual for Bava's technical skills to be acknowledged even in lukewarm reviews of his films – a review of *6 donne per l'assassino* in *La stampa* attributed what modest virtues it was deemed to possess to 'the highly refined technique of the director' rather than the 'ricketiness' of an 'awkward script' (Vice 1964: 4), while *Corriere della sera* found *Operazione paura* to be 'ably conducted by Mario Bava' without making any great claims for it (Anon. 1966: 6).

Even more interesting is a review of *5 bambole per la luna d'agosto* by Alessandro Cappabianca that appeared in the film journal *Filmcritica* the previous year to Autera's review of *Ecologia del delitto*. Here, arguably, was a Bava film in need of a sympathetic reviewer with its wild crash zooms, mechanical and derivative storyline, dull characters, and kitsch designs. His review is worth quoting at length:

> In *5 bambole per la luna d'agosto*... the *giallo* mechanism is filtered through a comic book look, accentuated by utterly banal script and dialogue, with extremely mediocre actors; with the complete inconsistency of characters, any interest in their eventual fate means less; precisely because of this, mind you, the undoubted protagonist becomes Bava's enjoyment in feeding the figurative flames to the visionary limit... or even trying to abolish the distinguishing features of things, through the constant use of out-of-focus shots, in view of their total disappearance. Which in fact happens, in the most stylistically exact moment in the whole film, when a sequence closes on the bodies of the sleeping survivors piled up on the floor of a room, and immediately after we see the same room, completely empty, sanitized, clean, showing itself to the eyes of the rescuers.
>
> (Cappabianca 1970: 194)

This stands at the opposite pole to the *Monthly Film Bulletin* review of *Ercole al centro della terra* that initially seemed to be praising Bava's colourful effects only to dismiss them as a non-style. Here, ostensible negatives – banal script, mediocre actors – are turned into positives because they clear the way for Bava to find 'solutions at the limits of virtuosity' (ibid.: 195). This kind of iconoclastic formalism – bad taste as visionary cinema – requires an auteur figure, an assumed aesthetic strategy that sounds a lot like the 'self-sabotage' that features in later readings of the film. If ever a Bava film was nothing but style, it is *5 bambole per la luna d'agosto,* but some critical ingenuity (and presumed authority) is needed for any case to be made for it as *good* style – 'style beyond narration, then, beyond characters, absolutely beyond kitsch and in spite of the kitsch. On the opposite bank to the innovators, at a pre-intellectual level (but isn't art *technè*?), Bava also makes cinema-cinema' (ibid.: 195). 'One of the most enduring notions (of auteurism)', writes Paolo Noto, 'is that the auteur plays the role of a genius against the system; that is, an artist able to unhinge... the narrative and representative conventions imposed by the cultural industry' (2016: 212). The 'Bava' implicit in Cappabianca's review is a kind of anti-artisan, unmaking the craft of storytelling and cinematic construction (the excessive use of zooms and focus), having already established his mastery of it in his earlier films. *Filmcritica* was one of the more receptive Italian film journals to genre cinema (ibid.: 213). An earlier review of *Diabolik* had been ambivalent (Mancini 1968, reproduced in Altariva 2008: 115), but Bava was now finding a similar receptiveness from some younger critics.

Diabolik received more press attention in Italy than most Bava films. It was a Dino De Laurentiis production which would bring on board some distinguished collaborators, most notably costume designer Piero Gherardi, who was uncredited on the film but whose involvement had been well publicized. Moreover, it was a high-profile project, promoted as an event, with a larger budget than Bava was accustomed to. *Diabolik*, created by Angela Giussani in 1962 and written with her sister Luciana, revolutionized Italian comics and spawned the *filone* of the so-called *fumetti neri*. By the time the film was made, the comic was something of a phenomenon – *Corriere d'informazione* felt that a different director, 'one of fantasy and humour', was needed for such a project, objecting that Bava was 'only a technician' (Anon. 1968c: 11). An earlier attempt had been made by producer Tonino Cervi and director Seth Holt to bring the character to the screen, a troubled production that was shut down and started again from scratch by De Laurentiis. Alain Delon had been (rather optimistically) linked with the role, but Jean Sorel had begun playing it in the Cervi-Holt version, with Elsa Martinelli as his partner Eva Kant. Bava began shooting with Catherine Deneuve in the Eva role, before replacing her with Marisa Mell. *Nazione sera* claimed that Mell would wear '14 of the craziest and most colourful outfits ever seen' (1967, reproduced in Altariva 2008: 55), emphasizing Gherardi's involvement. This was not the kind of coverage something like *Operazione paura* could expect. Bava was interviewed about the film's (rather superficial) countercultural take on the character – blowing up the tax office and undermining the government. To an extent, he played along, suggesting that Diabolik should be called 'Protestik'. But finally, Bava could not help himself – 'all cinema is made for infantile brains', he told Lietta Tornabuoni in *L'europeo* (1967: 73). In turn, this was how Tornabuoni characterized Bava – 'No one despises the cinema like this gentleman of around fifty years, tall, suntanned, witty, with a large Roman nose and a beautiful basset hound' (ibid.). This might not have been the publicity De Laurentiis was hoping for – his director announcing that he would rather be making horror films and that in any case the cinema was for idiots. The film's reviews were as mixed as one might expect of a slice of *cinema d'evasione* (escapist cinema) adapted from a comic book, but even some of the film's detractors felt it held its own against the James Bond films. While Luigi Cavicchioli in *Domenica del Corriere* would only grudgingly concede that it was 'no better and no worse' (1968, reproduced in Altariva 2008: 88), Leo Pestelli in *La stampa* was willing to go further in declaring it 'more dynamic' than 007 (1968: 8). Tullio Kezich acknowledged Bava's input as a 'specialist' who 'manoeuvres well between subterranean caverns with cybernetic equipment and a black jaguar followed by helicopters' but could not overcome the 'intrinsic poverty' of the material, its comic book source a 'champion of cultural underdevelopment' (1983 [originally 1968]: 188).

Several reviews of *Diabolik* returned to the subject of those 'crazy' critics across the alps who thought Bava a genius. According to *Film mese*'s reviewer, French critics placed him alongside Terence Fisher, Roger Corman and John Gilling as 'un maestro del cinema d'evasione' (F.M. 1968: 9).

Tommaso Chiaretti, reviewing the film in *Noi donne* magazine, referred to his reputation amongst 'foreign intellectuals, the French for example' (1968, reproduced in Altariva 2008: 111), likening the Bava cult to the surrealists' idolizing of Fantômas. But Chiaretti was unconvinced by the cultural elevation of Bava or *Diabolik* – 'we are in a world of explicit infantile fantasies', he grumbled, unimpressed by the director's 'lack of cultural inhibitions and bad taste'. Above all, he lacked 'impegno' (commitment), 'an element not to undervalue', and here is one of the differences between certain forms of Italian and French criticism. While there is a danger of generalizing here, it is the difference between a criticism marked by cinephilia and sheer aesthetic pleasure, and a criticism (shaped particularly by neorealism) that emphasized *impegno* and was often suspicious of formalism and aestheticism, let alone *cinema d'evasione*. The title of Franco Valobra's review in *Men* magazine, 'Mario Bava è meglio di *Diabolik*' (Mario Bava is better than Diabolik), suggests a more sympathetic evaluation but is more indicative of how little he thought of the film. Valobra was as dismissive of the director's presumed French reputation as Chiaretti but acknowledged that he possessed 'a high level of technical skill, a sense of irony, of taste' (1968, reproduced in Altariva 2008: 113). Ultimately, however, he credited Bava with not taking himself too seriously, knowing 'to make a film called *Diabolik* and not (for his and our luck) The Divine Comedy' (ibid.) – in other words, knowing his place.

Tullio Kezich would make one of the more exaggerated claims about Bava's reputation across the alps in a review of *Il rosso segno della follia* in *Panorama* – 'in France certain critics put him on the same level as Fellini, and call him the great Bava' (1970, quoted by Acerbo and Pisoni 2007a: 284). But Kezich was more sympathetic to Bava than some other Italian critics, and even liked the film for its 'figurative quality and the elegance of certain almost surrealist solutions' and Laura Betti's 'calculated' performance, even if he found the material derivative and over-familiar. And rather than cast French critics as simply misguided in the enthusiasm he had exaggerated, he pondered why Bava had been so coolly received at home, limited to 'marginal success'. His answer was a familiar one, based on the foreignness of fantasy to Italy – 'the indigenous tradition, figurative and literary, doesn't have an equivalent to Bosch or E.A. Poe; in Italy our monsters are imported goods like the *giallo* or Science Fiction' (ibid.). Or the Western, one might add, which did not seem to have needed an indigenous tradition in order to succeed in Italy, even if Sergio Leone had to initially pose as 'Bob Robertson' in film credits. As we shall see, Bava's French reputation was rather less secure than Italian critics made it sound, but the idea of a French Bava cult seemed to be a pretext for re-considering Bava as a filmmaker, not always as kindly as Kezich did. Nevertheless, the notion of Bava as a 'maestro' of some sort was starting to appear here and there. A (positive) review of *5 bambole per la luna d'agosto* in *Cinema d'oggi* referred to Bava as a 'master of the horror film', returning after 'an absence, very long for fans of the genre' (Anon. 1970: 10). No nationality was attributed to these horror fans, and while the film's box office fortunes did nothing to suggest that Bava was catching on with Italian audiences – Argento's arrival was imminent – it was no longer assumed that they were solely foreign eccentrics. The previous year saw the first issue of Italy's first horror film magazine, *Horror,* which included an interview with Bava. A specifically *Italian* Bava cult would grow over the next three decades, via magazines such as *Amarcord* and *Nocturno,* and the TV series *Stracult* (Rai 2, 2000–) inspired by Marco Giusti's 1999 book *Stracult: Dizionario dei film italiani stracult* which re-framed much of Serie B cinema as a cult cinema to be re-evaluated. Specialist DVD labels such as Raro and Nocturno's CineKult series would follow.

Barbara Steele at the Midi-Minuit: Bava and the 'crazy French'

One frustrating question remains to be asked: Who directed the admirable *Masque du Démon?*
    Michel Caen, reviewing *Ercole al centro della terra* (1962: 62)

French film criticism of the late 1950s/early 1960s gained a reputation for valorizing, if not the indefensible then at least that which was predominantly seen by some to be trivial, insubstantial, merely entertaining at best – for failing to distinguish between the low and the high. As a broad critical shift, auteurism would be the lasting monument to this critical tradition, but certain critical choices remained contentious – the French enthusiasm for Jerry Lewis was a source of amusement for American critics for years. There was also an earlier surrealist tradition of being attracted to 'low' genres, such as the Fantômas novels (Walz 2000), traces of which could be found in some of *Positif's* critics like Ado Kyrou. If Italy's Serie B directors were more highly regarded in France than they were at home, the same was largely true also of Terence Fisher, Roger Corman and others who worked in low brow genres – *Midi-Minuit Fantastique* even took William Castle seriously. At the same time, for those invested in rehabilitating horror and fantasy cinema, French critics could be cast as validating pioneers – who else would have devoted the first issue of a serious film journal to Terence Fisher in the early 1960s? Thus, the French Bava cult that Italian critics were increasingly mystified, amused, annoyed or intrigued by rang true – well, they *would* adore him, wouldn't they? Bava even perpetuated this view of the over-serious, over-analytical French himself, claiming to have been quizzed by *Cahiers du Cinéma* about the ending of 6 *donne per l'assassino,* which he claimed not to be able to remember (quoted by Pezzotta 2013: 8). In fact, *Cahiers* never interviewed

Bava – there was little sustained interest in him at the journal after his debut – and as Curti (2019: 112) suggests, this was perhaps more an instance of Bava choosing to play the role of the uncultured artisan.[5] If the story was fictitious (he might just have got *Cahiers* confused with *Positif*), it would also betray that he actually did remember his own films quite well. Certain French critics were receptive, if not always to Bava himself, then certainly to the kind of cinema that Bava made – let us again call it Bava-Freda-Cottafavi – and one Bava film in particular did find a rapturous critical reception. Overall, however, he was less idolized than one might expect.

Rolando Caputo paints a seductive, if 'embellished', picture of a particular kind of movie house in Paris and the cinephilia that flourished there:

> Imagine a movie theatre in the Paris of the early 1960s, perhaps located towards the periphery, or alternately in the district of Pigalle. No matter, what is important is that it be a second-run movie house, somewhat tawdry, with a small seating capacity and almost never full. It shows less than quality prints... At some point it's quite likely to screen a series of Hercules spectaculars... A Sunday matinee might possibly be a double-bill consisting of the titles *Le Corps et le Fouet* [*La frusta e il corpo*] and *Les Trois Visages de la Peur* [*I tre volti della paura*]. What is certain is that critics of different persuasions will encounter one another here and argue the respective merits of their favoured filmmaker.
>
> (1997: 56)

La maschera del demonio arrived in Paris in March 1961, screening at three cinemas – the Saint-Michel, the Scarlett and the cinema that has become perhaps most closely associated with French enthusiasm for *fantastique* cinema, sufficiently so to lend its name to the first French film journal devoted to the genre, the Midi-Minuit (1939–85). Bava's film had a relatively short stay at the Midi-Minuit, from 29 March to 11 April, when it was replaced by *Les mains d'Orlac/The Hands of Orlac* (1960). It arrived one year too early for the film journal that seemed made for Bava, *Midi-Minuit Fantastique,* but was greeted with great enthusiasm by the surrealist-inclined *Positif,* who placed Barbara Steele on the front cover, and, perhaps more surprisingly, *Cahiers du Cinéma.*[6] It may be that these two reviews alone informed the Italian perception of Bava's reputation in France. Both reviews were spread over five pages (*Cahiers* reviewed it alongside *The Time Machine,* but Bava's film was discussed at far greater length). Jean Paul-Torok spent part of his review imagining a hypothetical attempt to get to grips with the sort of film that confounded critical judgement – 'Magnify the irrational, the eroticism. One will deplore the rejection of the horror film in France. End by claiming that *La Masque du Démon... is* the true cinema' (1961: 25). The limitation of this approach, he argued – not 'condemnable' in itself – was of 'making people who don't take this sort of thing seriously shrug their shoulders' (ibid.). But his conclusion suggested that the most appropriate way to respond to the film was simply to fall under its spell:

> When aesthetic admiration is absolutely fused with desire and terror, it is impossible to account for. Where are your vaunted intelligence and your cultivated taste when everything in you freezes and is fascinated before revelations of utmost horror? Beneath the flowing robes of this young woman with so beautiful a countenance there appear clearly the tatters of a skeleton. Is she any less desirable? Before these metamorphoses of the vampire, in this double postulation of desire and fear, who are the monsters? It is in us that the demon is masked.
>
> (ibid.: 28)

'Bava has the soul of a painter', wrote Fereydoun Hoveyda in *Cahiers du Cinéma*, 'Bava's film is the pictorial poetry of the irrational communicated by virtue of the mise-en-scène' (1961: 56). If anything, Hoveyda made greater claims for Bava himself than Torok – 'Mario Bava finally proves to us that fear does not exclude beauty' (ibid.: 54) and 'has given the fantastic back to the cinema' (ibid.: 55). Not until *Diabolik* did *Cahiers* praise Bava unequivocally again, Jean Naboni enjoying his 'peremptory, naïve and cynical poetry' (1968: 73). Luc Moullet, later a Bava admirer, reviewed *La ragazza che sapeva troppo* over two pages – subsequent Bava reviews tended to be brief and sometimes anonymous – but with less enthusiasm than he would later show for the director, opening by suggesting that Bava's historical-mythological films had dispelled the hopes raised by *La maschera del demonio,* consigning him to being seen as 'a skilled director of photography, but incompetent in every other area' (1964: 73). *La ragazza,* he claimed, was 'a conventional parody that never rises to the level of critique' (ibid.: 74). Harsher words would follow – the anonymous reviewer of *6 donne per l'assassino* jeered that Bava's mask had fallen and that his new film showed 'six poor *ragazze* who don't know where to find an author' (Anon. 1965c: 90).

By the time *Midi-Minuit Fantastique* appeared, there was probably some uncertainty about which films could be attributed to Bava in the meantime – the confusing credits on the Italian versions of *Ester e il re* and *Le meraviglie di Aladino* also appeared on their French releases and both films would have disappointed anyone expecting more of what *La maschera* had delivered. But there was less doubt over *Ercole al centro della terra* being a Bava film, reviewed by editor Michel Caen in the first issue. 'Even after *Les Mille et Une Nuits* [*Le meraviglie di Aladino*], we still felt there was hope for Mario Bava', he wrote (1962: 62). 'Alas, his latest vampires, and there are plenty of them – in the Italian cinema, vampires are always plural – are enough to discourage the true fans who have been schooled in the works of Browning,

Lambert Hillyer, Terence Fisher... and Mario Bava!' Danny Peary, in his review of *Black Sunday* in *Cult Movies* nearly twenty years later, wondered 'if there were really two Mario Bavas' to explain why he never made another film anywhere near as good (1981: 35), and Caen seemed to be asking a similar question when he concluded by wondering who had directed Bava's debut. Looking at the magazine's choices of cover, one might suspect that Caen and others had retrospectively concluded that their enthusiasm for Bava's debut was less for its director than its star. Barbara Steele was the only person to appear on the cover more than once – issues 10–11 and 17, which also included an extensive picture gallery of her, one of the photos showing her reading the magazine. She was also interviewed by Caen in issue 12. Unlike Freda, Corman and particularly Fisher (who was interviewed more than once), Bava was never interviewed by *Midi-Minuit Fantastique*. *Positif* was the first French film journal to interview him in 1972, one of his more upbeat interviews. His name never appeared on the cover of *MMF*, although issue 13 (November 1965) featured a publicity still of Evi Marandi from *Terrore nello spazio*. The first *MMF* writer to praise Bava was an Italian, Goffredo Fofi, in his critical overview of Italian horror in the seventh issue (September 1963). But in the following issue, normal service resumed as Bernard Eisenschitz looked at Bava's three most recent films, opening by suggesting that the follow-ups to *La maschera del demonio* had made it look increasingly like a 'lucky accident' and were 'hard blows to a reputation as "a very great talent" bestowed too quickly on just one work' (1964: 62). He found *I tre volti della paura* derivative of Corman but was more enthusiastic about at least the first half hour of *La frusta e il corpo*, 'without doubt Bava's best work' and deserving of 'a place in an anthology of sadistic-erotic cinema' (ibid.). In the next issue, Jérôme Caulandre would re-evaluate one of the films dismissed by Eisenschitz, *La ragazza che sapeva troppo,* producing an eccentric Freudian reading of the film as being about 'the loss of a young woman's virginity' (1964: 119). But it was the Sadean and the erotic that brought Bava back into critical approval. *Cahiers'* anonymous critic had loathed *6 donne per l'assassino,* but the title of Alain Doremieux's review called it 'Un Rêve Fou' – a crazy dream. Surrealism, De Quincey's 'Murder Considered as One of the Fine Arts', Buñuel and Dali's *L'age d'Or* and the 'elegance' of Vincente Minnelli were the reference points in a review that declared that 'this film – the latest by Mario Bava shown in Paris – takes up residence in the fourth dimension of black poetry and neurotic dreams' (Doremieux 1965: 57). He concluded, 'Arranged by Bava with the unrestrained baroquism which doesn't exclude a rigor and strictly architectural coherence, it becomes this marvellous sabbath, this black mass, this diabolical ceremony that is *Six Femmes Pour L'Assassin*' (ibid.: 58). *MMF*'s readers were clearly equally enthusiastic – in the 1964 Readers Poll that appeared in issue 13 (November 1965), Bava's film came in sixth place, two places ahead of Freda's *Lo spettro*. Bava was about to enter a more uneven and uncertain period, and would not feature in the magazine again until *Diabolik*, but the coverage was sparse – a production still in issue 17 (where it was named *Diabolik contre L'inspecteur Ginko*) and given two stars ('interesting, curious') in issue 21 (April 1970) without a review – one more than its sister film *Barbarella* ('mediocre'), one less than *Dracula Has Risen From the Grave*.

In 1984, Pascal Martinet published the first full-length monograph on Bava, in a series that included volumes on Jean-Pierre Melville, Josef von Sternberg, Billy Wilder, Ingmar Bergman and – closer to Bava in spirit – Roger Corman. Martinet's book was a serious-minded auteurist account of Bava's films that seemed to confirm France as the natural home for his critical validation. In the same year, however, Stefano Della Casa and Carlo Piazza published *Il Cinema Secondo Mario Bava*, a less professional-looking publication with the look of a photocopied fanzine but equally serious in approach – it included essays by Teo Mora and Mario Giusti. The gulf between the two countries' perception of Bava had narrowed in the intervening years and his re-evaluation was more widespread.

'Smashing Balderdash': Bava's UK reception

This might be described as the triumph of mind over matter, or of Bava over a shoe-string budget and appalling dubbed dialogue.
Monthly Film Bulletin review of *Terrore nello spazio*
(Anon. 1968b: 204)

In 1967, UK distributor Miracle Films issued a press release ahead of the release of *Curse of the Dead*, the UK title of *Operazione paura*, with the headline 'Complete, Uncut version of Mario Bava's new Horror film to be seen in England'. Bava was described as 'the Italian director who shot to fame when his outstanding horror film "Black Sunday" ran into censorship troubles' (Harris 1967). The press release thus used two points of appeal – an uncensored film by a much-censored filmmaker and a horror auteur with a growing critical reputation in the UK:

Over the past few years Bava has built for himself a reputation that ranks with that of the truly great horror directors of all time, Tod Browning, James Whale, Terence Fisher and Roger Corman. His films have achieved extremely good reviews, not only in specialist 'Horror' magazines, but in some of the national newspapers and magazines such as 'Films and Filming' and 'The Monthly Film Bulletin'.

(ibid.)

This was PR, of course, that slightly inflated his critical reception (even the positive reviews usually had some caveats), but it is certainly true that both magazines cited had paid close attention to Bava and regarded him as a filmmaker to watch. *Operazione paura* would get some of Bava's best English-language reviews, as if to prove the distributor right. 'Narrative has never been Bava's strong point', conceded Tom Milne in British Film Institute periodical *Monthly Film Bulletin*, 'but with *Operazione Paura* he has happily found a story in which atmosphere is everything, and the result is even more splendid visually than *Sei Donne per l'Assassino* (the colour is exquisite throughout)', producing a 'cross between *La Belle et la Bête* and *The Turn of the Screw* as one imagines Franju might imagine it' (1967: 104–5). Miracle Films' press release was shrewdly pitched, clearly aware of interest in Bava amongst both horror fans – eager to see the as-yet unreleased *Black Sunday,* which would finally appear (cut) the following year – and cinephiles perhaps already keeping an eye out for his other films. *Operazione paura* has never achieved the classic status of *La maschera del demonio* – perhaps because it lacks the shock value of the earlier film (there was little for the censor to cut) but also because it was harder to see – but it has long been a favourite amongst Bava's admirers, with Teo Mora declaring it his masterpiece (1978: 178) and critics like Milne being able to cite Cocteau and Franju (a few years later, he might have added Fellini).

The initial banning of *Black Sunday* probably played an important role in the UK Bava cult. Stills from the film appeared in horror magazines and books about the horror genre. Although *Monthly Film Bulletin* was not able to review the film until 1968 (a largely positive piece by Tom Milne), Bava's name figured prominently in their reviews of his other films, even if he was not always being praised. The anonymous review of *Ercole al centro della terra* was unmoved by its 'limited box of tricks', but *Gli invasori* was found to be 'savagely effective in its gothic way and enhanced by Mario Bava's luridly filtered photography and fluid camera technique, and his effortlessly eclectic direction (Lang, Fuller maybe – certainly Kurosawa in Gunnar's arrow-transfixed death à la Mifune-Macbeth' (Anon. 1963b: 86).[7] Peter John Dyer reviewed *La frusta e il corpo* (heavily cut as *Night is the Phantom,* an English title only marginally less nonsensical than the US *What!*) twice – under his own name in the trade magazine *The Daily Cinema* and then anonymously for *Monthly Film Bulletin.* The *MFB* review gives the impression of being forced under torture to admit to liking it – 'slow, repetitive, verging on parody. Censor or distributor cuts have rendered much of the plot incomprehensible, though one doubts it ever made much sense… And yet it grows on one in retrospect' (Anon. 1965a: 40). Trade papers allowed more space for critics, if they chose, to assess a film on its own terms – as well as its commercial prospects – and his earlier review was more enthusiastic. 'Commendably compulsive – if a shade arty – box-office attraction' was his judgement, with Daliah Lavi 'outstanding' in the lead, 'magnificent' sets and locations, and 'an ace director of the genre' (Dyer 1965: 5). Dyer's most-quoted comment about a Bava film was in characterising 6 *donne per l'assassino* as ushering in 'a new era in Italian film-making – the Red Telephone era' (1966: 18). But this was another of those curious reviews that, to an invested reader, somehow dismissed the film while making it sound marvellous – Bava's 'most expensive-looking and decorative horror film to date' was 'a very good (i.e. characteristic) example of Bava's work' but 'a less good example of the murder thriller genre' (ibid.). Bava's virtuosity with the mobile camera fell on fallow ground, his camera 'tracking and panning through the vast, deserted fashion-house long after every ounce of suspense has been sucked out of the situation' (ibid.). Here was a film critic protesting a bit too much, if ever there was one.

If Dyer often managed to turn what sounded like praise into dismissal, fuelling a suspicion that he liked the films more than he was willing to say,[8] for Milne the Bava cup was usually at least half full. While 5 *bambole per la luna d'agosto* was 'by no means Bava at his best', Bava's camerawork made the film 'a pleasure to watch even when the plot flags and the zooms proliferate' (1972: 157). Only *Ecologia del delitto* (released belatedly as *Bloodbath* and cut by 14 minutes so that it was more of a blood-trickle) seemed to exhaust his patience. He judged it 'mechanical in the extreme', clearly preferring the more poetic side of Bava to gruesome body counts being 'gloatingly' observed (1980: 88). But overall, the critical view of Bava in *Monthly Film Bulletin* was the most common one in early English-language accounts – a filmmaker capable of brilliance who nevertheless 'always seemed to be promising more than he delivered' (Strick 1986a: 17). In 1991, *Monthly Film Bulletin* merged with *Sight and Sound,* a magazine that would once have had no room for the likes of Bava and was initially resistant to French auteurism, but which became more diverse in coverage and critical opinion. Before its relocation, *MFB* ran a three-part overview of Italian 'exploitation' cinema by Kim Newman in 1986, while Tom Milne and Philip Strick looked at Bava and Cottafavi films that were either coming out on video or available as 16mm prints. Strick again confirmed the unevenness of Bava's work but acknowledged that his working conditions should not be discounted in any critical evaluation – some of his best sequences the result of 'triumphant ingenuity in the face of remarkable odds' (1986b: 59). Some of these sequences even survived deteriorating prints, like this one from *Terrore nello spazio*:

> Quite one of the finer moments in baroque cinema (even in a standard-ratio 16mm print turning gently pink with age) begins with the toppling grave markers, three sculpted splinters capsizing in a sea of mist from which emerge the resurrected astronauts tearing at their amniotic plastic shrouds.
>
> (ibid.)

Newman, a younger critic and novelist more heavily invested in the horror genre and cult cinema, would provide less qualified praise in a review of a 16mm print of *Black Sabbath*, calling *I wurdalak*, in particular, 'a little masterpiece' (1986b: 24) – the film's flaws were solely those that AIP had contributed to *Il telefono*. A generational shift was taking place in the perception of Bava, even if it was not necessarily a dramatic one in the UK. For critics like Milne and Strick, Bava was an interesting and sometimes brilliant filmmaker, but there were better ones of his kind. For Newman and others, he was a founding figure and genre master – his promotion from cameraman to director the point at which Italy 'developed a really distinctive horror genre of its own' (Newman 1986a: 22).[9]

Movie, the auteurist antagonist to *Sight and Sound,* expressed some admiration for Cottafavi, but Bava never seemed to cross their radar. However, he would be a presence in one of the most interesting British film magazines during the 1960s and 1970s. While not obliged to review all his films, *Films and Filming* was receptive to the cinema of Bava-Freda-Cottafavi and 'Continental' genre cinema more generally. The magazine was launched with a dual aim, one of which would likely have been more evident to some readers than others, especially as it had to initially hide in plain sight – to produce a film magazine that was intelligent but less stuffy than *Sight and Sound's* original incarnation but also to deliberately target a queer male readership through a judicious choice of film stills and covers, as well as adverts, personal contact ads and, increasingly, focusing on matters of representation in reviews (Giori 2009; Bengry 2011). More diverse in its coverage and critical perspectives than *Sight and Sound,* one of its most distinctive and iconoclastic contributors was Raymond Durgnat, who had written about *Black Sunday* long before its UK release in a special issue of *Motion* called *Companion to Violence and Sadism in the Cinema* which featured Barbara Steele's hole-studded face on the front cover. 'There is no real horror without beauty, as Keats would have said if he could have beheld *Black Sunday*', he wrote (quoted by Miller 2014). If this is reminiscent of the French take on Bava, Durgnat was also a contributor to *Midi-Minuit Fantastique* and *Positif.* Like other Bava admirers, Durgnat found him maddeningly inconsistent – 'his films, like Corman's, zigzag from fascinating to awful, for much the same reasons' (1997 [originally 1965]: 54). Reviewing *Evil Eye,* he wrote:

> Mario Bava, like Roger Corman, is an intelligent director who's often betrayed by his subjects. Too often… he seems ready to take on only slightly rehashed clichés and try to "do something with them" by little variations of style when he would do far better to tear up his scripts and have them re-written by a first-class writer into something that will aid and abet his fertile visual gifts rather than bog them down.
>
> (ibid.)

This is not the most realistic view of Bava's working context – where was he going to find a 'first-class writer' in Serie B cinema, which generally had much better directors than writers, even if such a luxury was available to him? Corman at his best could draw on accomplished genre practitioners like Richard Matheson, Charles Beaumont and Ray Russell to write scripts. And 'doing something with' rehashed clichés arguably accounts for a good deal of Bava's output, perhaps even most of it. But Durgnat was ultimately on Bava's side – 'if Bava needs a really good scriptwriter, he certainly deserves one' (ibid.), he concluded. Dave Hutchinson expressed a similar view in his review of *Diabolik* – 'One wonders what heights Bava would reach with a story equal to his imagination' (1969: 45). *La frusta e il corpo* was, unsurprisingly, more to Durgnat's taste – a couple of years earlier, it would surely have been a candidate for his *Companion to Violence and Sadism in the Cinema*:

> The film's qualities survive censorship, and will encourage those, who since *Black Sunday* (still completely banned in this country) and *Hercules at the Centre of the Earth*, have seen Bava as a director of Corman's class.
>
> (1997 [originally 1965]: 54)

Durgnat paid particular attention to form and style in Bava's film, and was amongst the few, along with Spinazzola, to appreciate his use of colour – 'Several complex long shots are "composed" in terms, not only of space-and-form, but of colour-areas created by different-colour spotlights, a first use, to my knowledge, of "colour cubism" which has considerable possibilities' (ibid.).

An interesting review of *Shock* by Eric Brown in *Films and Filming* placed the film in the context of both its UK double-bill with the Spanish *La novia ensangretada/The Blood Spattered Bride* (1972), a film Brown found so ridiculous that he reviewed it in the form of a comic poem, and S.S. Prawer's book *Caligari's Children* (1980), which he had recently discussed on Radio 4 programme *Kaleidoscope* – 'the cumulative shock effects of the Bava film go as far as is legitimately possible, to effect catharsis (some might think, indeed, a little beyond)' (1980: 34). In the year of Bava's death, his final theatrical film would also be well reviewed in *Monthly Film Bulletin,* even if it was a relatively subdued cinematic swansong.

By way of contrast, it is worth considering how Bava films were reviewed in the UK trade press, less invested in evaluating directorial reputations and geared more towards a film's commercial prospects. They remind us of the ostensible ephemerality of the films, part of a veritable tidal wave of dubbed Italian genre films arriving in British cinemas – peplums, horror films, thrillers, Science Fiction, Mondo-sexy *di notte* documentaries. If there were horror fans waiting to see *Revenge of the Vampire* (as it was eventually re-named), this was of little concern to the reviewer of *Kine Weekly* – 'Preposterous claptrap, but quite well done and spooky enough to please unsophisticated customers' (Anon. 1968a: 152). As with Dyer and Milne in *Monthly Film Bulletin,* there was a certain amount of consistency in the reviewers of Bava's films in *The Daily Cinema* – Margaret Hinxman (later of the *Daily Mail*) initially and then Marjorie Bilbow, a witty and particularly astute critic of the kinds of popular cinema that 'quality' critics often saw as being beneath them. And yet neither seemed to particularly register Bava as an organizing presence across the different films they reviewed, even when Bilbow attributed the success of *Revenge of the Vampire* to the (unnamed) director:

> Competently acted, but it is the director's skill at building up suspense which lifts the film out of the rut. Unexpectedly, he offers a passage of rare and terrifying beauty when the ghostly coach with its vampire driver races noiselessly through the forest.
>
> (Bilbow 1968a: 14)

Bilbow reviewed three Bava films in 1968 without registering them as being by the same director. 'Smashing balderdash' was her view of *Terrore nello spazio* (Bilbow 1968a: 8), while she judged *Diabolik* '(a)cceptable fare for the undemanding' (1968c: 5) with no indication that she had admired an earlier film by the same director. Her review of *Il rosso segno della follia* in *CinemaTV Today* summed it up as a 'good-for-a-giggle shocker that should prove popular with uncritical adults' (1973: 20) – like Robin Wood, she was more impressed by its double-bill partner, *The Creeping Flesh*. 'Good-for-a-giggle' seemed to be her view of most of the Bava films she reviewed, in an often-infectious style best represented by her review of *Terrore nello spazio*:

> deliriously inconsistent and lavishly bedecked with complicated machinery, simple horrors, and fiendishly clever-sounding technical jargon. Cheerfully naïve pseudo-science providing thrills for the uncritical while stimulating tolerant hilarity in the more sophisticated… Most of the time it is barely possible to distinguish between the identically dressed characters who take part and even less possible to work out whether they are coming or going, living or dead (or both). But who cares? It's fun.
>
> (Bilbow 1968a: 8)

Apart from the rather condescending distinction between the 'uncritical' and the 'sophisticated' viewer, there is not much to object to here – this is as legitimate a way of responding to the film as the cinephile appreciation of Bava fashioning cinematic gold from plastic rocks and dry ice. Bava's films have probably prompted as many giggles as admiring gasps over the years, and Bilbow's review captures the different ways in which the Italian Serie B tidal wave registered on UK screens. 'The Italians are great ones for making mock British-type thrillers', wrote Hinxman in her review of *Evil Eye*, released on a double-bill with AIP's *Comedy of Terrors* (1963), 'and, here, a contingent of six script-writers have stirred up a lively imitation of "Agatha Christie"' (Hinxman 1965: 5). She found the film '(r)ather jaunty' and *Ercole al centro della terra* '(l)usty and colourful action-hokum' (1962: 10). But while both critics were often amused by the storylines and acting, they were often taken with the films' production values. 'Visually, the film's a knock-out', wrote Hinxman of *6 donne per l'assassino*, 'Dramatically, it's a let-down' (1966: 5). Her enjoyment of the film's luxurious settings is palpable – 'everyone lives in huge, period apartments, stacked with bizarre knick-knackery' (ibid.), while Bilbow enjoyed the look of *5 bambole per la luna d'agosto*, even though she could barely follow, or much care about, its narrative:

> Visually speaking, this is quite something. The no-expense-spared interiors simply ooze with an atmosphere of opulent vulgarity and decadence, and the cast have the glossy good looks of the well fed.
>
> (Bilbow 1971: 12)[10]

This anticipates certain aspects of the contemporary cultification of the *giallo all'italiana* that stresses their retro-kitsch pleasures and capturing of contemporaneous fashions and interior designs. What is interesting about Bilbow's reviews is the way that genre and cinephile seriousness give way to the material luxury and pulp preposterousness of the films. 'Smashing balderdash' was essentially what the bulk of *filone* cinema was aiming for, until more political concerns found their way into certain Westerns and *polizieschi*.

'A spine-chilling "gasser"': Bava at the grindhouse

In 1968, one day before Halloween, *Variety* reviewed *Operazione paura* under its US title, *Kill, Baby… Kill!* Distributed by Europix Consolidated, it had in fact been circulating in the United States for two years but was now being reviewed 'for the record' as 2nd feature on a double-bill at a 42nd Street grindhouse. However, the unusually effusive tone of the review suggests that there was more motivating the reviewer than dutifully ticking off the film:

> (The) film demonstrates once again, as some European critics think, that in director Mario Bava lies one of Italy's most important film talents though he specializes in genre product. 'Kill Baby Kill' is a small masterpiece of its kind, comparing favourably with the late Val Lewton horror programmers of the '40s.
>
> (Byro 1968: n.p.)

As in the UK the year before, *Operazione paura* provided the opportunity to single out Bava as a filmmaker of note. The tone is unusual because, as in the UK, Bava's films had not generally been approached as 'Mario Bava films' by the trade press, even though *Black Sunday* had been something of a sensation. 'This is the way they used to be made, during the great period of motion picture horror films', *The Hollywood Reporter* enthused of Bava's debut (Powers 1961: 3), while *The Motion Picture Herald* and *Film Daily*, whose reviewer attended a screening where the audience reportedly 'shrieked with abandonment' (H.M. 1961: 8), both reviewed the film enthusiastically. *Variety* generally inclined towards the tongue-in-cheek in their reviews of Italian horror films, including *Black Sunday* – 'After painstakingly vamping 'til ready for the prize transformation, Miss Vampira succumbs to that age-old occupational hazard of the plasma-gulping profession – crucifixion' (Tube 1961: n.p.). The reviewer wondered if Steele always knew whether she was playing Asa or Katia, and while mood, atmosphere and Bava's photography were praised, the film was summed up as an 'Italo shock package, long on production, short on scriptwork' (ibid.). *Variety* thought that *La frusta e il corpo* was likely to provoke 'more laughs than gasps' (Hogg 1965: n.p), whlle *6 donne per l'assassino* was merely 'Okay', but 'backgrounded by expensive sets which add a certain quality not always distinguishable in films of this sort' (Whit 1965: n.p.). Production values were often a source of praise, even in otherwise indifferent or dismissive reviews. *The Hollywood Reporter* could not make much sense out of *6 donne per l'assassino* overall but noted its 'beautiful photography in Technicolor' and thought that the 'beauty of the Roman settings, lushly lit and photographed, also makes the perverseness more real' (Powers 1965: 3). Their foreignness was mainly registered in the dubbing, often a source of amusement, but there were other ways in which cultural difference might be felt. Franco and Ciccio made the biggest impression on *Variety*'s reviewer in *Dr Goldfoot and the Girl Bombs,* but not in a positive way – 'Two Italian comedians, supposedly very popular in their own country, are the film's greatest drawback' (Murf 1966: n.p.). If the review of *Operazione paura* suggested a heightened interest in Bava, this had not been evident in *Variety*'s review of *Diabolik,* a more high-profile project in Italy, a few months earlier – 'Bizarre sets, poor process work, static writing and limp direction spell pure formula for lowercase grind bookings' (Murf 1968: 28). A review of *Ecologia del delitto* at the Sitges Festival in 1971 (under the title *Antefatto*) called it 'Bava's newest blood-and-gore thriller' (Anon. 1971: n.p.) – the name of the director and the kinds of films he was associated with had stuck, even if the film was consigned to being a 'double-bill horror filler'.

Bava would, not too surprisingly, generate more interest in horror film magazines, not least *Castle of Frankenstein,* whose writers included Joe Dante, one of the future gatekeepers of his reputation – in his *Trailers from Hell* video for *Terrore nello spazio,* he attests to the risk to health and life sometimes involved in venturing into 42nd Street grindhouses to catch the latest Bava film. More adult in approach than *Famous Monsters of Filmland*, *Castle of Frankenstein* quickly identified Bava and Italian horror films as something to look out for. Issue 4 included a feature on *Black Sunday*, mainly a lengthy illustrated synopsis, but identifying it as 'one of the best horror thrillers of recent years' – 'It is a pity that we have not seen more Italian and European terror movies in this country, as they have generally been equal to ours' (Anon. 1964: 32). The magazine regularly featured capsule reviews, some of them by Dante. 'Fabulous comic strip sci-fi shows director Mario Bava at his most visually inventive', enthused the anonymous reviewer of *Terrore nello spazio* (probably Dante), 'Bava's swell yet economical visuals make it a fascinating trip' (Anon 1974b: 42) while *Ecologia del delitto* was 'another masterpiece in a career studded with real if obscure achievements' (Anon. 1974a: 46). By the early 1970s, Bava had one acknowledged horror 'classic' to his name – *Black Sunday* would appear in William K. Everson's *Classics of the Horror Film*, an 'ultra-stylish return to black and white' positioned as an antidote to the perceived vulgarity of Hammer's colour gothics (1974: 207).[11] But he also had the allure of the 'obscure' – even *Variety* had had to venture into the grindhouse to belatedly review *Operazione paura*. On the other hand, genre magazines faced with Bava's 1970s output sometimes found them a trickier prospect. A review in *Cinefantastique* thought *Ecologia del delitto* was Bava's 'most complete failure to date' and Bava himself 'a director and expert cinematographer whose work is constantly being maimed by the unreasonably low standards set by his own lousy scripts' (Frentzen 1975: 36). As one might expect, Tim Lucas was more sympathetic to the later *Shock*, but nevertheless characterized Bava's later work as 'spotty' (1979: 20) – few people would do more to re-evaluate that 'spotty' output than Lucas himself, in articles for *Fangoria* and his own magazine *Video Watchdog*, and ultimately his book. Prior to Lucas, arguably the seminal English-language auteurist account of Bava's films was Silver and Ursini's 'Mario Bava: the Illusion of Reality', first published in 1975 and revised and reprinted several times after that. What had sometimes been niggling caveats for previous Bava admirers now became obstacles that 'the expressive power of his directorial style' was more than capable of transcending:

> That one man working against such limitations could become one of the most striking of genre stylists may seem hard to believe. The proof, beyond the often stilted, dubbed performances, creaky sound effects, and tinny music, beyond the panned and scanned, retimed and sometimes reedited videos, is in the images themselves. No matter how feeble the character development may be or how far-fetched the plot, Bava's visual style is the cornerstone of a sensory package that envelops the audience and sends them on a journey into undiscovered country.
>
> (Silver and Ursini 2000: 109)

Ultimately, however, the making of whatever reputation Bava currently has in the United States was cemented by those American film directors who identified Bava as a 'master' of his generic domain – it has become a default in almost any critical case made for the director to cite the approval of Dante, Burton and, above all, Scorsese. In the 2007 Italian language collection *Kill Baby Kill! Il cinema di Mario Bava*, it is the American filmmakers – Corman, Burton, John Landis, Sam Raimi – who generally offer the highest praise. Amongst the Italian filmmakers who comment, Monicelli is indulgently amused by Bava's elevation. Umberto Lenzi, on the other hand, is entirely unwilling to join in with the eulogization of Bava, claiming not to have seen any of the films he is asked about and characterizing Bava's legacy as 'scarce' (Acerbo and Pisoni 2007c: 134). Lenzi was an artisan of *filone* cinema not unlike Bava and a very capable one, but there is more evidence of envy than judgement here. One does not even have to particularly like Bava's films to see that they have found some sort of lasting place, however niche, in film culture.

According to Kenneth Craik, reputations go through three stages – a lifetime reputation, a transitional posthumous reputation comprising the surviving lifetime network and new members attracted by biographical and critical writing, and a purely posthumous reputation stage that consists solely of those who know the person indirectly (2009: 182). Given that cinema is a relatively young medium, few canonical filmmakers have reached that third stage, but in any case, artistic reputations are less reliant on people personally knowing them than, say, political figures. Bava's lifetime reputation was relatively modest but by no means negligible – his posthumous reputation has been more a matter of extending a 'living, dynamic reputation network whose members demonstrate a substantial commitment to speaking, writing, and reading about that person' (ibid.: 182). Bava's reputation network, in its transitional posthumous phase, consists of critics/biographers (Lucas, Pezzotta *et al.*), filmmakers that include surviving peers and contemporary admirers (some of them esteemed), surviving family (Lamberto and Roy), fans and scholars of horror and Italian genre cinema, cinephiles attracted to stylized and obscure films, blu-ray labels specializing in cult cinema, institutions such as the British Film Institute and the French Cinématheque. In Italy, there is even some modest mainstream recognition. This is a considerably smaller reputational network than the likes of Fellini or Hitchcock, and possibly even Argento's. But it is a much more substantial one than that of Cottafavi, once seen as Bava's superior, maybe even deservedly so, but whose reputation networks never seemed to fully take root beyond the French critical cult surrounding him. Reputation networks can be seen to inflate or do insufficient justice to an artist's standing, thus the complaints that someone is either overrated or underrated – both have been said of Bava, although he is still more likely to be seen as an underrated director. As we have seen, other factors play a role in addition to active reputation gatekeepers – the availability of the films, the quality of the transfers or prints of those films. Bava's films have benefitted enormously from the remediation of once hard-to-see films. But at the same time, not all reputation networks themselves enjoy the same power and influence. No one, not even Lamberto Bava, has been more active in growing and maintaining Bava's posthumous reputation than Tim Lucas (although the collective work of magazines like *Nocturno* has been similarly impactful). Pezzotta, his Italian equivalent, has always been more measured in his appreciation of the filmmaker. Lucas has written for a range of publications, including *Sight and Sound,* but his reputation was built primarily through cult-oriented film magazines, most notably his own *Video Watchdog,* much loved and missed by cult cinephiles as well as being the imprint for his Bava book. Meanwhile Sergio Leone – already a better-known and more critically acclaimed Italian genre director in a more respectable genre – has Sir Christopher Frayling, Rector and Professor at the Royal College of Art, as his main English-language reputation gatekeeper. This is not to say that Frayling is 'better' than Lucas, but he clearly occupies a more elevated position in the hierarchy of consecration when establishing that Leone is 'worthy' of the critical attention of an esteemed figure who is an academic with a strong public presence. Lucas's book, by contrast, is the meticulous labour-of-love of the invested cinephile, most likely addressing the converted (but extending their knowledge considerably) in a luxury limited print run of a book that would undoubtedly have been a huge risk (at least in its print form) for a more established publisher. In other words, while making considerable claims for Bava as a filmmaker, it operates entirely in terms of him being a cult, niche filmmaker who will always be appreciated most by a discerning few.

The story of Bava's developing reputation – or reputations – is also the story of the mutation of cinephilia and cult connoisseurship, whether encountering extraordinary but imperfect films in unpromising theatres or late night on TV, or collecting box sets and special editions of films and genres once seen to be disposable. There has been a reciprocal validation in the cult canonization of 'Italian horror' and 'the giallo' and Bava as a founding figure of both. The reason that Bava became the lasting figure out of Bava-Freda-Cottafavi, *i tre volti della Serie B,* is not because he proved over time to be the best of the three filmmakers – although that is both arguable and a matter of individual taste – but because his films, individually and as a directorial canon, were better positioned to be accommodated by these shifts in taste, canon-formation and technological remediation. In 2014, interviewed on the fortieth anniversary of Bava's birth, Pezzotta expressed some irritation that 'cinephile children of a trash-ist ignorance' now knew Bava's films by heart but had never heard of Antonio Pietrangeli or Luigi Comencini (Anon. 2014). Six years later, in an English-language article for *Offscreen,* he imagined himself telling 'Finnish or Texan kids' obsessed with

Bava that they should watch directors more 'important' to the history of Italian cinema, such as Alberto Lattuada, Francesco Rosi and Damiano Damiani (2020b). This appears to bring us back to where we started with Monicelli (another director possibly unknown to young Bava fans) and the problem that the cult filmmaker creates for questions of cultural value and where someone like Bava sits in whichever canon we choose to erect or challenge. Either way, if we are going to ask why Bava was once undervalued, if indeed he was, then that question cannot be separated from the question of why he clearly – *per fortuna,* as Monicelli said – no longer is.

Notes

1   Any claims regarding the growth of the Bava cult would inevitably be impressionistic, but it is not unreasonable to presume that the readier availability of the films and the market for 'obscure' films on Blu-ray has won new converts.

2   In his essay on the peplum, Vittorio Spinazzola refers to 'Francisci Cottafavi Freda' as if it was the name of a *filone* within the larger genre of the *storico-mitologici* film.

3   Of the Bava films released in the 1970s, only *Il rosso segno della follia* made less money, but then that film was not released twice.

4   Autera would single out the 'consummate professionalism of Mario Bava' in his review of *La venere d'Ille* eight years later (1979: 19).

5   Bava might have noticed that more mainstream filmmakers – John Ford, for example – enjoyed deflating auteurists in this way. Not everyone was as cooperative as Hitchcock.

6   French trade papers also liked the film. *Les Cinématographie Française* called it a 'veritable anthology of the terror film' – 'unlike a number of films of similar inspiration, "Le Masque du Démon" is both well staged and well played (also very well photographed) and at no point does it make one laugh' (J.G. 1961: 31). *Le Film Francais* compared it with Roger Vadim's *Et Mourir de Plaisir...* (1960) and Fisher's *Dracula*, but thought that 'the Italian work seems to have raised the stakes in horrors and terrifying scenes (here it is forbidden to those under 12 years)' (Y. 1961: 19). Both were greatly impressed by Barbara Steele.

7   Judging by their respective tone, I suspect that the *Ercole* review was by Peter John Dyer and the *Gli invasori* one by Milne. Dyer tended to be waspish about Bava, even though one suspects that he liked his films, while Milne was usually more sympathetic (and inclined to mention more 'legitimate' filmmakers as points of reference).

8   Dyer achieved some small notoriety with Hitchcock scholars by calling *Psycho* 'a very minor work' in his original *Sight and Sound* review. I mention it here not to discredit him but as an indication that critical opinion and the film canon was in a state of particular flux during this period.

9   For more on critical practices at *Monthly Film Bulletin,* see McDonald (2016).

10 David Quinlan evaluated the film similarly in *Films and Filming*, but not only framed it as a Bava film but also acknowledged that the director had his admirers. 'Pictorially, things are fine', he wrote, 'but even the most avid Bava fan will have to admit that, lacking the pace to conceal its implausibilities, the plot never fully works' (1972: 41–2).

11 Bava had already featured in Ivan Butler's *The Horror Film* (1967), which offered qualified praise for *Black Sunday* and *6 donne per l'assassino*, and the first edition of Carlos Clarens' book on horror published the same year.

Afterword

FilmTV is an Italian weekly magazine that combines film and TV listings with articles, reviews and commentary on contemporary media and culture. The cover of the issue dated 2 June 2020 featured original artwork recreating a scene from a film that would be well known to aficionados of *stracult* (super-cult) Italian cinema – a figure in a featureless mask, fedora hat and a trenchcoat with upturned collar with his arm around the neck of a screaming woman. The issue marked the fortieth anniversary of Bava's death with several articles – one by Pezzotta characterizing him as a 'bored mannerist' (2020a: 8–10) – and a reproduction of the original *locandina* for *6 donne per l'assassino*. Bava's films were characterized as 'seminal', long 'misunderstood', while he was a filmmaker with a legacy. None of this signals that he had become a household name in Italy, or indeed anywhere else – while by no means a heavyweight journal, *FilmTV*'s articles are aimed at a culturally literate audience. But it is evidence of the way he retains his currency as a brand name for a cinema of conspicuous style, atmosphere, decadence and violence, perhaps the most recognizable name associated with Italy's Serie B cinema. In addition to their circulation in box sets and on streaming services, atmospheric or violent set pieces from Bava's films are also congenial to YouTube, where you will also find eager cinephiles analysing and trying to account for his distinctive style of filmmaking or providing a rundown of his best films. Brief extracts from Bava films are converted into gifs on social media, whether capturing a zoom into Melissa Graps or Diabolik driving his black Jaguar. He is often described as an 'influential' filmmaker, but that influence is diffuse, sometimes acknowledged (Burton, a grudging Argento), sometimes inferred (*Toby Dammit, Alien*, the slasher film), sometimes the mere dropping of a cultish name. Most telling has been his take up by art cinema, the artisan that aesthetes love, whether in *Toby Dammit*, Pedro Almodóvar's *Matador* (1986), which opens with a character masturbating to scenes from *6 donne per l'assassino*, or the 'neo-giallo', which draws more broadly on the Italian thriller, but within which Bava remains a major (or even pioneering) figure. Bava was and is 'influential' in a way that did virtually nothing for his career as a filmmaker, but we might nevertheless say that a flickering Bava(esque) *filone* has been running through cinema for some time.

I want to end by coming back to Bava's status as artisan-auteur. He is an auteur in the sense that his name resonates, invokes a particular kind of cinema and became belatedly marketable in home media cultures. But the filmmaker-as-artisan always brings us back to the matter of creative labour, to what filmmakers can do, and have done, in particular circumstances. The artisan reminds us of filmmaking as work, as a set of technical and aesthetic challenges and a body of films as a sometimes-unpredictable career. The figure of the auteur retains its romantic allure, but artisans deserve our attention, too. Bava reminds us that such artisans need not be directors, even if that was one of their roles – there is also Bava the lighting cameraman or operator, Bava the maestro of effects, Bava the fixer of problem films. Was Bava a 'good' director in the conventional sense, or the best-case scenario of a great technician flourishing in genres where style, atmosphere and spectacle were enough? The artisan, and his fellow artisans, gave these 'unimportant' and ephemeral films aesthetic qualities that still hold our attention today. When I have screened *La maschera del demonio* to students, they have often wanted to know: how on earth, in pre-CGI 1960, was Barbara Steele aged before the camera in a single take? Many of Bava's trucchi seem to have lost none of their magic – the miraculous scale of Diabolik's hideout or some of the environments in *Terrore nello spazio*. Time might even have enhanced that magic.

Bava's films require too many allowances to be made – for variable acting, turgid dialogue, narratives not so much lacking as demoted in the cinematic hierarchy of affect – for him ever to be fully legitimized. But cult reputations often prove to be relatively stable, and his films still have a great deal to tell us about the endurance of ephemeral art, the eccentricities of Italy's *cinema di profondità* and the filmmaker as artisan. The place of the 'most discreetly mysterious of authors' (O'Brien 1993: 169) in contemporary film culture, however niche, seems as important as ever, whether as 'maestro of the macabre', bored mannerist or *grande artigiano*.

SELECT FILMOGRAPHY

List of abbreviations

d. Director
sc. Script
m. Music
ph. Director of photography
p.c. Production company
l.p. Leading players
Note: I have used the year of release except in those cases where there is a
    significant gap (two years or more) between production and release.

Films

I vampiri (Italy 1957) d. Riccardo Freda (and Mario Bava, uncredited); sc. Piero
Regnoli, Rijk Sijöstrom; ph. Mario Bava; m. Roman Vlad; p.c. Titanus, Athena
Cinematografica; l.p. Gianna Maria Canale, Dario Michaelis, Antoine Balpetré,
Carlo d'Angelo, Wandisa Guida, Paul Müller.

Le fatiche di Ercole/Hercules (Italy 1958) d. Pietro Francisci; sc. Ennio De Concini,
Pietro Francisci, Gaio Fratini; ph. Mario Bava (also Special Effects); m. Enzo
Masetti; p.c. Oscar Film, Galatea; l.p. Steve Reeves, Sylva Koscina, Gianna
Maria Canale, Ivo Garrani, Mimmo Palmara, Arturo Dominici, Lidia Alfonsi.

*La morte viene dallo spazio/Death Comes from Outer Space/The Day the Earth
Exploded* (Italy/France 1958) d. Paolo Heusch; sc. Marcello Coscia, Alessandro
Continenza; ph. Mario Bava (also Special Effects); m. Carlo Rustichelli; p.c.
Royal Film, Lux Film, Lux Compagnie Cinématographique de France; l.p. Paul
Hubschmid, Madeleine Fischer, Fiorella Mari, Ivo Garrani.

Ercole e la regina di Lidia/Hercules Unchained (Italy/France 1959) d. Pietro
Francisci; sc. Pietro Francisci, Ennio De Concini; ph. Mario Bava (also
Special Effects); m. Enzo Masetti; p.c. Galatea, Lux Film, Lux Compagnie
Cinématographique de France; l.p. Steve Reeves, Sylvia Lopez, Sylva
Koscina, Gabriele Antonini, Sergio Fantoni, Mimmo Palmara, Primo
Carnera.

Caltiki, il mostro immortale/Caltiki – the Immortal Monster (Italy/France 1959)
d. Robert Hampton [Riccardo Freda] (and Mario Bava, uncredited); sc. Philip
Just [Filippo Sanjust]; ph. John Foam [Mario Bava] (also Special Effects); m.
Roberto Nicolosi; p.c. Galatea, Climax Pictures; l.p. Didi Sullivan [Didi Perego],

Daniela Rocca, Gérard Herter, Giacomo Rossi Stuart, Arthur Dominick [Arturo Dominici].

La battaglia di Maratona/The Giant of Marathon (Italy/France 1959) d. Jacques Tourneur (and Mario Bava and Bruno Vailati, uncredited); sc. Ennio De Concini, Augusto Frassinetti; ph. Mario Bava; m. Roberto Nicolosi; p.c. Galatea, Titanus, Société Cinématographique Lyre, Lux Compagnie Cinématographique de France; l.p. Steve Reeves, Mylène Demongeot, Sergio Fantoni, Alberto Lupo, Ivo Garrani, Philippe Hersent, Daniela Rocca.

La maschera del demonio/The Mask of Satan/Black Sunday/Revenge of the Vampire (Italy 1960) d. Mario Bava; sc. Ennio De Concini, Mario Serandrei (Mario Bava, Marcell Coscia, Dino De Palma, uncredited); ph. Mario Bava; m. Roberto Nicolosi (US version Les Baxter); p.c. Galatea, Jolly Film; l.p. Barbara Steele, John Richardson, Andrea Checchi, Ivo Garrani, Arturo Dominici.

Ester e il re/Esther and the King (Italy/US 1960) d. Raoul Walsh (English credits), Mario Bava (Italian credits); sc. Raoul Walsh, Michael Elkins, Ennio De Concini; ph. Mario Bava; m. Angelo Francesco Lavagnino, Roberto Nicolosi; p.c. Galatea; l.p. Joan Collins, Richard Egan, Daniela Rocca, Sergio Fantoni, Dennis O'Dea, Rick Battaglia, Renato Baldini, Gabriele Tinti, Rosalba Neri.

Le meraviglie di Aladino/The Wonders of Aladdin (Italy/France/US 1961) d. Henry Levin (English credits), Mario Bava (Italian credits); sc. Paul Tuckaoe, Silvano Reina, Franco Prosperi, Pierre Very; ph. Tonino Delli Colli; m. Angelo Francesco Lavagnino; p.c. Lux Film, Lux Compagnie Cinématographique de France, Embassy Pictures; l.p. Donald O'Connor, Noëlle Adam, Milton Reid, Mario Girotti, Fausto Tozzi, Vittorio De Sica, Aldo Fabrizzi, Michèle Mercier.

Ercole al centro della terra/Hercules in the Centre of the Earth/Hercules in the Haunted World (Italy 1961) d. Mario Bava; sc. Alessandro Continenza, Franco Prosperi, Duccio Tessari, Mario Bava; ph. Mario Bava; m. Armando Trovajoli; p.c. Spa Cinematografica; l.p. Reg Park, Leonora Ruffo, Christopher Lee, George Ardisson [Giorgio Ardisson], Franco Giacobini, Ida Galli.

Gli invasori/Fury of the Vikings/Erik the Conqueror (Italy/France 1961) d. Mario Bava; sc. Oreste Biancoli, Piero Pierotti, Mario Bava; ph. Mario Bava; m. Roberto Nicolosi; p.c. Galatea, Critérion Film, Société Cinématographique Lyre; l.p. Cameron Mitchell, Giorgio Ardisson, Ellen Kessler, Alice Kessler, Françoise Cristophe, Andrea Checchi.

La ragazza che sapeva troppo/Evil Eye (Italy 1963) d. Mario Bava; sc. Ennio De Concini, Enzo Corbucci [Sergio Corbucci], Eliana De Sabata, Mino Guerrini, Franco Prosperi, Mario Bava; ph. Mario Bava; m. Roberto Nicolosi (US version Les Baxter); p.c. Galatea, Coronet Film; l.p. Letìcia Román, John Saxon, Valentina Cortese, Dante Di Paolo.

I tre volti della paura/Black Sabbath (Italy/France 1963) d. Mario Bava sc. Marcello Fondato, Alberto Bevilacqua, Mario Bava (and Ugo Guerra, uncredited); ph. Ubaldo Terzano; m. Roberto Nicolosi (US version Les Baxter); p.c. Emmepi Cinematografica, Galatea, Société Cinématographique Lyre; l.p. Michèle Mercier, Lidia Alfonsi (*Il telefono*), Boris Karloff, Susy Andersen, Mark Damon (*I wurdalak*), Jacqueline Pierreux [Jacqueline Soussard], Milli Monti [Milly], Harriet Medin (*La goccia d'acqua*).

La frusta e il corpo/The Whip and the Body/What/Night is the Phantom (Italy/
France 1963) d. John M. Old [Mario Bava]; sc. Julian Berry [Ernesto Gastaldi],
Robert Hugo [Ugo Guerra], Martin Hardy [Luciano Martino]; ph. David
Hamilton [Ubaldo Terzano]; m. Jim Murphy [Carlo Rustichelli]; p.c. Vox Film,
Leone Film, Francinor, Pip; l.p. Daliah Lavi, Christopher Lee, Tony Kendall
[Luciano Stella], Isli Oberon [Ida Galli], Harriet White Medin, Alan Collins
[Luciano Pigozzi].

6 donne per l'assassino/Blood and Black Lace (Italy/France/West Germany 1964)
d. Mario Bava; sc. Marcello Fondato, Giuseppe Batilla, Mario Bava; ph. Ubaldo
Terzano; p.c. Emmepi Cinematografica, Georges de Beauregard, Monachia
Film (Top-Film on German prints); l.p. Eva Bartok, Cameron Mitchell, Thomas
Reiner, Arianna Gorini, Mary Arden, Lea Krugher [Lea Lander], Claude Dantes,
Dante Di Paolo, Massimo Righi, Franco Ressel, Francesca Ungaro, Luciano
Pigozzi, Harriet White Medin.

La strada per Forte Alamo/The Road to Fort Alamo/Arizona Bill (Italy/France
1964) d. John M. Old [Mario Bava]; sc. Vincent Thomas [Vincenzo Gicca
Palli], Charles Price [Franco Prosperi], Jane Brisbane [Livia Contadi]; ph. Bud
Third [Ubaldo Terzano]; m. Piero Umiliani; p.c. Protor Film, Piazzi Produzione
Cinematografica, Comptoir Français du Film Production; l.p. Ken Clark, Jany
Clair, Michel Lemoine.

Terrore nello spazio/Planet of the Vampires (Italy/Spain 1965) d. Mario Bava;
sc. Ib Melchior, Alberto Bevilacqua, Callisto Cosulich, Mario Bava, Antonio
Román, Rafael J. Salvia, based on 'Una notte di 21 ore' by Renato Pestriniero;
ph. Antonio Rinaldi; m. Gino Marinuzzi jnr.; p.c. Italian International Film,
Castilla Cooperativa Cinematografica; l.p. Barry Sullivan, Norma Bengell, Ángel
Aranda, Evi Marandi.

Ringo del Nebraska/Savage Gringo/Nebraska Jim (Italy/Spain 1966) d. Anthony
Román [Antonio Román] (and Mario Bava, uncredited); sc. Jesús Navarro,
Antonio Román, Adriano Bolzoni; ph. Gugliemo Mancori; m. Nino Oliviero;
p.c. Italian International Film, Castilla Cooperativa Cinematografica; l.p. Ken
Clark, Yvonne Bastien, Peter Carter [Piero Lulli].

I coltelli di vendicatore/Knives of the Avenger (Italy 1966) d. John Hold [Mario
Bava] (and Leopoldo Savona, uncredited); sc. Alberto Liberati, Giorgio
Simonelli, Mario Bava; ph. Antonio Rinaldi; m. Marcello Giombini; p.c.
Saro Patané for Sider Film; l.p. Cameron Mitchell, Fausto Tozzi, Lissa [Elissa
Pichelli], Jack Stuart [Giacomo Rossi Stuart].

Operazione Paura/Kill, Baby … Kill!/Curse of the Dead (Italy 1966) d. Mario Bava;
sc. Romano Migliorini, Roberto Natale, Mario Bava; ph. Antonio Rinaldi; m.
Carlo Rustichelli (and Roman Vlad, uncredited); p.c. Ful Film; l.p. Giacomo
Rossi Stuart, Erika Blanc, Fabienne Dali, Piero Lulli, Max Lawrence [Luciano
Catenacci], Giana Vivaldi [Giovanna Galletti].

Le spie vengono dal semifreddo/Dr Goldfoot and the Girl Bombs (Italy/US
1966) d. Mario Bava; sc. Castellano [Franco Castellano], Pipolo [Giuseppe
Moccia] (US version Louis M. Heyward and Robert Kauffman); ph. Antonio
Rinaldo; m. Lallo Gori, 'Bang Bang Kissene' by De Paolis, Castellano and
Pipolo (US version Les Baxter); p.c. Italian International Film, American
International Pictures; l.p. Franco Franchi, Ciccio Ingrassia, Vincent Price,
Fabian, Laura Antonelli.

Diabolik/Danger: Diabolik (Italy/France 1968) d. Mario Bava; sc. Dino Maiuri, Brian Degas, Tudor Gates, Mario Bava; ph. Antonio Rinaldi; m. Ennio Morricone; p.c. Dino De Laurentiis Cinematografica, Marianne Production; l.p. John Phillip Law, Marisa Mell, Michel Piccoli, Adolfo Celi, Terry-Thomas.

Il rosso segno della follia/Un hacha para la luna de miel/Hatchet for the Honeymoon/Blood Brides (Spain/Italy 1968–69 – released 1970) d. Mario Bava; sc. Santiago Moncada, Mario Musy, Mario Bava; ph. Mario Bava; m. Sante Romitelli; p.c. Mercury Produzione Films, Pan Latina Films; l.p. Stephen Forsyth, Laura Betti, Dagmar Lassander, Femi Benussi, Jesús Puente.

Quante volte ... quella notte/Four Times That Night (Italy/West Germany 1969 – released 1972) d. Mario Bava; sc. Carl Ross, Mario Moroni, Guido Leoni; ph. Antonio Rinaldi; m. Lallo Gori; p.c. Delfino Film, Hape Film; l.p. Daniela Giordano, Brett Halsey, Pascale Petit, Dick Randall, Brigitte Skay.

5 bambole per la luna d'agosto/5 Dolls for an August Moon (Italy 1970) d. Mario Bava; sc. Mario Di Nardo; ph. Antonio Rinaldi; m. Piero Umiliani; p.c. Produzione Atlas Cinematografica; l.p. William Berger, Ira von Fürstenberg, Edwige Fenech, Maurice Poli, Teodoro Corrà, Howard Ross [Renato Rossini].

Roy Colt e Winchester Jack/Roy Colt and Winchester Jack (Italy 1970) d. Mario Bava; sc. Mario Di Nardo; ph. Antonio Rinaldi; m. Piero Umiliani; p.c. Produzione Atlas Cinematografica, Tigielle 33; l.p. Brett Halsey, Charles Southwood, Marilù Tolo, Teodoro Corrà, Isa Miranda.

Ecologia del delitto/Antefatto/Reazione a catena/Carnage/Twitch of the Death Nerve/Last House – Part 2/Bay of Blood/Bloodbath (Italy 1971) d. Mario Bava; sc. Filippo Ottoni, Mario Bava, Joseph McLee [Giuseppe Zaccariello]; ph. Mario Bava; m. Stelvio Cipriani; p.c. Nuova Linea Cinematografica; l.p. Claudine Auger, Luigo Pistilli, Claudio Volonté, Laura Betti, Leopoldo Trieste, Isa Miranda.

Gli orrori del castello di Norimberga/Baron Blood (Italy/West Germany 1972) d. Mario Bava; sc. Vincent Fotre, Willibald Eser, Mario Bava (English version Vincent G. Fotre, William A, Bairn); ph. Antonio Rinaldi; m. Stelvio Cipriani (AIP version Les Baxter); p.c. Leone International Film, Dieter Geissler; l.p. Joseph Cotton, Elke Sommer, Massimo Girotti, Antonio Cantafora, Rada Rassimov, Alan Collins [Luciano Pigozzi], Nicoletta Elmi.

Lisa e il diavolo/Lisa and the Devil (Italy/Spain/West Germany 1972) d. Mario Bava; sc. Mario Bava, Giorgio Maulini, Romano Migliorini, Roberto Natale (Chicca Rusicka, uncredited); ph. Cecilio Paniagua; m. Carlo Savina; p.c. Euro America Productions (Alfredo Leone), Tecisa, Roxy Film; l.p. Elke Sommer, Telly Savalas, Alessio Orano, Alida Valli, Espartaco Santoni, Sylva Koscina.

Cani arrabbiati/Semaforo rosso/Kidnapped/Rabid Dogs/Wild Dogs (Italy 1974 – not screened in any version until 1996) d. Mario Bava; sc. Alessandro Parenzo, Cesare Frugoni, based on 'Kidnapped' by Ellery Queen; ph. Emilio Varriani; m. Stelvio Cipriani (all versions, but different score in *Kidnapped*); p.c. Loyola Films (original production); l.p. Riccardo Cucciolla, Maurice Poli, George Eastman [Luigi Montefiori], Don Backy [Aldo Caponi], Lea Lander.

La casa dell'esorcismo/The House of Exorcism (Italy/Spain/West Germany 1975) d. Mario Bava (Italian release), 'Mickey Lion' (international release); sc. Mario Bava, Giorgio Maulini, Roberto Natale, Alberto Cittini, Alfredo

Leone; ph. Cecilio Paniagua; m. Carlo Savina; p.c. Leone International Film, Euro America Productions, Tecisa, Roxy Film; l.p. Elke Sommer, Telly Savalas, Robert Alda.

Shock (Transfert Suspense Hypnos)/Beyond the Door II (Italy 1977) d. Mario Bava (and Lamberto Bava, uncredited); sc. Lamberto Bava, Francesco Barbieri, Paolo Brigenti, Dardano Sacchetti; ph. Alberto Spagnoli; m. Libra; p.c. Laser Film; l.p. Daria Nicolodi, David Colin jnr., John Steiner, Ivan Rassimov.

Television

Odissea/The Odyssey (Italy/France/West Germany/Yugoslavia 1968) d. Franco Rossi, Mario Bava (Piero Schivazappa, uncredited); sc. Giampiero Bona, Vittorio Bonicelli, Fabio Carpi, Luciano Codignola, Mario Prosperi, Renzo Rosso; ph. Aldo Giordani; m. Carlo Rustichelli; p.c. Dino De Laurentiis Cinematografica, Rai Radiotelevisione Italia, Ortf, Bavaria, Jadran Film; l.p. Bekim Fehmiu, Irene Papas, Samson Burke.
Note: A 105 minute version was released theatrically in 1969 as *Le avventure di Ulisse*.

La venere d'Ille (Italy 1978 – broadcast in 1981) d. Mario Bava, Lamberto Bava; sc. Lamberto Bava, Cesare Garboli, from the story by Prosper Mérimée; ph. Nino Celeste; m. Ubaldo Continiello; p.c. Pont Royal Film TV, Rete 2 for the series *I giochi del diavolo – Storie fantastiche dell'Ottocento*; l.p. Marc Porel, Daria Nicolodi, Fausto De Bella.

BIBLIOGRAPHY

Acerbo, G. (2007), 'Gli anni maledetti', in G. Acerbo and R. Pisoni (eds.), *Kill Baby Kill! Il Cinema di Mario Bava*, 183–5, Rome: Un Mondo a Parte.

Acerbo, G. and Pisoni, R. eds. (2007a), *Kill Baby Kill! Il Cinema di Mario Bava*, Rome: Un Mondo a Parte.

Acerbo, G. and Pisoni, R. (2007b), 'Censurate Nevenka! Intervista a Ernesto Gastaldi', in G. Acerbo and R. Pisoni (eds.), *Kill Baby Kill! Il Cinema di Mario Bava*, 87–9, Rome: Un Mondo a Parte.

Acerbo, G. and Pisoni, R. (2007c), 'Il Vecchio e il nuovo: intervista a Umberto Lenzi', in G. Acerbo and R. Pisoni (eds.), *Kill Baby Kill! Il Cinema di Mario Bava*, 133–4, Rome: Un Mondo a Parte.

Aldridge, M. (2016), *Agatha Christie on Screen*, London: Palgrave.

Alloway, L. (1969), 'The Long Front of Culture', in J. Russell and S. Gablik (eds.), *Pop Art Redefined*, 41–3, New York and Washington: Praegers Publishers.

Alloway, L. (1970), 'The Development of British Pop', in L. R. Lippard (ed.), *Pop Art*, 26–7, London: Thames and Hudson.

Alloway, L. (1971), *Violent America: The Movies 1946–1964*, New York: Museum of Modern Art.

Alloway, L. (1975), *Topics in American Art Since 1945*, New York: W. W. Norton & Company.

Altariva, R., ed. (2008), *Diabolik: Cronistoria di un Film*, Sassuolo: Diabolik Club.

Altman, R. (1999), *Film/Genre*, London: BFI.

Andrews, D. (2013), *Theorizing Art Cinemas: Foreign, Cult, Avant-Garde, and beyond*, Austin: University of Texas.

Anon. (1960), 'La maschera del demonio', *Intermezzo*, 15 (16–17): 13.

Anon. (1963a), '*Ercole al centro della terra (Hercules in the Centre of the Earth)*', *Monthly Film Bulletin*, 30 (348): 21.

Anon. (1963b), '*Gli invasori (Fury of the Vikings)*', *Monthly Film Bulletin*, 30 (353): 86.

Anon. (1964), 'Black Sunday', *Castle of Frankenstein*, 4: 32–7.

Anon. [Peter John Dyer] (1965a), '*La frusta e il corpo (Night is the Phantom)*', *Monthly Film Bulletin*, 32 (374): 40.

Anon. (1965b), '*La ragazza che sapeva troppo (The Evil Eye)*', *Monthly Film Bulletin*, 32 (375): 58.

Anon. (1965c), '*Sei donne per l'assassino*', *Cahiers du Cinema*, 165: 88–90

Anon. (1966), 'Rassegna cinematografica (Operazione paura)', *Corriere della sera*, 8 (August): 6.

Anon. (1968a), 'Revenge of the Vampire', *Kine Weekly*, 3165: 152.

Anon. (1968b), '*Terrore nello spazio (Planet of the Vampires)*', *Monthly Film Bulletin*, 35 (419): 204.

Anon (1968c), 'Diabolik', *Corriere d'informazione*, (27–28 January): 11.

Anon. (1969) 'Review: *Danger Diabolik*', *Monthly Film Bulletin*, 36 (421): 31–2.

Anon. (1970), '*5 bambole per la luna d'agosto*', *Cinema d'oggi*, 31 (March): 10.

Anon. (1971), 'Antefatto (Before the Fact – The Ecology of a Crime)', *Variety*, (27 October).

Anon. (1974a), 'Frankenstein's MovieGuide', *Castle of Frankenstein*, 20: 46.

Anon. (1974b), 'Frankenstein's MovieGuide', *Castle of Frankenstein*, 22: 42.

Anon. (2014), 'Cento anni fa nasceva Mario Bava: intervista al critico di cinema Alberto Pezzotta', *Eni Polo Sociale*, available at http://www.enipolosociale.com/speciale-cento-anni-fa-nasceva-mario-bava-intervista-al-critico-di-cinema-alberto-pezzotta/ (accessed 17 March 2021).

Anon. (2019), 'Five Questions for Peter Strickland', *Time Out* 2536, (25 June–1 July): 49.

Argento, D. (2019), *Fear*, Godalming: FAB Press.

Autera, L. (1970), 'Rassegna cinematografica (Roy Colt e Winchester Jack)', *Corriere della sera*, 15 (November): 15.

Autera, L. (1971), 'Rassegna cinematografica (Ecologia del delitto)', *Corriere della sera*, 15 (December): 13.

Autera, L. (1979), 'Rai-TV padrona a Sorrento', *Corriere della sera*, 9 (October): 9.

Balmain, C. (2002), 'Mario Bava's *The Evil Eye*: Realism and the Italian Horror Film', *Post- Script: Essays in Film and the Humanities*, 21 (3): 20–31.

Bartolini, C. (2017), *Il cinema giallo-thriller italiano*, Rome: Gremese.

Bartolini, C. (2019), 'Laissez Bronzer Le Giallo', *Nocturno,* 195: 18–24.

Baschiera, S. and Di Chiara, F. (2010), 'Once Upon a Time in Italy: Transnational Features of Genre Production 1960s–1970s', *Film International*, 8 (6): 30–9.

Baschiera, S. and Hunter, R. (2016), 'Introduction', in S. Baschiera and R. Hunter (eds.), *Italian Horror Cinema*, 1–14, Edinburgh: Edinburgh University Press.

Baxter, J. (1970), *Science Fiction in the Cinema*, New York and London: A.S. Barnes and co./A. Zwemmer Ltd.

Belton, J. (1980/1981), 'The Bionic Eye: Zoom Esthetics', *Cineaste*, 11 (1): 20–7.

Bengry, J. (2011), 'The Queer History of *Films and Filming*', *Little Joe: A Magazine about Queers and Cinema, Mostly*, 2: 31–41, available at https://www.academia.edu/3284715/The_Queer_History_of_Films_and_Filming?email_work_card=view-paper (accessed 24 April 2020).

Bergfelder, T. (2005), *International Adventures: German Popular Cinema and European Co-Productions in the 1960s*, New York and Oxford: Berghahn Books.

Bergfelder, T. (2020), 'Notes on the German Crime Film', in T. Bergfelder, E. Carter, D. Göktürk and C. Sandberg (eds.), *The German Cinema Book*, 56–67, London and New York: BFI/Bloomsbury.

Berns, S.D. (1961), 'Black Sunday', *Motion Picture Herald*, 222 (5): 20.

Bettinson, G. (2015), *The Sensuous Cinema of Wong Kar-Wai: Film Poetics and the Aesthetics of Disturbance*, Hong Kong: Hong Kong University Press (Kindle edition).

Bilbow, M. (1968a), 'Revenge of the Vampire', *The Daily Cinema*, 9530 (7 June): 14.

Bilbow, M. (1968b), 'Planet of the Vampires', *The Daily Cinema*, 9602 (20 November): 8.

Bilbow, M. (1968c), 'Danger: Diabolik', *The Daily Cinema*, 9613 (16 December): 5.

Bilbow, M. (1971), 'Five Dolls for an August Moon', *Today's Cinema*, 9940 (17 September): 12.

Bilbow. M. (1973), 'Blood Brides', *CinemaTV Today*, 10014: 20.

Bini, A. (2011), 'Horror Cinema: The Emancipation of Women and Urban Anxiety', in F. Brizio- Skov (ed.), *Popular Italian Cinema: Culture and Politics in a Postwar Society*, 53–82, London and New York: I.B. Tauris.

Bocchi, P.M. (2020), 'Baviani, Bavosi, Bavette', *FilmTV*, 28 (22): 11.

Böhme, G. (2017), *The Aesthetics of Atmospheres*, Abingdon: Routledge.

Bondanella, P. and Pacchioni, F. (2017), *A History of Italian Cinema*, New York and London: Bloomsbury.

Bordwell, D. (1985), *Narration in the Fiction Film*, London: Routledge.

Bordwell, D. (1989), *Making Meaning: Inference and Rhetoric in the Interpretation of Cinema*, Cambridge, MA and London: Harvard University Press.

Bordwell, D. (2000), *Planet Hong Kong: Popular Cinema and the Art of Entertainment*, Cambridge, MA, and London: Harvard University Press.

Bordwell, D. (2001), 'Aesthetics in Action: *Kungfu*, Gunplay, and Cinematic Expressivity', in E. Yau (ed.), *At Full Speed: Hong Kong Cinema in a Borderless World*, 73–93, Minneapolis: University of Minnesota Press.

Bordwell, D. (2008), *Poetics of Cinema*, New York and London: Routledge.

Botting, F. (1996), *Gothic*, London: Routledge.

Bourdieu, P. (1993), *The Field of Cultural Production*, Cambridge: Polity Press.

Brizio-Skov, F. (2011), 'Dollars, Bullets and Success', in F. Brizio-Skov (ed.), *Popular Italian Cinema: Culture and Politics in a Postwar Society*, 83–106, London and New York: I.B. Tauris.

Brizio-Skov, F. (2014), 'Spaghetti Westerns and Their Audience', in P. Bondanella (ed.), *The Italian Cinema Book*, 181–7, London: BFI.

Brown, E. (1980) 'Shock', *Films and Filming*, 26 (7): 34.

Bruni, D. (2017), '"La tua cultura è che una tinta". Gli "equivoci" del giallo nel primo cinema sonoro (1930–1944)', *Bianco e Nero*, 587: 47–65.

Bruschini, A. and Piselli, S. (2010), *Giallo + Thrilling All'Italiana (1931–1983)*, Florence: Glittering Images.

Bruschini, A. and Tentori, A. (1992), *Profondo Tenebre: Il Cinema Thrilling Italiano 1962–1982*, Bologna: Granata Press.

Bruschini, A. and Tentori, A. (2013), *Italian Giallo Movies*, Rome: Profondo Rosso.

Bryce, A. (1991), 'One Step away from the County Line: Harry Alan Towers Interviewed', *Shock Xpress*, 1: 84–91.

Burke, F. (2011), 'The Italian Sword-and-Sandal Film from *Fabiola* to *Hercules and the Captive Women*', in F. Brizio-Skov (ed.), *Popular Italian Cinema: Culture and Politics in a Postwar Society*, 17–51, London and New York: I.B. Tauris.

Buscombe, E. (1981) [originally 1973], 'Ideas of Authorship', in J. Caughie (ed.), *Theories of Authorship*, 22–34, London: Routledge/BFI.

Butler, I. (1967), *The Horror Film*, London and New York: A. Zwemmer/A.S. Barnes.

Buxton, D. (1990), *From The Avengers to Miami Vice: Form and Ideology in Television Series*, Manchester: Manchester University Press.

Byro (1968), 'Kill Baby Kill (Operazione Paura)', *Variety*, (30 October).

Caen, M. (1962), 'Hercule Contre Les Vampires', *Midi-Minuit Fantastique*, 1: 61–2.

Camilleri, A. (2013/2019), 'Difesa di un colore', reprinted in A. Camilleri (2019), *Km 123*, 139–154, Milan: Mondadori.

Canova, G. (2017), 'Più furti che delitti. Uno sguardo intermediale sulla genesi del giallo in Italia', *Bianco e Nero*, 587: 30–46.

Cappabianca, A. (1970), '5 bambole per la luna d'agosto', *Filmcritica*, 21 (206): 194–5.

Caputo, R. (1997), 'Blood and Black Celluloid: Some Thoughts on the Cinema of Mario Bava', *Metro*, 110: 55–9.

Castaldi, S. (2010), *Drawn and Dangerous: Italian Comics of the 1970s and the 1980s* (Kindle edition), Jackson: University Press of Mississippi.

Caulandre, J. (1964), 'La Fille qui en Savait Trop', *Midi-Minuit Fantastique*, 9: 119–20.

Censi, R. (2017), 'In Limbo', in F. Ganzo (ed.), *Jacques Tourneur*, 192–6, Paris: Čapricci.

Censi, R. (2020), 'Controlocandina', *FilmTV*, 28 (22): 54.

Ceretto, Alberto (1965), 'Da Hollywood a Roma per un giallo-intersediale', *Corriere della sera*, 22 (April: 17).

Chandler, R. (1950/1984), 'The Simple Art of Murder', in *The Chandler Collection Volume Three*, 175–92, London: Picador.

Cherry, B. (2009), *Horror*, London and New York: Routledge.

Childs, M. and Jones, A. (1981), 'City of the Living Dead', *Cinefantastique*, 11 (1): 11.

Church, D. (2015), 'One on Top of the Other: Lucio Fulci, Transnational Film Industries, and the Retrospective Construction of the Italian Horror Canon', *Quarterly Review of Film and Video*, 32 (1): 1–20.

Church, D. (2016), *Disposable Passions: Vintage Pornography and the Material Legacies of Adult Cinema*, New York and London: Bloomsbury.

Cicioni, M. and Di Ciolla, N., eds. (2008), *Differences, Deceits and Desires: Murder and Mayhem in Italian Crime Fiction*, Newark: University of Delaware Press.

Clarens, C. (1971), *Horror Movies: An Illustrated Survey*, London: Panther.

Clarke, F.S. (1976), 'The House of Exorcism', *Cinefantastique*, 5 (2): 35.

Codelli, L. (2014), 'Bava Le Diabolik', *Positif*, 639: 96–7.

Conterio, M. (2015), *Black Sunday*, Leighton Buzzard: Auteur/Devil's Advocates.

Corsi, B. (2001), *Con qualche dollaro in meno: Storia economica del cinema italiano*, Rome: Editori Riuniti.

Cozzi, L. (2004), *Mario Bava: Master of Horror*, Rome: Mondo Ignoto srl/ Profondo Rosso.

Cozzi, L. (2016), *La famiglia Bava: Cento anni di cinema*, Rome: Profondo Rosso.

Craik, K.H. (2009), *Reputation: A Network Interpretation*, New York: Oxford University Press.

Curti, R. (2002), 'The Wild, Wild World of Diabolik and Co.: Adults-only Comic Books on Screen in the 1960s', available at http://offscreen.com/view/diabolik (accessed 8 July 2016).

Curti, R. (2014), 'Mario Bava's Legacy: Afterword', in T. Howarth (ed.), *The Haunted World of Mario Bava*, 200–4, Baltimore: Midnight Marquee Press.

Curti, R. (2015a), *Italian Gothic Horror Films, 1957–1969*, Jefferson, North Carolina: McFarland (Kindle edition).

Curti, R. (2015b), 'Color Me Blood Yellow: The Italian *Giallo* from the Page to the Screen', in T. Howarth (ed.), *So Deadly, So Perverse: 50 Years of Italian Giallo Films*, 17–26, Baltimore and London: Midnight Marquee Press.

Curti, R. (2016), *Diabolika: Supercriminals, Superheroes and the Comic Book Universe in Italian Cinema*, Baltimore: Midnight Marquee Press.

Curti, R. (2017), *Italian Gothic Horror Films, 1970–1979*, Jefferson, North Carolina: McFarland (Kindle edition).

Curti, R. (2019), *Blood and Black Lace*, Leighton Buzzard: Auteur/Devil's Advocates.

Curti, R. and Di Rocco, A. (2014), 'Maledizione! The True Story behind Seth Holt's Accursed Version of Diabolik', *Video Watchdog*, 176: 22–35.

De Chiara, F. (2016), *Peplum: Il cinema italiano alle prese col mondo antico*, Rome.

Della Casa, S. (1997), 'Mario Bava: A Career Overview', *Metro*, 110: 39–44.

Della Casa, S. and Piazza, C. (1984), *Il Cinema Secondo Mario Bava*, Turin: Edizioni Movie Club.

Desser, D. (2005), 'Hong Kong Film and the New Cinephilia', in M. Morris, S.L. Li and S. Chan (eds.), *Hong Kong Connections: Transnational Imagination in Action Cinema*, 205–21, Durham, NC, and Hong Kong: Duke University Press/ Hong Kong University Press.

Dickinson, K. (2007), 'Troubling Synthesis: The Horrific Sights and Incompatible Sounds of Video Nasties', in J. Sconce (ed.), *Sleaze Artists: Cinema at the Margins of Taste, Style and Politics*, 167–88, Durham and London: Duke University Press.

Diffrient, D. S. (2014), *Omnibus Films: Theorizing Transauthorial Cinema*, Edinburgh: Edinburgh University Press.

Doherty, T. (1988), *Teenagers and Teenpics: The Juvenilization of American Movies in the 1950s*, Boston: Union Hyman.

Dool (1965), 'Planet of the Vampires', *Variety*, (8 December).

Doremieux, A. (1965), 'Six Femmes pour l'Assassin: Un Rêve Fou', *Midi-Minuit Fantastique*, 12: 56–8.

Dumontet, C. (1998), 'Bloody, Scary and Sexy', in C. Dumontet (ed.), *Ghosts, Vampires and Kriminals: Horror and Crime in Italian Comics*, 6–20, London: National Art Library/Victoria and Albert Museum.

Dunnett, J. (2010), 'Supergiallo: How Mondadori Turned Crime into a Brand', *The Italianist*, 30 (1): 63–80.

Dunnett, J. (2011), 'The Emergence of a New Literary Genre in Interwar Italy', in G. Pieri (ed.), *Italian Crime Fiction*, 6–26, Cardiff: University of Wales.

Durgnat, R. (1997 [originally 1965]), 'Night Is the Phantom and The Evil Eye', *Metro*, 110: 53–4.

Dyer, P. J. (1965), 'Night Is the Phantom', *The Daily Cinema*, 9020 (27 January): 5.

Dyer, P. J. (1966), 'Sei donne per l'assassino (Blood and Black Lace)', *Monthly Film Bulletin*, 33 (385): 18.

Dyer, R. (1997), *White: Essays on Race and Culture*, Abingdon and New York: Routledge.

Dyer, R. (2015), *Lethal Repetition: Serial Killing in European Cinema*, London: BFI/Palgrave.

Eco, U. (2008) [originally 1984], 'Casablanca: Cult Movies and Intertextual Montage', in E. Mathijs and X. Mendik (eds.), The Cult Film Reader, 67–75, Maidenhead: Open University Press/McGraw-Hill.

E.F. (1971), 'Ecologia del delitto', Corriere della sera, (15–16 December): 13.

E.G.L. (1964), 'Sei donne per l'assassino', Bianco e nero, 25 (6): 48–9.

Ehrenreich, A. (2017), 'Niente affatto una nicchia: la distribuzione e la commercializzazione del genere giallo', Bianco e Nero, 587: 113–26.

Eisenschitz, B. (1964), 'Les Trois Derniers Films de Mario Bava', Midi-Minuit Fantastique, 8: 62–3.

Elley, D. (1984), The Epic Film: Myth and History, London, Boston, Melbourne and Henley: Routledge and Kegan Paul.

Erickson, G. (1999), 'Danger: Diabolik - The Guiltiest Pleasure of Them All!', DVD Savant, available at http://www.dvdsavant.com/s71diabolik.html (accessed 9 June 2017).

Everson, W. K. (1974), Classics of the Horror Film, Secausus, NJ: Citadel Press.

Fish, S. (1980), Is There a Text in This Class? The Authority of Interpretive Communities, Cambridge, MA and London: Harvard University Press.

Fisher, A. (2014), Radical Frontiers in the Spaghetti Western: Politics, Violence and Popular Italian Cinema, London and New York: I.B. Tauris.

Fisher, A. (2017), 'Italian Popular Film Genres', in F. Burke (ed.), A Companion to Italian Cinema, 250–66, Chichester: John Wiley and Son.

Fisher, A. (2019), Blood in the Streets: Histories of Violence in Italian Crime Cinema, Edinburgh: Edinburgh University Press.

F.M. (1968), 'Diabolik' (review), Film Mese: Mensile di critica cinematografia, 2 (13): 9–10.

Fofi, G. (1963), 'Terreur en Italie', Midi-Minuit Fantastique, 7: 80–3.

Forgacs, D. (1996), 'Cultural Consumption 1940s to 1990s', in D. Forgacs and R. Lumley (eds.), Italian Cultural Studies: An Introduction, 273–90, Oxford: Oxford University Press.

Foucault, M. (1984), 'What is an Author?', in P. Rabinow (ed.), The Foucault Reader, 101–120, New York: Pantheon Books.

Frayling, C. (1981), Spaghetti Westerns: Cowboys and Europeans From Karl May to Sergio Leone, London: Routledge and Kegan Paul.

Frentzen, J. (1975), 'Twitch of the Death Nerve', Cinefantastique, 4 (3): 36.

Freud, S. (2004 [originally 1919]), 'The Uncanny', in D. Sandner (ed.), Fantastic Literature: A Critical Reader, 74–101, Westport: Praeger.

Fujiwara, C. (2007), 'Boredom, Spasmo, and the Italian System', in J. Sconce (ed.), Sleaze Artists: Cinema at the Margins of Taste, Style, and Politics, 240–58, Durham and London: Duke University Press.

Galt, R. (2011), Pretty: Film and the Decorative Image, New York: Columbia University Press.

Gervasini, M. (2020), 'Un macabre rinascimento', FilmTV, 28 (22): 51.

Ginsborg, P. (1990), A History of Contemporary Italy 1943–1980, London: Penguin.

Giori, M. (2009), '"A sensible film magazine for intelligent filmgoers": Notes for a History of Films and Filming (1954–1990)', available at https://www.academia.edu/2023952/_A_sensible_magazine_for_intelligent_film-goers._Notes_for_a_History_of_Films_and_Filming_1954-1990 (accessed 24 April 2020).

Gomarasca, M. and Pulici, D. (2004), *Genealogia del delitto: Guida al cinema di Mario e Lamberto Bava*, Milan: Nocturno Dossier.

Grazzini, Giovanni (1968), 'Rassegna cinematografica (*Diabolik*)', *Corriere della sera*, 27 January: 13.

G.T. (1992), 'Estate, horror all'italiana', *Corriere della sera*, 21 (July): 41.

Guins, R. (2005), 'Blood and Black Gloves on Shiny Discs: New Media, Old Tastes and the Remediation of Italian Horror Films in the United States', in S. J. Schneider and T. Williams (eds.), *Horror International*, 15–32, Detroit: Wayne State University.

Gunning, T. (2008), 'Making Fashion Out of Nothing: The Invisible Criminal', in M. Uhlirova (ed.), *If Looks Could Kill: Cinema's Images of Fashion, Crime and Violence*, 22–30, London: Koenig Books.

Günsberg, M. (2005), *Italian Cinema: Gender and Genre*, Houndmills and New York: Palgrave Macmillan.

H.M. (1961), 'Black Sunday', *The Film Daily*, 118 (35): 8.

Hanich, J. (2010), *Cinematic Emotions in Horror Films and Thrillers: The Aesthetic Paradox of Pleasurable Fear*, New York and Abingdon: Routledge.

Hardy, P., ed. (1985), *The Aurum Film Encyclopedia: Horror*, London: Aurum Press.

Harris, E. J. (1967), 'Complete, Uncut Version of Mario Bava's New Horror Film to Be Seen on England', Miracle Films Press Release.

Hebdige, D. (1988), *Hiding in the Light: On Images and Things*, London and New York: Comedia/Routledge.

Heffernan, K. (2007), 'Art House or House of Exorcism? The Changing Distribution and Reception Contexts of Mario Bava's *Lisa and the Devil*', in J. Sconce (ed.), *Sleaze Artists: Cinema at the Margins of Taste, Style and Politics*, 144–63, Durham and London: Duke University Press.

Hills, M. (2011), *Blade Runner*, London and New York: Wallflower/Columbia University Press.

Hinxman, M. (1962), 'Hercules in the Centre of the Earth', *The Daily Cinema*, 8683 (5 November): 10.

Hinxman, M. (1965), 'The Evil Eye', *The Daily Cinema*, 9049 (5 April): 5.

Hinxman, M. (1966), 'Blood and Black Lace', *The Daily Cinema*, 9162 (5 January): 5.

Hogg (1965), 'What', *Variety*, (May 26).

Hoveyda, F. (1961), 'Les grimaces du démon', *Cahiers du Cinéma*, 20 (119): 53–7.

Howarth, T. (2014), *The Haunted World of Mario Bava*, 2nd edn Baltimore: Midnight Marquee Press.

Howarth, T. (2015), *So Deadly, so Perverse: 50 Years of Italian Giallo Films Volume 1 1963–1973*, Baltimore: Midnight Marquee Press.

Hubner, L. (2011), 'Introduction: Valuing Films', in L. Hubner (ed.), *Valuing Films: Shifting Perceptions of Worth*, Houndmills and New York: Palgrave Macmillan

Hughes, H. (2011), *Cinema Italiano: The Complete Guide from Classics to Cult*, London and New York: I.B. Tauris.

Hunt, L. (1992), 'A (Sadistic) Night at the Opera: Notes on the Italian Horror Film', *Velvet Light Trap*, 30: 65–75.

Hunt, L. (1993), 'What Are Big Boys Made of? *Spartacus, El Cid* and the Male Epic', in P. Kirkham and J. Thumin (eds.), *You Tarzan: Masculinity, Movies and Men*, 65–83, London: Lawrence and Wishart.

Hunt, L. (2016), 'Kings of Terror, Geniuses of Crime: *giallo* cinema and *fumetti neri*', in S. Baschiera and R. Hunter (eds.), *Italian Horror Cinema*, 145–59, Edinburgh: Edinburgh University Press.

Hunt, L. (2018), *Danger: Diabolik*, London and New York: Wallflower Press.

Hunter, R. (2010), '"Didn't you used to be Dario Argento?": The Cult Reception of Dario Argento', in W. Hope (ed.), *Italian Film Directors in the New Millennium*, 63–74, Cambridge: Cambridge Scholars Press.

Hunter, R. (2016), '*Preferisco l'inferno*: Early Italian Horror Cinema', in S. Baschiera and R. Hunter (eds.), *Italian Horror Cinema*, 15–29, Edinburgh: Edinburgh University Press.

Hutchings, P. (2000), 'Authorship and British Cinema: The Case of Roy Ward Baker', in J. Ashby and A. Higson (eds.), *British Cinema, Past and Present*, 179–89, London and New York: Routledge.

Hutchings, P. (2001), *Terence Fisher*, Manchester: Manchester University Press.

Hutchings, P. (2012), 'Resident Evil? The Limits of European Horror: *Resident Evil* versus *Suspiria*', in P. Allmer, E. Brick and D. Huxley (eds.), *European Nightmares: Horror Cinema in Europe Since 1945*, 13–23, New York and Chichester: Wallflower Press.

Hutchings, P. (2016), 'Bavaesque: The Making of Mario Bava as Italian Horror Auteur', in S. Baschiera and R. Hunter (eds.), *Italian Horror Cinema*, 79–92, Edinburgh: Edinburgh University Press.

Hutchinson, D. (1969), 'Review: *Danger Diabolik*', *Films and Filming*, 15 (7): 31–2.

Ince, K. (2005), *Georges Franju*, Manchester: Manchester University Press.

Jancovich, M., Reboll, A.L., Stringer, J. and Willis, A. (2003), 'Introduction', in M. Jancovich, A.L. Reboll, J. Stringer and A. Willis (eds.), *Defining Cult Movies: The Cultural Politics of Oppositional Taste*, 1–13, Manchester: Manchester University Press.

Jenks, C. (1992), 'The Other Face of Death: Barbara Steele and *La maschera del demonio*', in R. Dyer and G. Vincendeau (eds.), *Popular European Cinema*, 149–62, London and New York: Routledge.

Jones, A. (1998), 'Mario Bava: Blood and Black Celluloid', *National Film Theatre Programme* (August): 16–23.

J.G. (1961), 'Le Masque du Démon', *La Cinematographie Française*, 1912: 5.

J.G. (1968), 'Danger: Diabolik', *Le Film Francais*, 1241 (19 April): 18.

Kannas, A. (2013), 'No Place Like Home: The Late-Modern World of the Italian *Giallo* Film', *Senses of Cinema*, 67, available at http://sensesofcinema.com/2013/uncategorized/no-place-like-home-the-late-modern-world-of-the-italian-giallo-film/ (accessed 22 August 2019).

Kannas, A. (2017), 'All the Colours of the Dark: Film Genre and the Italian *giallo*', *Journal of Italian Cinema and Media Studies*, 5 (2): 173–90.

Kannas, A. (2020), *Giallo! Genre, Modernity, and Detection in Italian Horror Cinema*, Albany: State of New York Press.

Kapsis, R. E. (1989), 'Reputation Building and the Film Art World: The Case of Alfred Hitchcock', *The Sociological Quarterly*, 30 (1): 15–35.

Kapsis, R. E. (1992), *Hitchcock: The Making of a Reputation*, Chicago and London: University of Chicago Press.

Karola (2003), 'Italian Cinema Goes to the Drive-In: The Intercultural Horrors of Mario Bava', in G. D. Rhodes (ed.), *Horror at the Drive-In: Essays in Popular Americana*, 211–37, Jefferson, NC, and London: McFarland.

Kezich, T. (1983), *Il millefilm: Dieci anni al cinema 1967–1977*, Milan: Oscar Mondadori.

Kezich, T. and Levantesi, A. (2004), *Dino: The Life and Films of Dino De Laurentiis*, New York: Miramax Books.

King, G. (2019), *Positioning Art Cinema: Film and Cultural Value*, London and New York: I.B. Tauris.

Klinger, B. (2008), 'The DVD Cinephle: Viewing Heritages and Home Film Cultures', in J. Bennett and T. Brown (eds.), *Film and Television after DVD*, 19–44, London and New York: Routledge.

Koven, M.J. (2006), *La Dolce Morte: Vernacular Cinema and the Italian Giallo Film*, Lanham, Maryland, Toronto and Oxford: Scarecrow Press.

Lagny, M. (1992), 'Popular Taste: The peplum', in R. Dyer and G. Vincendeau (eds.), *Popular European Cinema*, 163–80, London and New York: Routledge.

Ian. (1960), 'Rassegna cinematografica (La maschera del demonio)', *Corriere della sera*, 13 (August): 6.

Lane, J. F. (1998), 'Vittorio Cottafavi Obituary: Lost Hero of Italian Film', *The Guardian*, 30 December, https://www.theguardian.com/news/1998/dec/30/guardianobituaries (accessed 7 April 2020).

Lippi, G. and Codelli, L. (1976), *Fant'Italia: 1957–1966 Emergenza Apoteosi e Riflussi del Fantastico nel Cinema Italiano* (XIV Festival Internazionale del Film di Fantascienzia), Trieste: La Cappella Underground.

Locatelli, M. (2017), 'Lo zoom interminabile. Il giallo all'italiana nell'epoca delle emozioni', *Bianco e Nero*, 587: 100–12.

Lowenstein, A. (2016), 'The *Giallo*/Slasher Landscape: *Ecologia del Delitto, Friday the 13th*, and Subtractive Spectatorship', in S. Baschiera and R. Hunter (eds.), *Italian Horror Cinema*, 127–44, Edinburgh: Edinburgh University Press.

Lucas, T. (2007), *Mario Bava: All the Colors of the Dark*, Cincinatti, Ohio: Video Watchdog.

Lucas, T. (2008), 'Death on the Runway: Mario Bava's *Blood and Black Lace* and Arne Mattsson's *Mannequin in Red*', in M. Uhlirova (ed.), *If Looks Could Kill: Cinema's Images of Fashion, Crime and Violence,* 170–9, London: Koenig Books.

Lucas, T. (2012), 'Continental Op', *Video Watchdog*, 168: 16–39.

MacDonald, R. L. (2016), 'Elevating the Film Review: Critics and Critical Practice at the *Monthly Film Bulletin*', *Film Studies*, 14 (1): 93–111.

Malausa, V. (2005), 'Dignité Burlesque', *Cahiers du Cinema*, 607: 30–1.

Maiuri, D., Degas, B., Gates, T. and Bava, M. (1967), *Diabolik* Screenplay (Fourth Version).

Martinet, P. (1984), *Mario Bava*, Paris: Edilig.

Mazzei, L. and Valentini, P. (2017), 'Se l'Italia fosse un colore', *Bianco e Nero*, 587: 11–17.

McDonagh, M. (2010), *Broken Mirrors/Broken Minds: The Dark Dreams of Dario Argento*, Minneapolis: University of Minnesota Press.

McDonagh, M. (2013), '*Dressed to Kill*: American Giallo', Arrow Films (Blu-ray booklet): 8–19.

McGee, M. T. (1996), *Faster and Furioser: The Revised and Fattened Fable of American International Pictures*, Jefferson and London: McFarland.

Meek, S. (1980), 'Shock Transfert-Suspense-Hypnos (Shock)', *Monthly Film Bulletin*, 47 (556): 95.

Miccichè, L. (1975), *Il cinema italiano degli anni '60*, Venice: Marsiglio Editore.

Miller, D. A. (2021), *Second Time Around: From Art House to DVD*, New York: Columbia University Press (Kindle edition).

Miller, H. K. (2014), '1963 and All That: Raymond Durgnat and the Birth of the Great British Phantasmagoria', *Sight and Sound*, 24 (9), available at https://www.bfi.org.uk/news-opinion/sight-sound-magazine/features/poetry-motion (accessed 24 April 2020).

Milne, T. (1967), '*Operazione Paura (Curse of the Dead)*', *Monthly Film Bulletin* 34 (402): 104.

Milne, T. (1972), 'Cinque bambole per la luna d'agosto', *Monthly Film Bulletin*, 39 (463): 156–7.

Milne, T. (1980), 'Antefatto (Bloodbath)', *Monthly Film Bulletin*, 47 (556): 88.

Milne, T. (1986), '*Ercole alla conquista di Atlantide (Hercules Conquers Atlantis)*', *Monthly Film Bulletin*, 53 (624): 18–19.

Mittell, J. (2004), *Genre and Television: From Cop Shows to Cartoons in American Culture*, New York and London: Routledge.

Monicelli, M. (2007), 'Inseguendo Totò e Fabrizi', in G. Acerbo and R. Pisoni, (eds.), *Kill Baby Kill! Il Cinema di Mario Bava*, 37, Rome: Un Mondo a Parte.

Mora. T. (1978), *Storia del cinema dell'orrore Vol. 2*, Rome: Fanucci Editore.

Morris, G. (1985), *Roger Corman*, Boston: Twayne Publishers.

Moscati, C. (2001), *Franco & Ciccio: due comici dalla strada*, Genoa: Edizione Lo Vecchio.

Moullet, L. (1964), 'De la disponibilité', *Cahiers du Cinéma*, 26 (154): 73–4.

Moullet, L. (1997), 'Fear and Stupor' [originally *Cahiers du Cinema* 486, December 1994], *Metro* 110: 51–2.

Murf (1966), 'Dr Goldfoot and the Girl Bombs', *Variety*, (November16).

Murf (1968), 'Danger: Diabolik', *Variety*, (15 May): 28.

Murf (1972), 'Baron Blood', *Variety*, (25 October).

Naha, E. (1982), *The Films of Roger Corman: Brilliance on a Budget*, New York: Arco Publishing Inc.

Narboni, J. (1968), 'Diabolik', *Cahiers du Cinema*, 202 (June/July): 73.

Naremore, J. (2008), *More Than Night: Film Noir and Its Contexts*, rev. edn, Berkeley, LA and London: University of California Press.

Needham, G. (2003), 'Playing with Genre: Defining the Italian *giallo*', in S. J. Schneider (ed.), *Fear without Frontiers: Horror Cinema across the Globe*, 135–44, Godalming: FAB Press.

Neremberg, E. (2012), *Murder Made in Italy: Homicide, Media, and Contemporary Italian Culture*, Bloomington and Indianapolis: Indiana University Press.

Newman, K. (1986a), 'Thirty Years in Another Town: The History of Italian Exploitation', *Monthly Film Bulletin*, 53 (624): 20–4.

Newman, K. (1986b), 'Black Sabbath', *Monthly Film Bulletin*, 53 (624): 24–5.

Newman, K. (1986c), 'Thirty Years in Another Town: The History of Italian Exploitation II', *Monthly Film Bulletin*, 53 (625): 51–5.

Newman, K. (1986d), 'Thirty Years in Another Town: The History of Italian Exploitation III', *Monthly Film Bulletin*, 53 (626): 88–91.

Newman, K. (2002), 'Psycho-Thriller, qu'est que c'est?', in S. Chibnall and J. Petley (eds.), *British Horror Cinema*, 71–81, London and New York: Routledge.

Nicoli, M. (2017), *The Rise and Fall of the Italian Film Industry*, New York and London: Routledge.

Noto, P. (2016), 'Italian Horror Cinema and Italian Film Journals of the 1970s', in S. Baschiera and R. Hunter (eds.), *Italian Horror Cinema*, 207–21, Edinburgh: Edinburgh University Press.

O'Brien, D. (2013), '*Hercules* versus *Hercules*: Variation and Continuation in Two Generations of Heroic Masculinity', in L. Bayman and S. Rigoletto (eds.), *Popular Italian Cinema*, 183–99, Houndmills and New York: Palgrave Macmillan.

O'Brien, D. (2014), *Classical Masculinity and the Spectacular Body on Film*, Houndmills and New York: Palgrave Macmillan.

O'Brien, G. (1993), *The Phantom Empire: Movies in the Mind of the 20th Century*, New York and London: W.H. Norton.

O'Leary, A. and O'Rawe, C. (2011), 'Against Realism: On a "certain tendency" in Italian Film Criticism', *Journal of Modern Italian Studies*, 16 (1): 107–28.

Olney, I. (2013), *Euro Horror: Classic European Horror Cinema in Contemporary American Culture*, Bloomington: Indiana University Press.

Orwell, G. (1944/1986), 'Raffles and Miss Blandish', in *Decline of the English Murder and Other Essays*, 63–79, Harmondsworth: Penguin.

Parry, M. (1983), 'The Spawn of *Psycho*', *Halls of Horror*, 25: 15–21.

Paulicelli, E. (2016), *Italian Style: Fashion and Film from Early Cinema to the Digital Age*, New York, London, Oxford, Delhi and Sydney: Bloomsbury.

Peary, D. (1981), *Cult Movies*, London: Vermillion.

Pestelli, L. (1968), 'Diabolik strizza l'occhio anche a chi ignora i fumetti', *La Stampa*, (31 January–7 February): 8.

Pezzotta, A. (2007), 'Il regista nascosto', in G. Acerbo, G. and R. Pisoni, R. (eds.), *Kill Baby Kill! Il Cinema di Mario Bava*, 99–102, Rome: Un Mondo a Parte.

Pezzotta, A. (2013), *Mario Bava*, 3rd edn, Milan: Il Castoro Cinema.

Pezzotta, A. (2020a), 'Mario Bava: Il manierista annoiato', *FilmTV*, 28 (22): 8–10.

Pezzotta, A. (2020b), 'Forty Years without Bava: Myths and Discoveries', *Offscreen*, 24 (11–12), available at https://offscreen.com/view/forty-years-without-bava-myths-and-discoveries-by-alberto-pezzotta (accessed 18 March 2021).

Pezzotti, B. (2016), *Investigating Italy's Past through Historical Crime Fiction, Films and TV Series: Murder in the Age of Chaos*, New York: Palgrave Macmillan.

Pirie, D. (1977), *The Vampire Cinema*, Feltham: Quarto.

Pirie, D. (2009), *A New Heritage of Horror: The English Gothic Cinema*, London and New York: I.B. Tauris.

Piselli, S., Bruschini, A. and Morrocchi, R. (2008), *Cinefumetto: Nerosexy/Fantastique/Western/Saderotik/Estetica Pop Italiana 1960–1973*, Florence: Glittering Images.

Po, M. (1980), 'Mario Bava: era l'artigiano del cinema horror', *Corriere della sera*, 29 April: 20

Porro, M. (1998), 'Addio Cottafavi, un "padre" del nostro cinema mitologico', *Corriere della sera*, 16 (December): 38.

Powers, J. (1961), 'Vampire Drama in Old Tradition', *The Hollywood Reporter*, 164 (3): 3.

Powers, J. (1965), 'Blood and Black Lace', *The Hollywood Reporter*, 186 (1): 3.

Pulici, D. (2017), 'Prefazione', in C. Bartolini, C. (ed.), *Il cinema giallo-thriller italiano*, 5–7, Rome: Gremese.

Quinlan, D. (1972), 'Five Dolls for an August Moon', *Films Illustrated*, 2 (14): 41–2.

Rea, L. (1999), *I colori del buio: Il cinema thrilling italiano dal 1930 al 1979*, Florence: Igor Molino Editore.

Rigby, J. (2016), Euro Gothic: Classics of Continental Horror Cinema, Cambridge: Signum Books.

Ruddell, C. and Ward, P. (2019), 'Introduction', in C. Ruddell and P. Ward (eds.), *The Crafty Animator: Handmade, Craft-Based Animation and Cultural Value*, 1–15, Cham, Switzerland: Palgrave Macmillan.

Rushing, R. A. (2016), *Descended from Hercules: Biopolitics and the Muscled Male Body On Screen*, Bloomington and Indianapolis: Indiana University Press.

Sconce, J. (1995), 'Trashing the Academy: Taste, Excess, and an Emerging Politics of Cinematic Style', *Screen*, 36 (4): 371–93.

Scorsese, M. (2019), 'I Said Marvel Movies Aren't Cinema. Let Me Explain', *New York Times*, 4 November, https://www.nytimes.com/2019/11/04/opinion/martin-scorsese-marvel.html (accessed 7 November 2019).

Shiner, L. (2001), *The Invention of Art: A Cultural History*, Chicago and London: University of Chicago Press.

Siegel, M. (2011), 'The Nonplace of Argento: *The Bird with the Crystal Plumage* and Roman Urban History', in J. D. Rhodes and E. Gorfinkel (eds.), *Taking Place: Location and the Moving Image*, 211–32, Minneapolis: University of Minnesota Press.

Silver, A. and Ursini, J. (2000 [originally 1975]), 'Mario Bava: The Illusion of Reality', in A. Silver and J. Ursini (eds.), *The Horror Film Reader*, 95–109, New York: Limelight.

Silvestri, R. (2007), 'Scusi, dov'è il West?', in G. Acerbo, G. and R. Pisoni, R. (eds.), *Kill Baby Kill! Il Cinema di Mario Bava*, 109–12, Rome: Un Mondo a Parte.

Smith, A. (2018), *The Distribution and Exploitation of Popular European Film in British Cinemas*, PhD dissertation, University of Sussex.

Smith, M. (1999), 'Gangsters, Cannibals, Aesthetics, or Apparently Perverse Allegiances', in C. Plantinga and G. M. Smith (eds.), *Passionate Views: Film, Cognition, and Emotion*, 217–38, Baltimore: Johns Hopkins University Press.

Solomon, J. (2014), 'The Muscleman Peplum: From *Le fatiche di Ercole* (1958) to *Hercules and the Princess of Troy* (1965)', in P. Bondanella (ed.), *The Italian Cinema Book*, 163–71, London: BFI/Palgrave Macmillan.

Spadoni, R. (2014a), 'Horror Film Atmosphere as Anti-Narrative (and Vice Versa)', in R. Nowell (ed.), *Merchants of Menace: The Business of Horror Cinema*, 109–28, New York, London, New Delhi and Sydney: Bloomsbury.

Spadoni, R. (2014b), 'Carl Dreyer's Corpse: Horror Film Atmosphere and Narrative', in H. Benshoff (ed.), *A Companion to the Horror Film*, 151–67, Malde, MA: Blackwell.

Spadoni, R. (2020), 'What Is Film Atmosphere?', *Quarterly Review of Film and Video*, 37 (1): 48–75.

Spinazzola, V. (1963), 'Ercole alla conquista degli schermi', in V. Spinazzola (ed.), *Film 1963*, 75–111, Milan: Feltrinelli.

Spinazzola, V. (1964), 'Cinema italiano 1963', in V. Spinazzola (ed.), *Film 1964*, 11–54, Milan: Feltrinelli.

Stanfield, P. (2008), 'Maximum Movies: Lawrence Alloway's Pop Art Film Criticism', *Screen*, 48 (2): 179–93.

Stein, E. (1989), 'Hercules in the Haunted World', *The Village Voice*, 25 (July): 71.

Stollery, M. (2019), 'Filmland's Forgotten Man: Paul Rotha and Reputation Studies', *Film History*, 3 (1): 57–82.

Strick, P. (1986a), '*Ercole al centro della terra (Hercules in the Centre of the Earth)*', *Monthly Film Bulletin*, 53 (624): 17–18.

Strick, P. (1986b), '*Planet of the Vampires*', *Monthly Film Bulletin*, 53 (625): 59–60.

Telotte, J. P. (1991), 'Beyond All Reason: The Nature of the Cult', in J.P. Telotte (ed.), *The Cult Film Experience: Beyond all Reason*, 5–17, Austin: University of Texas Press.

Thompson, H. (1968), 'The Bliss of Mrs Blossom/Danger: Diabolik', *The New York Times*, (12 December): 62.

Thrower, S. (1996), '*Giallo*', in K. Newman (ed.), *The BFI Companion to Horror*, 136–7, London: Cassell.

Thrower, S. (2018), *Beyond Terror: The Films of Lucio Fulci*, rev. edn, Godalming, Surrey: FAB Press.

Tornabuoni, L. (1967), 'Diabolik protesta', *L'europeo*, (13 July): 57–60.

Torok, J. P. (1961), 'Le cadaver exquis: Le Masque du Démon', *Positif*, 40: 24–8.

Tube (1961), 'Black Sunday', *Variety*, (22 February).

U.bz (1981), 'Freda, Bava & c., l'horror italiano', *La stampa*, 4 (April): 21.

U.bz (1982), 'Un thriller tutto da vedere (ma non è per niente horror)', *La stampa*, 23 (July): 23.

V. (1963), 'Rassegna cinematografica (La frusta e il corpo)', *Corriere della sera*, 30 (August): 8.

Van Leeuwen, E. J. (2019), *House of Usher*, Leighton Buzzard: Auteur Publishing/Devil's Advocates.

Venturini, S. (2001), *Galatea S.p.A. (1952–1965): Storia di una casa produzione cinematografica*, Rome: Associazione Italiana per le ricerche di storia del cinema.

Venturini, S. (2014), *Horror italiano*, Rome: Donzelli Editore (Kindle Edition).

Vice (1964), 'Sullo schermo (6 donne per l'assassino)', *La stampa*, 15 (May): 4.

Vitali, V. (2016), *Capital and Popular Cinema: The Dollars Are Coming!* Manchester: Manchester University Press.

Volta, O. (1972), 'Entretien avec Mario Bava', *Positif*, 138: 44–8.

Wagstaff, C. (1992), 'A Forkful of Westerns: Industry, Audiences and the Italian Western', in R. Dyer and G. Vincendeau (eds.), *Popular European Cinema*, 245–61, London and New York: Routledge.

Wagstaff, C. (1998), 'Italian Genre Films in the World Market', in G. Nowell-Smith and S. Ricci (eds.), *Hollywood and Europe: Economics, Culture, and National Identity 1945–95*, 74–85, London: BFI

Wagstaff, C. (2014), 'Production around 1960', in P. Bondanella (ed.), *The Italian Cinema Book*, 149–62, London: BFI.

Walz, R. (2000), *Pulp Surrealism: Insolent Popular Culture in Early Twentieth Century Paris*, Berkeley, LA and London: University of California Press (Kindle edition).

Whit (1965), 'Blood and Black Lace', *Variety*, (June 23).

Willemen, P. (2013), 'The Zoom in Popular Cinema: A Question of Performance', *Inter-Asia Cultural Studies*, 14 (1); 104–9.

Wood, M. (2005), *Italian Cinema*, Oxford and New York: Berg.

Wood, M. (2007), 'Italian Film Noir', in A. Spicer (ed.), *European Film Noir*, 236–72, Manchester: Manchester University Press.

Wood, M. (2014), 'Italian Film Genres and Mario Bava', in P. Bondanella (ed.), *The Italian Cinema Book*, 303–16, London: BFI/Palgrave Macmillan.

Wood, R. (1973), '*Hacha para la luna di Miel (Blood Brides)*', *Monthly Film Bulletin*, 40 (469) (February): 29.

Wood, R. (1986), *Hollywood from Vietnam to Reagan*, New York: Columbia University Press.

Y (1961), 'Le Masque du Démon', *Le Film Francais*, 18 (882): 19.

INDEX

CPSIA information can be obtained
at www.ICGtesting.com
Printed in the USA
LVHW081522170322
713719LV00005B/193